THE HOSPITABLE CANON

CULTURA LUDENS:
IMITATION AND PLAY IN WESTERN CULTURE

General Editors:

Giuseppe Mazzotta
(New Haven, Connecticut)
Mihai Spariosu
(Athens, Georgia)

4

Virgil Nemoianu and Robert Royal (eds)

The Hospitable Canon
Essays on literary play, scholarly choice, and popular pressures

THE HOSPITABLE CANON

ESSAYS ON LITERARY PLAY, SCHOLARLY CHOICE, AND POPULAR PRESSURES

Edited by

VIRGIL NEMOIANU
and
ROBERT ROYAL

JOHN BENJAMINS PUBLISHING COMPANY
PHILADELPHIA/AMSTERDAM

1991

Library of Congress Cataloging-in-Publication Data

The Hospitable canon : essays on literary play, scholarly choice, and popular pressures
/ edited by Virgil Nemoianu and Robert Royal.
   p.   cm. -- (Cultura ludens, ISSN 0882-3049 ; 4)
Includes bibliographical references and index.
1. Canon (Literature) 2. Popular literature -- History and criticism -- Theory, etc. 3.
American literature -- History and criticism -- Theory, etc. 4. English literature -- History and criticism -- Theory, etc. 5. French literature -- History and criticism -- Theory,
etc. I. Nemoianu, Virgil. II. Royal, Robert, 1949-   . III. Series.
PN56.C6H67   1991
809 -- dc20   91-8337
ISBN 90 272 4237 2 (Eur.)/1-55619-152-9 (alk. paper)   CIP

Table of Contents

Foreword

The present collection seeks to respond to a public need. Debates over the literary canons in the United States have become polarized, simplified, and politicized in ways that threaten to take them entirely outside the realm of thoughtful intellectual debate. Political and ideological figures from one side of the spectrum to the other are beginning to use academic deliberation as an excuse to promote convenient new code words in power struggles that would be better waged on their proper ground and in more openly partisan terms. It is, of course, not the first time, and doubtless will not be the last time either, that cultural or religious terminologies are drawn upon to embellish naked political-economic conflicts. We are not at all unaware of the very real and intimate interdependencies of cultural and intellectual matters with all other workings of society. Many of the contributors to this volume, however, seem to believe (as, in the editors' opinion at least, most reasonable people do also) that cultural and intellectual pursuits have an integrity, autonomy, and sphere of their own, that are precious and worth preserving, not only for their own sakes, but precisely for the good of that more comprehensive body of relationships that we call society.

This autonomous integrity of the cultural sphere, even if quite relative and limited (a possible, but not absolutely certain appraisal), continues to be a legitimate object of research and rational reflection. The study of literary canons, curricula, and value may not be an insulated pursuit, but that does not eliminate its own respectability and weight. Providing carefully researched and thoughtfully expressed insights on this field of human knowledge may, with a little luck, clarify disagreements and defuse tensions outside academies or (an even more difficult enterprise) inside them. Such moderating efforts are sorely needed since some of the more passionate participants in the debate seem, like Aufidius in *Coriolanus* (I, xi., 24-27), driven by fury to wash their "fierce hand in's heart" even in circumstances that go directly "against the hospitable canon."

This was the editors' chief purpose, and they are perfectly aware that such goals are never fully or finally attained. They have consoled themselves with the belief that, whatever its shortcomings, this collection advances a crucial cultural conversation in several ways. In fact, the subsidiary aims of the collection, by no means trivial in themselves, have certainly been achieved. Two of these deserve mention here. One is to draw attention to the comparatist and trans-national aspects of literary canonicity, something that is not often noticed in the discussions as they are currently conducted. The other is to remind readers of the multiple ways in which any literariness, and, even more so, the literariness of "canonized" works, is a ludic phenomenon: authors and critics, scholars and readers, contemporaries and the posterity are all caught up in a non-rational, but certainly joyful activity ("the ambivalent laughter of the people," to use Bakhtin's expression) when they engage in writing, reading, and listening. The democracy of play, one of the most durable and widest bonds uniting the human race, is no less real than are most fundamental biological and social needs, and in the case of literary canonicity it can be observed in full action.

Some of the contributors chose to approach the common issue by resorting to individual examples. Rosa Penna presents for the first time the syllabus J.L. Borges used in English literature: it is fascinating to follow the ways in which a leading figure of literary modernism (or is it post-modernism?) plays a kind of hide-and-seek with the canonical tradition, accepting and modifying it in creative ways. Lilian Furst, in a sowewhat similar vein, follows the meanderings of the ethical and the aesthetic in the case of some acknowledged classics of realism: rejection and acceptance on one plane seem in inverse ratio to one another, and yet only a mutual illumination (of the ethical and the aesthetic) makes them convincing to us and – almost as an afterthought – canonically plausible. Even more allegorical is Raymond Prier's analysis of the relationship of Lessing's *Laocoön* to both its predecessors and its later commentators: an exemplar of canonical misreading and fruitfulness. The thorough examinations of French and American curricular practices by Yves Chevrel and Glen Johnson are replete with surprising and, perhaps, reassuring conclusions. Anthologies of American literature strain and chafe towards self-imposed large purposes, but hardly ever destroy or exclude, Glen Johnson explains. French comparatism, with its "modern language" examinations, elaborate programatically alternatives to classical and national curricular patterns and develop traditions of their own, a kind of comparatist canon, one might say.

Others among the contributors take a more directly theoretical approach. Peter Walker explores how the critical discourse itself, after Arnold, and irrespective of methodological and ideological orientation, encouraged religious metaphorization of literary readings and valuation. Robert Royal shows even more directly how the aesthetic and political realms face each other and how both face ultimate questions. Christopher Clausen argues that beneath canonical choices lie existential, thematic, and archetypal structures that are incorporated in some works in ways that rightly gain and maintain attention. Virgil Nemoianu sets up levels of meaning in our usage of "canons" and related terms, and examines the relationship between them. Michael Cooke argues for the solidarity between the different provinces of literature and for a (playful indeed) interchangeability of margins and centers, particularly with regard to new or non-European literatures. Charles Altieri, who for a number of years has been one of the most respected specialists in canon discussions, presents the philosophical dimensions of the issue by examining the importance and limits of "difference" in any phenomenological grasp. Altieri's fruitful concept of the communicative role of literary canons as a historical grammar of forms and themes is put here, we think, to excellent use.

It was not the intention of the editors to seek consensus, definitive conclusions, or a common line of argument among the contributors. Nor can we easily discover much agreement behind their various differences in topic, approach, or orientation. Two underlying positions seem to be discernible, however, both well beyond the narrower issue of curriculum or canon. One is the belief in the intrinsic worth of and human need for literature, in addition to a scholarly affection for literature that stands in some contrast with the suspicion and distaste that inform many contemporary critical methodologies. The other is a calm tone of voice and an apparent desire to lower confrontation to controversy, passion to reason. Such common bonds, more than a shared ideology or cast-iron conclusions, seem promising and valuable for our academic institutions.

The editors wish to acknowledge the valuable support of the Ethics and Public Policy Center in Washington, D.C., and of its president, George Weigel, for this project. They also owe Gretchen Baudhuin an enormous debt of gratitude for her indispensable help and heroic dedication in turning the various contributions into a coherent book manuscript under inhuman time pressures.

The Editors

Canons and Differences

Charles Altieri

Virgil Nemoianu's invitation to contribute to this collection put me in a position to appreciate one of the stranger ironies of our profession. He requested the essay because he had been interested in another that I had written on the same subject. So here was one of those rare moments in the profession when one's work gets recognized. Unfortunately the recognition meant that I had to write something new, on which I feared I had no more ideas, on a subject where what I really wanted was to have more people read the old essay carefully.[1] There I thought I did have something to say, something which now I had in effect to unmake for the audience who will judge my ideas by this supplement. Academic decorum imposes the task of not repeating those few things one says in a lifetime that may bear repeating.

The ego has ways around this dilemma. For if one is to explain one's own failures and the stakes involved, one must begin by outlining the original case. Mine consisted of two basic arguments. The first concentrated on the kind of thinking we must allow ourselves if we are to make sense of what the traditional ideals of a canon propose. As with ethics, there is no obvious way simply to describe values as if they were subject to the same conditions as facts. Doing that will get us certain kinds of sociological analyses revealing who holds what positions and how those positions gain or lack social power. But it will not show us how people in fact care about values, what ends values serve for individuals who use them as means for self-representation and as appeals to their communities that they are worthy of certain identities, and how communities go about assessing those appeals. That process cannot rely on descriptions from the point of view of an outsider but must be cast in essentially circular forms. With regards to the nature of a literary canon one can only appeal to the specific culture for which the canon claims authority, seeking to develop common grounds for assessing the interests facilitated and blocked by

competing positions. Then having projected a version of these grounds, I
based my particular arguments on the interests that could be served by
honoring the curatorial and normative functions of a traditional ideal of a
literary canon. There are of course several different versions of that traditional ideal. Yet for my purposes the important issue is not the make-up of
any specific canon but the rationale for basing most of one's considerations in that discussion on values and models that have their significance
and force from the cultural circle itself formed by the range of candidates
for this kind of canonical status. In practice this means that the canon I
tried to defend is a complex web, looking very much like a version of
Quine's sense of embedded cultural networks. At the core, and relatively
unchangeable, are those few authors (not texts) like Dante, Sophocles,
Homer, and Shakespeare without whom we could have virtually no sense
of why the various Western canons had the appeal they did. To think
about a literary canon is to engage the cultural authority comprised in the
structure of permissions and challenges that these authors came to represent.[2] Then there are several interlocking relationships among texts which
take on importance because of the historical role they play in the development of certain imaginative forms or in defining certain values. Here a
good deal of change takes place, relative to the questions cultures ask and
to the purposes that might govern certain pedagogical or artistic practices.
Yet even here if we seek authority for certain works as representing the
canon our discussion is constrained in several ways by the history in which
those writers we admire express their admiration for other authors. As we
become educated within a general canon, we form a comparative framework that requires our answering certain questions in our valuations and
our engaging certain contrasts which have already been defined by those
acts of valuing one another's writing (as Wordsworth of Milton) which survive within the canon. And as we think about educating others in that
canon we ought be able to make possible the experience of that kind of
thinking. There is obviously no way to teach the canon that graduate students learn to general education students or to literary majors or to those
whose ambition is to be writers. But we can give them enough knowledge
of certain interrelations among those texts that they come to understand
how canons constrain and liberate the formation of values based on literary experience. And we can hope to give them a complex enough education within one traditional literary culture that it becomes possible for

them to appreciate what is involved in the fact that agents from other cultures have similar traditions.[3]

That education in a canon, that engagement in the imaginative sites provided by the shifting hierarchies and the discourses they engender, then can be seen as providing curatorial and normative roles that are fundamental to a wide variety of human interests within the general culture whose literary values can be said to have been in large part shaped by that canon. Therefore I thought it possible to articulate those interests by contrasting the values that seemed to me to follow from my stance with those that I saw governing contemporary criticism. One found there in 1982 widespread agreement that the major task of criticism was to submit all traditional idealizations to the kind of suspicious reading which would reveal how they were caught up in the particular interests and blindnesses of their historical situations. And then the canon becomes, in Gerald Bruns's terms, "not a literary category but a category of power" (*Canons* 81). However from my perspective such critical attitudes trapped themselves within third-person stances from which we can explain the functions that value claims seemed to produce within a society but not talk about the conditions for internalizing them. In contrast, the traditional canon presents values as claims upon our first-person capacities to present our actions as efforts to earn personal identities within certain communities, so one can claim for it at at least three competing cultural functions: it institutionalizes idealization as a force shaping our sense of what communities we wish to identify with and what selves to pursue; it challenges individuals and new movements in the arts to meet certain criteria of self-representation if they choose identities within certain communities, and it is capable of focusing those discussions about the ends of politics that are very difficult to develop if one's major interests lie in demystifying prevailing beliefs and resisting all cultural positivities.

Unfortunately these abstractions do not play very well in the current theoretical climate: they strike readers as thinly veiled conservatism allied with those who would resist expanding the canon to meet the range of new political constituencies in America; they offer naive evasions of the new historicist critiques of idealization and their insistence on specific social factors which make use of the past as norms in the present highly suspect; they maintain an elitist distinction from popular culture that is both unfounded and impractical given the real interests of most readers today; they do not face the reality of how canons are used primarily to institution-

alize the kinds of power resisted variously by feminist, Foucauldian, and
Marxist versions of critical practice, and they ignore the psychological and
ethical values which thinkers like Lacan and Lyotard have located in the
refusal of all claims to be the subject who knows what is good for another.
Yet the ego has ways around even this chorus of responses. For the una-
nimity of negative reactions is easily turned to one's own credit. The rhetorics of resistance begin to appear more like rhetorics of conformity, and
that conformity then makes it very important to have a model of the canon
that promises us alternative communities offering at least the possibility
that we can explore intellectual identities not bound to the specific ideologies prevailing in one's own marketplace.

The ambitious ego also has at its disposal the very useful strategy of
being able to admit limited errors. Then one earns the right to repeat once
again while also asking for a second chance. In this case that strategy is
necessary because I have seen three basic mistakes in the way my original
essay presented its case. The first I have already been attempting to rectify
by trying to be more precise on why the canon that I defend must remain
quite vague, more an ideal productive network of possibilities than a specific curriculum. Second, I was far too abstract in the contrastive language
that I used to set off my own claims. Thinking that the major antagonist to
the canon was the conjunction of poststructural semantics and cultural
relativism pervading many of these contemporary positions, I constructed
as my antagonist what I thought was the best logical case for demystifying
the forms of power that canons encode. My logic, however, proved to have
serious limits. I saw only the case for reading against texts and thus failed
to address those who treated such methods as a prelude to claims stressing
the need to read for new or different values. Finally, even though I argued
at length that questions about idealization cannot be resolved by direct argument but require imaginatively exploring the interests addressed by the
competing positions, I in fact proceeded as if the goal were less to reach
agreement than to expel some dangerous intellectual disease. I could only
imagine fighting imagined enemies rather than negotiating with those who
have different but equally pressing positive values.

Let me try now to make amends. I hope to show that the case for the
traditional canon which I have outlined (hereafter to be called "the traditionalist position," because its more appropriate name, "the missionary
position" might be misunderstood) satisfies a greater range and depth of
interests basic to literary studies than the alternatives, often in ways that

are in fact compatible with their very different priorities. On the one hand, the curatorial and normative functions posed by those traditional ideals create a climate in which those advocating more specialized canons must, and can, make that case in a more public language than they would if they addressed only their own tribe. On the other hand this scope makes it possible to continue the liberal dream that to a considerable degree we can actually appreciate one another's differences because we can see them against the background of some more abstracted, less historically local set of ideological claims than those which now constitute the differences. Speaking more generally, one can say that imagining the possible force of a traditional canon requires entertaining complex interactions between our capacities to make identifications and our experience of unrecuperable differences which are fundamental to any theoretical understanding of the issues underlying our debates. But one must also admit that one cannot tease out those possibilities of identification if one stays on the level of abstract theoretical arguments. There I would immediately resort to my claims that the dominant stances in contemporary criticism are severely limited by three crucial problems – a suspicion of all idealizations not directly connected to very specific interests, a somewhat glib equation between the force of culture in constituting values and a general cultural relativism, and a rather narrow model of self-interest that does not consider problems of self-correction or second-order identities. And my own stance would merely repeat what to them are anachronistic pieties. So instead I shall show how the traditionalist case can respond to the three concrete differences which for those relativist stances make it impossible to grant authority to received high cultural values. By confining the discussion to these issues I hope we can modify the traditional case by dropping those assertions not sufficiently responsive to those differences, but at the same time I want to show how much remains of the traditional case which has compelling claims upon us, perhaps especially if one wants to understand how literary experience can best foster our living within incommensurable social commitments. This is not to say that the competing sides will agree; it is to hope that they may learn from one another, that there may emerge sufficient mutual understanding to sustain compromise on practical decisions, and that we may be able to argue in ways allowing a less committed audience to make articulate and persuasive judgments on the issues.

I

Traditional appeals for a high canon have relied on hypotheses about some central core of human experience which pervades cultural change and which enables us to test and to preserve those works most fully expressive of that humanity. But for current criticism claims about that humanity stifle significant differences that develop over time while inordinately flattering and sustaining those who align themselves with the projected core. Thus we find Barbara Herrnstein Smith arguing that rather than speak of universal properties we should say simply that works endure primarily because they continue "to perform desired/able functions" ("Contingencies of Value" 31), usually functions that do not remain constant but adapt to evolutionary changes. The shift seems innocuous, but it provides a powerful means of isolating the two basic dangers in the traditional ways of claiming authority for those texts – that in order to make them "timeless we suppress their temporality" (32), and that we confuse the fact that texts have endured with the claim that they have some distinctive right to endure, when in fact the reasons for the endurance involve nostalgia, conservative political pressures, stock rhetorical needs, and the inertia of established power: "Since the texts that are selected and preserved by 'time' will always be those which 'fit' (and, indeed, have often been *designed* to fit) their characteristic needs, interests, resources, and purposes, that testing mechanism has its own built-in partialities accumulated in and thus intensified by time" (33).

What Smith puts analytically becomes much more assertive in the eloquent prose of Annette Kolodny:

> What we gain when we read the classics, then, is neither Homer's Greece nor George Eliot's England *as they knew it* but, rather, an approximation of an already fictively imputed past made available, through our interpretive strategies for present concerns. Only by understanding this can we put to rest that recurrent delusion that "the continuing relevance" of the classics serves as "testimony to perennial features of human experience." The only "perennial feature" to which our ability to read and reread texts written in previous centuries testifies is to our inventiveness – in the sense that all of literary history is a fiction which we daily re-create as we reread it. ("Dancing Through the Minefield" 505)

There is still considerable sense in this formulation. But as the passions intensify the claims begin to seem a bit too easy. Their very fit with the prevailing cultural climate clouds the complexity of the issues. Why must we speak of "suppressing" temporality in order to make texts timeless? Why must the idea of "fit" lead so readily into "partialities accumulated in and thus intensified by time," as if there could be no larger frame accounting for the fit or even demanding the canon because we so often fail to fit with the partialities of our own time? And finally what do we gain and lose by so quickly leaping from denying the canon's claims about the perennial into the confident claim that literary history is simply a fiction imputed on to other fictions – are there no alternative castings which might enable us to distinguish among kinds and uses of fictions, some of which define interpretive strategies that challenge or stretch "present concerns" or engage various existential criteria?

Kolodny's and Smith's anti-foundationalism proves very important for the traditionalist. If we have only fictions, and if we nonetheless must make significant distinctions among them, there are very good reasons for preserving those imaginative energies in our culture which have been devoted precisely to testing the long term claims that these fictions can make upon us. From this perspective Smith's use of the magical verb "suppress" provides the clearest marker of the very different assumptions about temporality that the two sides make, and it offers the most vulnerable feature of the contemporary stance. One need not search very long to come up with occasions where it seems necessary not only to reject Smith's claim but even to reverse it entirely. For rather than suppressing temporality, the canon honors some fictional constructs primarily because they are seen as giving a timeless rendering of a particular temporal situation, for example in the ways that the *Aeneid* came to represent the power and the pathos of Rome or perhaps that Rousseau's *Confessions* became for Hegel a paradigm for the limitations of Romantic consciousness. But to generalize from those examples would be to polarize the issues. Suppose then we say simply that while works from the past preserved by a canon flatten temporal differences, they also go a long way towards preserving both a feel for those differences and a sense of how specific differences take on long term significance. In making texts relatively timeless, and hence capable of representing large segments of cultural experience over considerable time units, we frame their temporality so that we can understand how the engagement in time might be extended into typological functions. Approaching the question of historicity this way enables us to attribute plausible reasons for shifting our attention from specific socio-historical contexts while at the same time enabling us to finesse terms with the ontological weight of "universal" or "permanent" or "perennial." One need simply argue that among their many other ways of meaning some texts manage to address aspects of problems which are likely to take place in a wide variety of social structures – for example in the challenges to authority and the questions of love and honor that shape the *Iliad* or in the needs for imaginative order leading the exiled Dante to develop his *Commedia*. Thus the crucial issue is not the truth of such works to some deep nature but their functional relevance for enabling those in other temporal frames to find their emotions engaged and minds provoked to sharper and perhaps fresher grasps of the problems rendered.[4]

It is tempting to point out that there is no more perennial theme in the traditional canon than the complaint against the kind of glib critical over-generalizations that we are dealing with here. But I will content myself with the more important observation that the very mythology of suppression and the need for imaginative alternatives to the positivities of the socially enforced canon is itself a constant motif in canonical texts like Ovid's *Metamorphoses*, Wordsworth's "Nutting," or Eliot's *Mill on the Floss*. Here then is a simple case of typological relevance. We can align the passions that engage us now with certain constructions from the past of-fering imaginative terms which help explain why we invest as we do in the rhetoric of suppression, and which suggest better imaginative terms than our theories do for resisting narrow definitions of how texts can be said to fit our preconceptions.[5] But at the same time the example requires our recognizing the very limited way in which such imaginative terms can assume cultural force. For because they exist within a complex and contra-dictory set of historical exemplars, these texts do not have the kind of authority from which we can make direct conclusions. They are confronted by other, equally canonical works committed to reinforcing the established canon against some version of what Arnold saw as the diseased sensibil-ities of his contemporaries.[6] So the power of the canon is less in the themes *per se* than in how the texts dispose imaginative energies in relation to the issues – not to provide answers but to elaborate what answers must take responsibility for. Yet what we lose in assertive force we gain in framing a model of persistence over time much more difficult to subsume under a rhetoric of temporal difference, suppression and fit with prevailing powers. For those powers are far too impatient to care about qualities; they want insistent ideological claims, and they try to inculcate a much narrower canon that really does fit with their interests in more direct ways. Against that backdrop, it becomes clear why we might have strong interests in reading through rather than reading against texts, since the first mode of reading is the best means we have to sustain the diversity which is our one stay against those powers. That lesson, I hasten to add, has the additional benefit of illustrating the possibility that despite our very different contemporary commitments we can share those ideals of interpretation that secure readings of the past sufficiently determinate in historical terms to distance the text from those political interests, and thus to make it available for a wide variety of significant challenges and applications in the present.[7]

So far we have been speaking about the semantic roles one can attribute to the possible presence of the past, in large part because that is the domain where contemporary critics feel most comfortable. But we cannot be content with this level of the canon's functioning. For we must also take up the fact that in many ways the canonical works do not simply earn their authority by the effectiveness we discover when we use them as aspects of a cultural grammar. There is also a presumption of possible authority, an implicit demand that we ought try the attitudes they preserve even if we see no obvious need. It is this presumption that most bothers critics like Smith and Kolodny, yet it is also this presumption that is basic to the canon functioning as the holistic, relational field which I have been describing, so there is no escaping the issue. Whether we grant that authority depends on how we understand the ways in which those works come to endure. Their semantic utility is one reason. But that is too easy to subsume under an abstract language of contingent fit, or perhaps even of arbitrary fictions, so we need more concrete grounds. I suggest then that these works endure primarily because they have engaged other minds whose achievements gained them the respect and admiration of writers and thinkers whom we continue to admire. Works have claims on us because we want to understand how they could have mattered to the degree that they did for those writers either who we still think have very strong claims from the past or whose contemporary stances engage us. The authority is analogous to the authority we attribute to persons who are highly honored within a community. Thus the authority is not the power to make specific demands on our behavior. Rather it is a claim on our reflective life to serve as part of what we consider when we deliberate on actions or even when we project the kinds of images that structure and direct our investments. Then if we imagine a range of such voices, each affiliated with other persons who have engaged them in ways that the canon preserves, we understand how taken together the works within that canon have considerable claims to authority in shaping both the contents of our literary educations and the questions we pose to those contents. Not only do they exemplify specific attitudes, they create an idealized context of judges whose relation to one another one can imagine internalizing in one's own dialogue with oneself and with what one proposes as the communities from which one desires to achieve particular identities.

I propose two practical tests for clarifying how this authority might function and how it is compatible with interests that many of us share. The first is essentially negative because I think it is necessary to show how claims for the traditional canon need not lead to abuses like the one that Annette Kolodny cites, where an Oxford-trained colleague justified a vote against a women's studies seminar by claiming that "if Kate Chopin were really worth reading, she'd have lasted – like Shakespeare" ("Minefield" 503). That works have endured for those writers who matter to us is a reason for using them as part of our discourse about values; it is not a reason to dismiss other works from consideration, especially works invoked for their contemporary relevance and works that one has non-literary grounds for seeing as really suppressed. Rather it is in the spirit of the traditional canon to seek out those works which can exemplify certain qualities that we feel are important for contemporary experience. Imagine Dante or Jane Austen or Shakespeare denying that. Moreover I think it fair to say that even though the choice to read Chopin in this case has no relation to the canon, the canon that one in fact relies on will have a great deal of influence on how one reads her. Obviously if we put her in the context of the traditional canon by arguing that she does deserve to be read with James and Wharton, we cannot simply read her for her sexual politics; we must concern ourselves with the quality of the sexual politics, with the ways in which the interpretive stances she brings to bear within the book carry over into our understanding of our options in the real world. Contrary to a now common assumption, it is likely that a rich experience of the traditional canon will keep us from false oppositions between an aesthetic framework and an existential one.[8] Consider again how the authors within the canon evaluated each other. Rarely do we find works treated as major only for their craft or for some abstract sense of formal beauty (unless it is the case that the writer, like Flaubert or Wilde, makes craft a thematic principle). Instead formal properties are means not ends. The prevailing criteria are the intensity of the world presented and the wisdom of what one does within and through those presentations.

But why can't one justify the reading of Chopin entirely in terms provided by contemporary theory, without reference to the canon? One can. However this possibility does not mean that such an enterprise, such a disposition of authority, is a wise one. In fact it will be by looking at that possibility that I think we best understand why the alternative of giving the traditional canon substantial authority in such discussions may be in most of our interests. This time our test case must be much more abstract. It seems clear that the biggest challenge now facing literary education is whether the proliferation of theories and their centrality in our understanding of understanding provide an equal or better structure for pedagogical and critical practices than we had when we relied on a roughly shared sense of canonical hierarchies and the associated materials necessary for particular specializations. Do we look to articulate ideas for our principles of order and value, or do we continue to place our faith in the various versions of educated sensibilities that were thought to be produced by becoming familiar with a range of exemplars loosely tied to general patterns in the history of style and the history of ideas?

I am very uncomfortable with the ways in which the ideal of educated sensibilities slips into class-based ideals of the gentleman or his surrogates. Yet if one follows this line one can at least hope to find in the canon substantial resistance to that narrow interpretation of imaginative empowerment. The other option, the new dispensation, seems to me even more dangerous because it lacks such internal correctives, except as the contingent war of competing powers, and because even at its most pluralistic it draws far too narrow and predictable a circle. In this dispensation all the authority derives from our sense of contemporary intellectual and political priorities. Our theories tell us both what works to read and how to read them. That leaves us precious little otherness, precious little ground either for confronting our own self-satisfactions, for framing alternative views of our ends, or for under standing the past in a way that challenges the assumptions that turn out to underly competing contemporary theories (and, as I hope one can see from our references so far to contemporary theory, there is a degree of shared belief that should prove frightening to theorists of resistance and difference). Consider how easy those critics we have been treating find it to map the many differences which the traditional canon encodes along a single axis distinguishing those works which somehow fit the biases of established cultural power and those which somehow promise freedom from or resistance to that cultural hegemony. At one pole this ignores the various ways that being suppressed by the main stream culture limits a group's imaginative scope, at the other it suppresses the diversity offered by authors like Dante, Blake, Pope, Milton, and Flaubert.

One cannot treat the traditional canon as if it were able to overcome all the blindness that comes with our contemporary interests, and one must yield to the claims by Kolodny and by Smith that the lines of connection posed between present and past stem from biased and limited versions of cultural history. Yet my view offers two basic checks on the urge to remake the world to fit our contemporary melodramas – it locates considerable authority in judgments made in other cultural contexts and it confronts our theorizing with the challenge that it account for the fact of endurance over time with something better than global claims about the past as our fiction. And it assumes that there can be no single conceptual structure or set of political interests that can best handle the complex demands that experience will make on us and, in literature at least, we on it. So even if one could show that the cultural history so represented was systematically blind to certain phenomena now very important to us, like the equality of genders and races, the range of terms it offers for thinking about our own historicity and modes of valuing our world seem to me clearly preferable to what we might get from a canon of those who are far more sensitive to one particular domain of experience but lacking larger frameworks. This is not ideal. But we are not limited only to that canon. And to the degree that we are, we at the least find it cultivating a sense of internal dialogue and a model of how authority resides in individual exemplars that seem to me very difficult to give up in favor of on the one hand particular thematic orientations and on the other very vague claims about the unrepresented.

II

My claims about interests, recurrences, and our capacities for making judgments that are affected by the typologies we invoke all presuppose a particular model of human agency that is by no means self-evident (or, because it seems self-evident demands investigation). These claims are all too obviously woven into the very canon that I am trying to defend. So here either I must admit that each of us simply repeats our different circles when we deal with fictions about values or I must show that there are levels within these circles where competing claims can be tested on grounds that do not invoke the authority of the canon one is trying to defend. I think these levels become visible if we shift our attention to a second set of claims to irreconcilable differences which leads contemporaries to reject the traditional canon. For here what I am calling claims to differences in space explicitly raise questions about the images of human needs, desires and powers that a canon can be said to represent and to foster. Faced with the pressure to come to terms with the various cultural groups each demanding a canon for their own perceived interests, I think it possible to claim that most of us are better served by letting the forms of identification which the traditional canon offers play a major role in our educational practices. For that model of potential identifications provides the best account of the complex relation between otherness and self-reflection basic to reading, provides a richer range of imaginative experience, and proposes more effective principles for connecting the powers that we exercise in reading to those we bring to bear in making some of our important practical judgments with respect to representing ourselves to our selves and determining possible relations with other persons.

Put in its most abstract form, this second challenge to the traditional canon concerns those differences in space rather than in time which can be said to expose that canon as far too narrow to acknowledge the needs and interests of the range of psychological types, sexual orientations and socio-political formations constituting even just contemporary life in America. As Lillian Robinson puts it, our educational models should be responsive to the criterion "of truth to the culture being represented, the whole culture and not the creation of an almost entirely male white elite" ("Treason Our Text" 577). Two basic arguments sustain the case. First, it is indubitable that over time the values that have cultural hegemony in various domains get developed as systems of names that do not apply equally to all groups within a society. As a result there will be those for whom traditional canons are little more than oppressive and alienating modes of naming which seem more like a trap than they do the structure of permissions I have been praising. Each effort to use the canon as a cul-

tural grammar becomes a sordid reminder of how what mediates voice
and subjectivity for some occludes it for others. Thus Annette Kolodny's
feminist claims also capture superbly the conditions holding for every
person who by virtue of occupying certain race and class positions finds
the "most cherished private experience 'hedged by taboos, mined with
false namings'" ("Minefield" 502).

The second argument then takes up the practical demands that follow
from the desire to repossess the language. Once one experiences that
alienation it seems absurd to devote oneself to mastering the received
canon. One must try to construct simultaneously principles of resistance to
that authority and new discourse communities providing positive alternatives. As our example of how these arguments develop I shall rely on feminist claims, but the same logic, although not the same specific arguments,
applies to many other groups. The best feminist theory need not rely on
essentially negative terms that locate the significant differences primarily
by pointing to areas of experience where the male names and processes
are clearly inappropriate. It has developed considerable but by no means
universal agreement on at least the following positive names for the differences that interest them: both the tradition of woman's writing and the
exigencies of female experience in our culture demand a canon characterized by a more open attitude to expressions of direct feeling, this canon
will explore and elaborate ethical principles like those developed by Carol
Gilligan, emphasizing the principles of care and avoidance of giving pain
to others, and it will pursue a less authoritative, more intimate and communal relation between author and audience (often shaped by the fact
that the literature directly mirrors what women know is distinctive to their
experience). On the basis of these new names and stances then, the different class can make its inroads on established power, at times by simply
bringing ironic pressure to bear on the hegemony that thinks it has no
other, so that there emerges within the master discourse a haunting
absence, a critical listener everywhere sceptical but nowhere allowing the
consolation of direct argument, and at times by what Lillian Robinson calls
using the master's tools to dismantle the master's house because those are
"the only ones you can lay your hands on" ("Canon Fathers and Myth Universe" 34).

The overall case here seems a compelling one. Yet several problems
continue to haunt it. On the practical level it is very difficult to decide how
much force to give the particular differences stressed by any one group's

canon, to say nothing about what happens when the different differences begin to pile up. Even if one grants that in each case the assertions locate conditions of value excluded by the dominant culture, one must begin to suspect the totalized way in which each claim to difference is proposed as an explanation of the group's alienation and as a locus for the powers necessary for relieving that alienation. For as our concerns for differences proliferate we face an extreme Balkanization where any effort to postulate causes of oppression or to develop large scale programs for change must be able to say that some differences are more important than others.[9] That then creates the need to show just how the difference one cites actually generates the consequences one claims for it, or to decide which among differences like those between genders, races, and classes is the most important factor. And, at the opposite pole, the more we insist upon differences, the more we must find ways of locating what those different groups share which will allow them to work together or at least not destroy one another. But how then do we insert that potential for sharing into the model of agency within which difference must play so powerful an explanatory force? And how do we correlate those claims for difference with those practical demands on us to think in terms that cannot at all be marked by the difference, demands ranging from the simple need to make mathematical calculations to the crucial arguments we muster for articulating the nature of justice and for defending political rights? Finally these same problems of identification and differentiation take disturbingly practical form as the group claiming difference manages to increase its power and thus must reflect on how it can and cannot let its access to the material resources of the mainstream culture influence its models for personal ethics.

Our addressing each of these issues will require our making explicit the ways in which the model of agency that we work with can negotiate between the degree to which we can stress the kinds of interests, needs, and powers best suited to talking about irreducible differences, and the degree to which we must emphasize the generic over the gendered and all that the gendered stands for in our overall discussion. I want to argue that while there are very good reasons to insist on supplementing the traditional canon in a variety of ways so that it addresses these differences, it is also crucial to see how there are levels on which its assumptions about both the powers and the needs of persons by virtue of shareable aspects of their humanity prove more central to most of our interests than the diverse models of difference which are offered as alternatives. So I shall try to develop my case by turning to an essay by Lawrence Lipking that I think best represents the contrary claims about agency by which one can justify rejecting the traditional canon.[10]

Lipking's case is simple and elegant. He argues that even though there is no explicit poetics for women's writing, there is enough evidence of careful reflection by women on the subject to allow our now tracing the outline of a theory therein embedded. He then concentrates on three points (which I slightly recast in order to bring out their most general features and to distance them from his efforts to make them conform to the thematics of abandonment):[11] 1) a woman's poetics must begin with "the possibility of never having been empowered to speak," (91) or as I prefer to put it, woman's writing cannot assume the high culture as its enabling background but is framed by fears of strangeness and/or presumption regarding that culture; 2) the major concern of that poetics is with the qualities of personal involvement attained in both the reading and the writing of literature, usually because the art can be seen as an extension of private life (94, where Lipking's stress on private contexts manages to include a sense of the primacy of "feeling" within his woman's poetic without trapping himself, and his subject, in a reified equation of female subjectivity with "feeling");[12] and 3) this poetics is acutely aware of writing and reading as acts which both depend on and reinforce a sense of concrete limited community (as opposed to the ideal of a polis or Longinian tribunal of great minds) within which it is plausible to imagine "a free sharing of meanings and interests, a place for meeting the world without defenses" – texts are not performances but "silent conversations or webs of relationship to which each reader might bring her own confidences" (97).

Here then a poetics clearly committed to certain qualities of agency provides the obvious grounds for an alternative canon. But that clarity also makes it evident how thin this model of agency is compared to what the traditional canon both relies on and promises to develop. We begin to see the force of the claim that once a model must rely so strongly on differences rather than seeking potential universals it has to exclude features which are almost as important as what it stresses to any sense of the complexity of our psychic make-up or of the possible uses to which we might put our reading. Lipking's canon would have to exclude those features of Louise Labé's poetry which reach for transcendental neoPlatonic resonances as well as much of the Victorian sense of public life fundamental to

George Eliot. The problem lies in how he must separate femaleness from some more general sense of human needs, and powers, if only to understand what particular claims this isolating will sanction. For whatever the reason, the consequences that emerge prove almost as limiting as if we had to define an alternative canon based on some common assumptions about maleness (where perhaps our only undebateable paradigms would be Hemingway and Mailer).

Let me propose a simple practical test which should make it possible for a wide variety of specific circles of value to find common ground: would even most women familiar with the alternatives be willing to replace the traditional canon at its various levels with one whose criteria for inclusion derived only from Lipking's general model of a woman's poetic? I think most answers would be negative – for reasons that lead both back to questions about agency and out to the various uses that a canon can play within a culture. Let me briefly elaborate four of those reasons. The first two take up different features of the possibility that a canon based on this poetic would be severely confining – in the content it transmitted and in the functions which it allowed the content to serve. Lipking's female poetic concentrates on those texts that we take to be continuous with private life and that enter into the kind of community we can imagine sharing private experiences. But I suspect most readers also want to engage imaginatively in the political and philosophical predicates that take form in public life, and most of us have at least some desires to explore the kinds of identity that using such predicates allows us to seek. So a canon responsive to those desires would not only reaffirm those differences in which we are heavily invested, it would also provide an imaginative grammar for trying out a range of imaginative positions to explore for the provisional identifications they can offer us, to use as ways of understanding other social agents, or to project as challenges against which one must better define one's own values. Second, these limitations are paralleled by an impoverished sense of the functions that canons perform and hence of the interests that they can satisfy. Lipking stresses those literary experiences that confirm one's identity within a supportive community of essentially like-minded individuals. This ignores the range of ways we might desire those identities which can only be achieved by imagining more remote and austere communities for whose approval we must perform up to certain limits. Many feminist critics would reply that such desires force us to confine ourselves to those disinterested and abstract reflective stances cultivated by a purely contemplative view of literary experience. But it seems both narrow and historically inaccurate to assume that we only fully participate in those works that either directly mirror our lives or that we can appropriate within that sphere. Rather we can participate intensely on many different levels in a text, whether that involves adapting our full personal investments to a process of momentarily bracketing our immediate concerns so that we can see ourselves from a distance, or engaging certain alienation effects, or encountering uncanny or sublime modes of presence which simply expel our naturalizing gestures (for example in late Beckett), or trying to understand what possible general typological and causal patterns might be manifest in certain ways of composing the art work. (We must remember that Kant's case for disinterest in the consequences of our ethical choices coexists with a very strong interest in being a rational person.) And when we move from how we experience art to what we make of those experiences, we have an interest in and power to engage the work as a provocation leading us to attempt extending our sense of personal identity by taking on the standards of various communities and exploring who we become as we gain distance from our professional and domestic filiations. At times such projections provide us ways of resisting the claims that the marketplace or intellectual fashion put upon us, at times they help us to understand how and why others can seek different kinds of differences.

The third reason for demanding more than Lipking's proposal allows us leads from psychology to aesthetics, or more precisely to what aesthetics can contribute to our psychology. For if we are to pursue an interest in these projective dimensions of our lives – into social space and into possible selves, we must demand a wider range of imaginative forms and ways of relating to the real than those which are cultivated within the intimate communities that Lipking imagines. If we are concerned primarily with the arts as extensions of private life we are likely to concentrate on either the domain of dream and fantasy or on intensely mimetic works. The novel, at best complemented by confessional and domestic versions of personal poetry, becomes our arbiter of imaginative resources, and we end up seriously undervaluing all those works which address more antithetical or eloquent or constructivist versions of art's relation to life. We banish as formalism or as experiments in style those imaginative worlds that locate values in the capacity to concentrate on structuring energies rather than dramatic scenes, and we distrust or treat as immature those allegorical or intensely rhetorical works which make visionary demands upon us.

The final dissatisfaction that might arise is more complex and more contentious, but also more useful in showing how our deep assumptions about agency shape our concerns for canons. On the simplest level it is tempting to argue that Lipking's canon clearly trivializes those aspects of our sense of person which might go into strong political commitments. By stressing woman as victim he also composes a canon whose primary traits are those of withdrawal from all public space, almost as if he were self-consciously echoing Nietzsche's version of moralities developed by a defeated culture. For the expressive interests and the sense of community he idealizes at best generate or sustain an affective politics which simply cannot suffice for analyzing how that community is influenced by social forces or how it might influence those forces. However, this objection also cuts against the canon I am trying to defend, since that canon is at best indirectly political. To expect a literary canon to serve political purposes is to risk more than one gains because the project requires us to suppress a wide range of works capable of serving alternative functions, yet it would at best yield imaginative terms less useful than many other discourses in helping us gain an adequate analytic grasp of the social and political situation. Yet there is another kind of quasi-political blindness in Lipking's case which does bring out by contrast the force of the traditional canon. One of the subjects basic to the discourse of this woman's community would be the phenomenon of oppression in all its practical forms. But by confining our imaginative framework to woman's writing and to a specific set of personal stances, this community would not have a full grasp of how we have come to have such investments in concepts of oppression or perhaps even of the full dynamics of oppression and of what becomes available as we manage to overcome that dynamics. Consider for example the ways in which a Dante or a Blake or a even a Joyce make visible the terms by which we come to enslave ourselves and, at the other pole, how those terms sustain by contrast the sense of paradisical self-possession that these writers build to – a sense, by the way, that Emily Dickinson also offers if we are allowed by our aesthetic to stress the constructivist features of her poetry. But if we confine ourselves to Lipking's homogeneous community, the art women build of their concrete encounters with oppression could not be sufficiently responsive to the religious roots of the related concepts or to the range of states which those religious roots envisioned as our reason for devoting ourselves to its overthrow. These women could not, in other words, make what H.D. does of the allegorical and mythic frameworks of their heritage or what Adrienne Rich develops from the models of assertive identity fostered by poets like Milton and Yeats.

III

What good is a deep imaginative grasp of oppression and its fictive opposites when the oppression is not materially changed? More to the point, how can I handle the fact that the canon I am defending, seems on the side of those oppressors because it relies on those traditional values and psychological principles which have the effect of maintaining a wide variety of economic and social injustices. This effect is not merely the result of abstract statements. Traditional canons play a substantial role in reproducing elites, who then try to keep for themselves the time, the education, and the social interrelations they can purchase with such social capital.[13] Thus we have then still to face the third, and probably the most difficult theme of difference responsible for contemporary distrust of claims for the traditional canon – the effect of those differences in status and class which are preserved and fostered by canonical hierarchies.

For the abstract analysis of these differences we need turn to John Guillory's use of theorists like Foucault, Macherey, and Bourdieu. Rather than concern ourselves with the specific content of competing claims about literary values we ought to examine the underlying discursive and social formations giving the very formulation about value its force. Then we will see that traditional claims about the canon serve ultimately to reproduce social relations in accord with the desires of the class that has social hegemony (494). Those class interests in discursive power have as their primary function the wielding of a "symbolic violence" (502) that imposes an "unproblematic image of a universalized literacy not exhibited by any social formation" (485). And once that violence takes hold it has the concrete effects so painstakingly traced by Bourdieu's analyses: the interests of those with cultural capital create a wide range of positions and beliefs that reinforce the prevailing economy while dispossessing those not favored by the prevailing model of literacy (494 ff.).[14]

Unfortunately I see no way to engage the issues on this level of abstraction. Once theorists are programmatic in their insistence that all questions about values are essentially moments within social struggle there is no way to make counterassertions without becoming as abstract as I did in my first essay on the canon. And even that does little more than confirm the polarities reinforcing the sense of irreducible struggle. We need concrete issues where the competing claims can be tested, and perhaps shareable interests elicited by the discussion. Therefore I shall turn here to those who confine their charges of symbolic violence to the particular issue of elitism, and I shall concentrate on that version of the charge which criticizes the defenders of the traditional canon for cultivating sharp distinctions between "serious" and "middle-brow" or "popular" literature. At stake is whether one can defend the modes of elitism fostered by claims for the authority of a traditional canon as not merely the imposition of values peculiar to intellectuals, often only to academic literary intellectuals, on a populace that would not on their own make even remotely similar choices.

Such a defense will not be easy. Its traditional intellectual sanctions have been severely challenged by those like Barbara Herrnstein Smith who argue convincingly that all idealizations must be understood as choices within contingent circumstances and so are to be evaluated only in empirical, functional terms. Thus hierarchies one might pose about literary works cannot be derived from hierarchies we attribute to some shared potential in human nature. Instead we are bound to the basic principles of the social sciences – that differences are simply differences, with any proposed hierarchy simply the effort of one interpretive community to dominate another. Those principles in turn carry a good deal of weight because their authority does not rest simply on abstractions. They are beginning to inspire a literary criticism willing to do the kind of painstaking analysis necessary to show that what the hierarchists dismiss as popular or sensational or mere fantasy in fact does substantial cultural work. Feminist scholars like Jane Tompkins, Kathy Davidson, and Janice Radway have insisted that we pay attention to the enormous influence such writing wields and that we see how "sentimental" fiction in fact served and serves educational roles for its audience.

Let us take as our example of the impact this work has on theorizing about the canon the following passage from Janice Radway's analysis of "the social construction of taste." Her specific subject is the editorial processes by which the editors at the Book-of-the-Month Club make decisions about the "serious" fiction they will offer to their members:

To dismiss the middle range as products of a fundamental insufficiency, therefore as the result of a certain incompetence, is to accomplish several other goals simultaneously, all of which have relevance to the self-interest of those making the distinction. It is to state, first, that there is a single hierarchy of value in which all verbal products are ranged and that all such works aspire to the highest position. It is also to affirm the validity and preeminence of that single set of criteria against which all works are measured and thus to insist that there is only one appropriate way to read. Finally it is to value reflexively and in a hierarchical way those individuals who are able to recognize such value and to appreciate it by reading properly. To label the club middlebrow, therefore, is to damn it with faint praise and to legitimate the social role of the intellectual who has not only the ability but also the authority to make such distinctions and to dictate them to others. ... The easy critical dismissal of the Club and other "popularizers" is an act of exclusion that banishes those who might mount even the most minimal of challenges to the culture and role of the contemporary intellectual by proclaiming their own right to create, use, and value books for different purposes. ... It seems probable, therefore, that for a significant number of Club members, books play quite a different role in their lives and serve other purposes than they do for people who make their living producing, analyzing, and distinguishing among cultural products. ("On the Uses of 'Serious' Fiction" 518-19)

Each of her three basic assertions raises serious questions for those defending the traditional canon. But in developing each one I think she takes on a good deal more ideological baggage than her sociological analysis can support, especially in her description of the arguments posed by the defenders of the traditional canon. So it becomes possible in considering each of those to set the record straight and make clear those functions which might justify an elitist position, if only within those domains where we speak of forming taste and interpretive abilities.

Radway's first claim is that proponents of a traditional canon seek a single rank ordered hierarchy of values for all literature. That is simply false, because it reifies what must be a much more supple and flexible process. The hierarchies that concern those proponents are much less like deciding where something is on a ranked list than they are like deciding relative to function whether something can play in a certain league. Within the league value is assumed, so that comparative discourses can take place in more complex and provocative ways, for which the paradigm might be the contrasts between Milton and Shakespeare or between Dryden and

Pope central to eighteenth century criticism. And because the mechanics of value are in effect functions of fields of relation rather than hierarchical lists, there is nowhere near the imperialism that Radway detects. If there is a problem with canonical hierarchies it is with how much they simply ignore rather than with how much they bother to rank. For the traditionalists tend to care only about a very limited set of functions connected to educational frameworks or mystiques of *Bildung* (including those by which writers train themselves), and hence with how texts can be said to create and foster those tastes which then are invoked as arbiters of educational policy.

This stress on education and this tendency towards Olympian distance then make Radway's second charge the much more important one – that a defense of the traditional canon entails proclaiming that "there is only one proper way to read." Here I must grant her point, but primarily on levels so abstract as to be almost tautological (that is, that there is for the canon only one way to read in the same sense that wearing clothes is the only proper way to dress). In fact the idealizing of educational functions is compatible with a wide range of readerly stances. The most we can charge is that traditionalists do believe there are some ways of reading which are not compatible with their sense of the social roles which the canon can foster. For my evidence with regard to these assertions I need only point to Radway's own evidence, where we see both that intellectuals have competing paradigms for reading which overlap with those beyond the academy and that those ways of reading cannot be equated with aestheticism or with a mania for ranking. In order to differentiate her editors from academic intellectuals she is careful to point out how they insist on moral categories like personality and how they refuse "the enshrinement of the aesthetic as something valuable in and for itself": "Having thus assured communion and participation, it [their view of the artistic] must provide the occasion for moral and ethical judgments which can be turned reflectively on the reader and later used as guidelines for behavior" (537). Such formulations however would satisfy most academic intellectuals who are not specialists in modern literature and not a few of those specialists who share a good deal of their demands on literature with Arnold and Lukács – I wish I had Radway's formulation for the conclusion of my own *Act and Quality*. So the result of her effort is not to reduce the canon to sociology but to demonstrate some of the competing values that generate controversy and make it necessary for individual intellectuals to take responsibility for their distinctive positions. That competition in turn requires our turning to more idealized and speculative contexts within which the necessary discriminations can be worked out. We can not simply point to who holds beliefs or gesture at covert interests the beliefs might serve, we must examine the formulations transforming those beliefs into functional accounts with claims on public interests.

Radway's third claim leads us into the terms we shall need for these functional judgments because it makes clear the limitations in treating phenomena like elitism primarily by focusing on the play of sociological forces involved in groups attempting to legitimate and extend their own powers. For there might in fact be good reasons for granting those groups the relevant powers, especially if in fact the powers involve significant checks and balances. Radway will not consider that. In her view canons are so hierarchical because their primary function is to legitimate the social power of intellectuals. But there seems to me no good reason why one cannot admit that canons legitimate intellectuals and then go on to ask whether that observation somehow delegitimates that legitimacy? Why should intellectuals not have desirable social functions? And what function better suits their training than the discipline of reflecting discursively on the values people hold and the reasons that might lead to changing those values. Of course if we consider such reflections to be a means to "dictate" those values, as Radway does, we will be less than sanguine about such authority. But that assertion seems a little strong, a result perhaps of the literary imagination inflating sociological research.

Suppose we test Radway's assertion by asking ourselves whether we would prefer to live in a society where there were no intellectuals responsible for getting us to consider the nature of our values, the limits of our "tribal" commitments, and the possible alternative values available to us? I cannot imagine very many of us choosing the world without intellectuals, even if it escapes elites. For the alternative would in fact not be without symbolic violence (it is no accident that critics of symbolic violence like Guillory provide no alternatives), it would merely lack forms of social reproduction enabling us to criticize and recast the symbolic forms governing the dominant forms of social life. There is no culture without cultural reproduction. But there can be different qualities of cultural reproduction and different levels of the cultures that we see playing against one another in these reproductive processes. So rather than making theatrical, global gestures against the inevitable, the obvious choice is to cultivate social institutions capable of developing and testing reasons for fostering or blocking the projected functions and dominant interests which specific social practices provide. The terms for such choices, I hasten to add, have already been developed by Enlightenment thinkers as they faced, and managed to pass on, the need to create a class of intellectuals capable of resisting those entrenched interests whose refusal of public argument led far beyond merely symbolic violence.[15]

Granting intellectuals these reflective functions would be extremely dangerous if Radway were correct in treating them as if they formed only one social group with a common ideology. That however seems to me very difficult to demonstrate. One must admit that most intellectuals are perforce committed to some form of communicative rationality, and they do tend to have the kind of stakes in the prevailing order that Herrnstein Smith points to. But the former is not an arbitrary construction of values, while the latter is hardly a disqualifying condition because it applies to almost all of us, and indeed perhaps should apply because if we are to call for change we should share the cost that our demands might exact. So there is no scandal in Radway's observation, not unless she can develop a plausible account of intellectuals that explains their possible social functions without granting them a commitment to the powers and practices necessary to cultivate some form of communicative rationality. Should we prefer that they have no ideals governing the form of their work so that there is no way to criticize party hacks or *agents provocateurs*? And can we really confine our reflections to a domain sufficiently abstract to be characterized only by their common interests? Their deepest common interest may be the constant presence of productive differences within those very general parameters. Consider for example the very different approaches to the concept of a canon with which we have been grappling, and then imagine including in our colloquy figures like Irving Howe, Leo Bersani, Robert Reich, Irving Kristol, William Bennett, or Andy Warhol. Yet all the figures we have been mentioning are intellectuals in the sense that their mode of production is the dissemination and consumption of ideas, and they all share pretty much the same structure of material benefits from that mode of production. But it would take a pretty complex argument to derive from that the further claim that they are determined by those similarities to make the same judgments about which aspects of the social institutions affecting literary taste we will foster and for what reasons.

For those claims we need to shift our attention from origins, even social origins, to the practical options that face us. Nothing that we have said changes the fact that the traditional canon is an elitist notion and does insist on basic distinctions between high culture and popular literature (distinctions based largely on the degree to which authors have some version of that canon in mind as part of their audience). So the only option a defender of that canon has is to stop apologizing for the fact and ask what shareable interests can be served by embracing that elitism. In this case the best answer may be to make it clear what interests are not very well served. For it seems to me simply an error to insist as most of its critics do that the traditional canon serves the interests primarily of those who hold economic power and positions of political influence in contemporary American society. The canon does not threaten those interests in any immediate material way and it is compatible with the bourgeois financial position of most academics. But that is as far as one can go. One needs simply imagine a discussion of Homer or Dante at Bebe Rebozo's villa in Bimini or on the ranch at Santa Barbara to realize how much difference there is between high culture and socio-economic hegemony, especially where literature is in question. Business does support the performing arts (tepidly), but it is difficult to see how it thereby gains more than a general respectability. The sad fact is that the dominant ideology is well in place in America because the majority are sufficiently well off to prefer to protect their gains over experimenting with change in any aspect of their lives. With such commitments to comfort, they simply do not want to be challenged by anything that might entail shifting the parameters of their self-regard. As evidence for that condition one needs simply to ask oneself whether in a nation with America's reading habits changes in canons would change the distribution of social power in any way that was not a reflection of changes that had already taken place (like the emergence of women in the work force)?

But changes in canons do affect individuals. So it is in the sphere of education and the cultivation of imaginative attitudes that the serious functional issues arise. We must ask how competing versions of the canon can play roles in a range of pedagogical practices – from the structuring of various levels of formal education, to the images of making ourselves better readers and perhaps better persons that we develop from our encounters with literature, to the writers' own concerns for mastering their art and projecting ideal audiences for their work. In this regard it becomes possible to argue that the traditional canon's frank embrace of elitism gives it direct access to two important and closely related functions. On the one hand that elitism demands resistance to prevailing mores. For it presents a range of attitudes and ideals and states of intensity preserved by the culture precisely because they are not available within contemporary practices and yet remain capable of haunting it with possibilities not realized. Then, on the other hand, the canon can offer a grammar promising as the reward for such resistance a set of models and provocations and communal identifications enabling us to explore new aspects of identity and give rich and contoured explanations for our choices.

Unfortunately claims like these have been around almost as long as the most ancient elements of the canon, so they become very difficult to trust. So how do we show that they have plausible claims upon us? In one sense there is no arguing the case; there is only setting forth the ideals as ideals, showing how there is nothing impractical about them, and asking people to reflect on those imaginative experiences that have led people they know to pursue values that the people come to respect or even to envy. But it may help to clarify the functions of those idealizations if we compare the possible claims on us of the high canon to those that might derive from alternative educational and artistic frameworks of values. Suppose then we ask the kinds of questions necessary to compare values – questions about what versions of education we can imagine actually governing our own goals or those of our children, about what we can imagine using as sources of wisdom and as principles through which we can imagine justifying our commitments to ways of reading, and even principles we can imagine making possible a better world once some of the necessary political changes get accomplished.

When I planned this essay I thought these comparisons would clinch my case. It seemed clear that most of the alternatives, especially the turn to "popular" literature, were so bound to the principles of cultural criticism that no one could defend actually basing first person identifications upon the specific texts. How could persons be satisfied to channel all the idealizing force attributed to the traditional canon into a body of work that they themselves almost always read not as their own imaginative projection and testing of ways of thinking and attaching to values but as sociological information? What we read as sociological information in order to expose blindness or indict late monopoly capitalism is not what we turn to

for wisdom or long term projections of attitudes to be cultivated and communities before whom to seek personal identities.

Of course I still think that such literature will not perform the necessary educational functions. But the case is by no means as clear as I had
hoped. For now many of the best critics no longer read that material primarily in third-person terms but ask us to see how it serves educational
roles for its audience and manages by qualities negated within the high
canon to develop large and morally significant cultural communities. If
one is to make the case I had planned, one must argue about different
qualities of first person experience and of the cultural grammars provided
by the various canons. For my case this entails two basic strategies. First I
must call attention to the difficulties critics still encounter in making first
person identifications with the educational roles that they trace in popular
writing. There remains a good deal of patronizing distance in even the best
of this criticism. (Radway, for example, manages in her last page to turn
respect for the editors into a ritual analysis of how those people remain
dominated from outside by "constraints that their own class is responsible
for calling into being.") And when others flamboyantly identify with the
principles of feeling cultivated by that literature, their prose can get downright embarrassing if they also try to use such values as means for accom-
plishing tasks like earning distance from other people or providing alternatives to argument. Then my second strategy becomes feasible. I suggest
that there are good reasons for that distance, reasons that inhere in the
difficulty of adopting any culture developed in opposition to hegemonic
values as one's exemplar within mainstream culture. For a literature
developed by those who resist what they take to be oppressive hegemonic
values will itself have to struggle with the degree to which the oppression
limits the nature and the depth of the alternative values that it proposes.
As we see perhaps most clearly in the fears of the early Anglo-Irish
Modernists, the literature of the oppressed provides marvelous imaginative freedom and modes of sympathy occluded in the high culture, but it
also has strong tendencies to escapist fantasies, to cynical and defensive
attitudes towards spiritual states that the mainstream culture can make
available, and to those forms of self-repetition that occur when there are
not strong critical traditions. Attitudes developed to survive oppression
may not offer the best principles for developing individual powers in a
more permissive society. In fact it may be precisely those cultural traditions which make it especially important also to have a traditional high

canon from a broader cultural base which enables one to stage one's own ambivalences in more comprehensive and often more intensely dramatic imaginative terms.

This high canon is not without its fantasies, its unwarranted cynicisms, and its repetitiousness. But it does have richer ways of handling its own limitations, primarily because in the West the traditional canon has an abstractness and a variety far less confining and much more flexible than one finds in any more local culture. There is almost no danger that one will identify solely with its terms because there is such historical distance and because there is so much contradiction within the canon that it serves more as grammar than as code of values, more as example of possible intensities and modes of self-representation than as vehicle imposing any particular model of behavior. Moreover this canon has negotiations over the idea and ideal of authority built into it – both in terms of what the works themselves seek and in terms of the critical arguments about those works which we also inherit. One can use those reflections on authority as part of one's account of one's own choices, so the logic of seeking identifications and testing identities is fundamental to the very educational processes encouraged by that canon. One might even say that what makes this canon preferable as a framework for making first person commitments to literary traditions is that it includes within it the principles that sanction its own elitist claims. Its model of self-representation is based on fostering resistance to established habits that do not make intense enough demands on our capacities, and its means for turning that resistance into positive achievements is to define processes by which we explore and test projected selves that we then come to represent as ideals we are committed to pursuing. Thus the canon must be elitist because it must hold out imaginative attitudes which do not reduce to sociological categories or allow us to distance ourselves comfortably from them by treating them as explainable within clear social parameters. The very idea of fostering better or richer selves requires our sustaining idealizable frameworks.

Now however I am driven to the most problematic aspect of my case – for whom does it make sense to propose so idealized a canon? By casting the canon as the means by which we in effect struggle for what can be elite in our own imaginative and practical lives I raise the doubt that there are indeed very few people who have either the intellectual interest, the leisure, or the desires appropriate to the picture I have been composing.

This picture might prove compelling for a Yeats or a Frye or a Burke, but not for most of those students and acquaintances whom we encounter in our practical lives. For them it is likely that the most we arbiters of academic literary standards can hope to provide is a bourgeois community filtered through some form of popular literature.

I am bourgeois enough to find this a compelling claim, especially since I despair of any substantial improvement in American political life and hope for little more than slightly more civilized conditions of cultural consumption and hence of our human interactions. But I am not sure that even that becomes possible when we let our cultural institutions ignore the traditions which define those standards of civility. More important, there remain significant shortcomings to this smug picture of student and civic complacency. In fact many people who go through liberal arts educations do have at least their abstract values changed. Ironically because America does not have traditions of student unrest, the roles students played in resistance to the war in Vietnam and especially in the less glamorous resistance to racial injustice must be attributed in large part to their educations (at least in the early years of those movements). And many of us do learn from the canon that our psyches have certain capacities for intensity, for moral identifications, and for living in relation to the values of idealized communities even though there is no marketplace payoff.

Perhaps then rather than reject the canon because we cannot imagine an audience for it, we ought to begin teaching it as if there were a significant potential audience eager to find literature serving as equipment for living and sufficiently disillusioned with the prevailing popular versions of that equipment to invest in new models for the psyche as well as new communities to which they give the power of conferring identities. Then the traditional canon will no longer appear either a form of symbolic violence or a repository of a set of dead monuments preventing us from taking up the real cultural work offered by demystified contemporary theory. Then we might without embarrassment impose some of our critical energies on the blindness in our rhetorics of blindness and the complacency in our myths of community through difference. And then when we ask for whom we propose the canon we can say that we propose it in the name of all those who care, or whom one as an educator imagines can and should be led to care, that we not let the humanities give all to its present and come to this:

> The traditional – idealist, humanist, genteel – tendency to isolate or
> protect certain aspects of life and culture, among them works of art and
> literature, from consideration in economic terms has had the effect of
> mystifying the nature – or, more accurately, the dynamics – of their
> value. In view of the arbitrariness of the exclusion, it is not surprising
> that the languages of aesthetics and economics nevertheless tend to
> drift toward each other and that their segregation must be constantly
> patrolled. ("Contingencies of Value" 17)

It seems to me that anyone sensitive to what might be called the Julian
Schnabel phenomenon would be a little less eager to see the borders
between the aesthetic and the economic erased. Some patrols are well
worth maintaining despite the considerable expense and risk, for reasons
that I think Smith's essay makes quite clear. Even though Smith is much
more generous in the predicates to which she will attribute value than
most of those using this economic language (perhaps in part because of
her own training in the traditional canon), the attitude here reveals what I
take to be two crucial reasons for the very defensiveness that she attacks,
and hence for preserving the instruments making that defensiveness possible. First there is a crucial equivocation between economics in the classical
sense, where all questions of exchange or function are part of one's parameters, and economics in the modern sense where there is sanctioned only
a very small set of motives for evaluating those exchanges.[16] Then there is
the work she asks that narrow language of motives to do. Is it really true
that the basic reason for resisting the language of economics, especially in
the second sense, is to protect the unholy trio of idealism, humanism, and
gentility (and are they linked here as alternatives or as appositives)? If we
turn to literary history, especially to the romantic and modern canon, we
find a range of authors all concerned with different ways that the language
of economic motive threatens not gentility (snake oil sellers can be gen-
teel) but our ability to describe and to care about the intensity and depth
and moral nature of those human actions that are not intended to be
measured in accord with the rationality of the economic calculator. In philosophy that tradition has led to John Rawls's powerful critique of even
the best utilitarian calculi, and in the arts it has been fundamental to the
entire range of experiments in positing other models for how we can
dispose ourselves towards the world and towards other people.

Notes

1. In the last section of my first essay I try to develop three abstract principles which
    usually govern the arguments used in addressing these challenges – arguments for
    the self-subsuming particularization by which the text tries to interpret the world it
    projects, for the representativeness of its grasp of the problems it confronts and the
    characters that it uses for embodying that grasp, and for the ways in which those
    exemplars become projectible in contemporary experience. These criteria matter
    for two reasons – they still impose significant and important demands on authors,
    and they at least begin to focus the kind of discussion that can try to answer
    challenges like John Guillory's which simply deny that the aesthetic can contribute
    to human freedom because that is a matter of material conditions. It seems to me
    that by trying to show how minds can come to richer senses of experience and begin
    to realize the demands on their own self-representations which a high culture
    establishes we also begin to show how lives can differ substantially in quality while
    sharing the same socio-economic conditions. If we wait for the changes he wants
    before we allow ourselves terms like freedom we will have to live for a long time
    with a terribly narrow and a terribly bitter vocabulary, and I see no prospects
    making it reasonable to pay that price. For Guillory's arguments see his "Canonical
    and Non-canonical: A Critique of the Current Debate," 487 and note 4.

2. I am indebted for this point to Kim Johnson Bogart in conversation.

3. This claim is not incompatible with Smith's insistence on a functional language.
    However, as I shall argue later, the claim cannot be sufficiently developed in terms
    of the particular functions that she sees the past playing for and in the present. For
    example, she assumes, like Kolodny, that any authority that the text may gain neces-
    sarily derives from its flexibility over time. That seems to me a severe oversimplifi-
    cation. Of course we must apply the text to different situations, so there will be
    translations that take place. But we can make that translation either because we
    read the text for different functions or because we try to understand what it said for
    its author and for other authors that engaged it and then we make our applications.
    In that case the text can have an authority which forces us to reconsider our own
    assumptions rather than simply impose them on what we read. In fact it is that kind
    of case which makes sense of the very idea of authority and of how writers try to
    dignify their own enterprises – consider how Wordsworth engaged Milton, or Yeats
    Shelley, or Eliot Dante reading Vergil.

4. I would like to cite in this regard an essay of mine which tries to show how re-
    covering Wordsworth from certain contemporary languages helps us understand an
    imaginative ideal of eloquence which promises in its turn to clarify and even to
    direct new directions in contemporary American poetry. For another, very different
    perspective on how the prevailing modes in contemporary criticism ignore or limit
    the actual concerns of contemporary writing see Marjorie Perloff, "Canons to the
    Right of us, Canons to the Left of Us."

5. Hazard Adams, "Canons: Literary Criteria/Power Criteria" is very good on how
    canonical works can have an antithetical force that challenges the present, especial-
    ly in so far as it wants to use predicates based on the workings of social power. But
    he confuses the overall resistance that the canon offers as a grammar of possibil-

ities with a demand that each text within the canon have this "antithetical" or "visionary" status – which is to confine us to a – antic canon, to make mystery or plurisignification the only model for ethical significance, and to ignore the degree to which canons matter because of the very precise, recuperable sense that the works make or definitiveness that their images muster. The canon itself can be antithetical because many of the works it preserves have other functions.

6. A recent essay by Brooke Thomas, "The New Historicism and the Privileging of Literature," provides a very good example of how these common interests become visible through the limitations that arise as we try to work out the possible claims that the new historicism can make about historical differences. Thomas takes most new historicism to task for not having a good answer to the positivist historian's question – why study so unrepresentative and fundamentally subjective a realm as literature if we desire to understand the historical shape of particular cultural complexes. As the historian Lee Benson put it, "No set of systematic propositions have yet been developed to define the relationship between literature and life, and ... historians, therefore, cannot now use literature as a valid and reliable indicator of public opinion" (25). So if we are to show how literature does "cultural work" we must be able to show that in history literature performs a distinctive social function. Then he tries to develop that function by concentrating on a particular kind of self-consciousness about language fostered by literary attitudes, because he can then show that such modes of attention manage to resist particular ideologies and thus help transform the present into a new future (33).

What fascinates me is how much Thomas must modify his own historicist assumptions towards versions of a perpetual present basic to defenders of traditional canons like Pound and Eliot in order to develop that social function for literature. To be sure, Thomas refuses to renounce the historicist language of social production as social critique, but this insistence obviously prevents him from developing the full range of modes of connection that have in fact been claimed in the past as literature's social function. In other words, Thomas wants to speak about social functions performed within history, but he wants contemporary theory to be the arbiter of what the social functions can be. Yet his case for criticism having to locate those social functions is far more powerful and more capacious than his narrow interpretation of those functions allows. For example in order to stress functions bound to concerns for language and ideological critique he can only attribute the present tense of literature to a spirit of play, rather than to the very processes of imaginative reflection (34-37). Then he takes from Benjamin a very suggestive model for a historical inquiry offering an "antifoundational foundation" from which we can reflect on our historical situation" (39): criticism must preserve the possibility of texts "bringing forth the time which recognizes them – that is our time – within the time that produced them" (43). But when he goes on to describe that relation he has only standard cliches from critics like Macherey stressing the capacity of the text's productive forces to so engage the present that it opens up the seams within the prevailing ideology and thus makes new expression possible. But on this basis he can do no more than promise on another occasion to develop a fuller analysis of temporality as his means of showing "what it is about literary texts that lends them to creating such a critical perspective on the present" (44). I suspect that if his case is to be adequate it will come out like the concerns of early

Eliot and Arnold, those reactionary antifoundationalists, who tried to show how it was much more than literary language, a spirit of play, or an emphasis on the seams in prevailing ideologies that gave the past its claims on the present. More important, this case will have to recognize the fact that critique only has significant force when this past not only reveals seams in the present but actually proposes alternative ways to think, ways that cannot arise within even a modified new historicism.

7.   Adams's essay makes a very interesting but I think mistaken point on this question of the role of literary criteria. He rightly thinks they tend to be applied too narrowly and thus seem to justify invoking the opposite claim that the real criteria for the canon are simply power criteria. He posits his ideal of the antithetical quality of canonical works as a contrary to that entire opposition. But by continuing the notion of single oppositions, rather than fields of complex predicates, he is forced into terms that take on an absoluteness incompatible with the variety that the canon offers. In fact Adams's oppositions lead him to something very close to a sense of the canon as a quasi-theological repository for transcendental experience. I must confess to sharing that form of secular religion, but I hope as a private vice and not as a theoretical ground, in part because once one invokes the transcendental one cannot, as Adams wants to do, also claim that the canon has ethical force. Once the works are given the status of being so different from ordinary experience, even to the degree of warranting a language of disinterest, one ends up with a version of the problem that Kant's own transcendental ethic has – how do you get back to empirical experience: either we can all treat one another as antithetical, and then the texts loose their specialness, or we must reserve that attitude for works of genius, which may include some lives, but then one has lost the universalizing terms of an ethic.

8.   Frank Lentricchia notes this problem of making a stress on single differences do explanatory cultural work in his exchange with Sandra Gilbert and Susan Gubar in *Critical Inquiry*. And indeed there is no better evidence for the problem. Their *No Man's Land* documents ad nauseam male fear and resentment of the emerging powers of woman writers, but offers no clear arguments as to how this fear and resentment in fact outweighs other factors in influencing the literature or even how it had influence in its own right. I try to show how similar problems of handling competing claims arise for the very different absolutizing of difference that one finds in Jean-François Lyotard's recent work in my essay "Towards a Postmodern Theory of Justice: Or how Lyotard teaches us to read Rawls."

9.   I am not unaware of the difficulties involved in this effort to explain female difference by resorting once again to male names. I even confess to the probability that I am more comfortable with Lipking because he argues in the old ways (and probably retains some of the old biases). But I also have what I hope are good reasons for this choice. At least I cannot be accused of misunderstanding Lipking because of my gender (at least so long as I acknowledge now that he is making a purely hypothetical case to which he does not subscribe as a general theory of the canon). And he is quite good in setting up the issues in a way that allows us to formulate arguments and make the kind of comparisons we need if we are to use testable reasons to justify our actions. Moreover in using his work we find ourselves testing the

relation between difference and shareable identifications about which I have just been speaking: to the degree Lipking proves an adequate spokesperson for the differences basic to a canon based on feminist principles, he provides a concrete example of how complexly woven those differences may be with other, perhaps more capacious features of human agency that can make and use provisional identifications. Finally, in so far as I know of feminist objections to his argument, they concentrate his claims about the centrality of abandonment and need, claims that I too find problematic, for reasons that are pertinent to our discussion. After making his general claims about a woman's poetic Lipking focuses on the ideas of Madame de Staël in order to develop the most melodramatic features of his case. But the very notion of developing a poetic or a canon on one person's principles, or on one thematic attitude, clearly misses the whole point of how canons must be embedded in history, and thus characterized by the kind of contradictions that historical contingency and a range of geniuses will produce.

10. Here is Lipking's synthetic statement: "Poetry is the expression of a life, personal, incomplete, and proportioned to a self; employing whatever language and conventions one has been allowed to acquire; presented in fragments, and achieving, through sharing the emotions of loneliness and abandonment, a momentary sense of not being alone" ("Aristotle's Sister" 101).

11. Jane Tompkins's "Me and My Shadow" is not so careful, so she provides a good example of the limitations inherent in that emphasis on a single psychological principle as the basis for a poetics, or critical stance, or model of self-representation. In her essay the emphasis on feeling is asked to perform the following tasks – to sanction a mode of discourse that does not share the old tone and level by which we create the sense that reality exists and that there is thus an "authority effect" by which some claims come much closer to approximating that reality (175), to declare her independence of epistemology and hence of her husband for whom that is more "his game" than it is hers (176), and to allow us to speak in terms of anger and love that we are taught "are mushy and sentimental and smack of cheap popular psychology": "The disdain for popular psychology and for words like *love* and 'giving' is part of the police action that academic intellectuals wage ceaselessly against feeling, against women, against what is personal" (178). Such openness on Tompkins's part strikes me as admirable. But even the openness becomes disturbing when we realize its dependence on the assumption that somehow the self we express immediately is the one to which one must attribute feelings, feelings which then must be set in opposition to the more reflective dimensions or our capacities for acting and expressing ourselves. While we all have such feelings, the terrible oversimplifications of her case suggest that it is not here that we in fact possess our individuality, not here that one can win independence in any way that has more content than the simple assertion, and not here that we fully appreciate who we are as emotional beings. What she calls a police action against popular psychology goes back at least to Dante's Paolo and Francesca and Shakespeare's Malvolio, that is back to the fear that those feelings which are not deeply considered are probably not those which distinguish the individual or individual relations from very gross emotional categories. There may be nothing in "reality" that sanctions intellectual's dismay with popular psychology, but there is a great deal in those rich experiences that are pre-

served in a canon, and indeed that reflective engagement on our lives provides, which indicates how reductive are the concepts of self, of other, and of the possible terms of community that those languages promulgate. If Tompkins wants her independence on those terms she is entitled to it, but to cheapen the domain of feeling or the concept of personal independence by relying on them is to make both literary criticism and popular culture far more banal domains than they can be – a large price to pay for independence.

12.   Barbara Herrnstein Smith nicely captures what the traditional canon seems to justify as social privilege:

> The characteristic resources of the culturally dominant members of a community include access to specific training and the opportunity and occasion to develop not only competence in a large number of cultural codes but also a large number of diverse (or "cosmopolitan") interests. The works that are differentially re-produced, therefore, will often be those that gratify the exercise of such competencies and engage interests of that kind: specifically works that are structurally complex and in the technical sense information-rich – ... However much canonical works may be seen to question secular vanities such as wealth, social position, and political power, "remind" their readers of more elevated values and virtues, and oblige them to "confront" such hard truths and harsh realities as their own mortality and the hidden griefs of obscure people, they would not be found to please long and well if they were seen to undercut establishment interests *radically* or to support the ideologies that support them *effectively*. (33-34)

13.   This is not the occasion for an extended analysis of those like Bourdieu who try to develop coherent aesthetics for different classes. But I cannot resist asking the reader to be wary of the degree to which a loose sense of the aesthetic is used to characterize "bourgeois or intellectual interests." In fact the most avant-garde aesthetics are as radical in their claims for presence and participation as is any popular aesthetic, but often on very different grounds – Mondrian is hard to link to popular arts – and very few artists or critics use the idea of the aesthetic in a positive sense without at least bringing in all the models of content that attach to the concept through figures like Schiller. Again, this is not to say there is not a popular aesthetic, but it is to warn us to be wary of the kinds of values we use to distinguish it from other stances when in fact the differences are often matters of means or degrees of abstraction, if it makes sense at all to speak of so intellectualized a term as aesthetics for popular arts. Is there an aesthetics of soap operas? Yet there is very much a structure of investments basic to that art form (so perhaps there is even a canon, or will be).

14.   It is these Enlightenment defenses of the intellectual that I think engender the counter-Enlightenment spirit giving thinkers like Foucault and Lyotard their historical mission. But neither they nor their followers have made much effort to provide a full positive alternative to the Enlightenment. And, more important, both seem to me to cast their critique in terms strongly dependent on some of the most arrogant and most problematic features of Enlightenment thinking. It was the En-

lightenment that cultivated (or imposed) the *frisson* of a lucidity which could revel in the seductions afforded by using reason to cause scandals about reason. And it was a particular contradiction in Enlightenment thought (registered in the last chapter of *Les Mots et Les Choses*) that proved most useful in furthering that sense of scandal. For one can employ this rhetoric of symbolic violence, tribalism, and resisting the power of all institutional discourses because of the two incompatible principles that many of those thinkers projected as the grounds of the social order – that there is some original being possessed of a "natural" freedom, and that this freedom is always already determined by a will to power that then manifests itself as opposition to a society's efforts to impose acculturating structures upon it.

15. I cannot insist strongly enough that my quarrel with Smith stems from respect for her formidable intelligence because the clarity she can muster exacts as serious a price in the domain of literary theory as her exemplars have in social theory. In lieu of a full argument on the points I raise let me at least try to support my claims against her on two levels. The first is her tendency to offer functional accounts that are so general that they simply dissolve controversy into a description of the options, as if once we understood those the issue could be left to the struggle of preferences, and the second is a corollary tendency for the accounts to be terribly thin in their sense of what is at stake in our concerns about values. So while the theory does not demand it, there is a constant aura of reductiveness in her description of the choices available and the consequences attendant upon the options.

For an example of the first problem consider some of the passages I have already quoted, or the description of the two possible trajectories that might ensue for a work once it is given canonical status (31), or this effort to reverse traditional ways of formulating questions about literary value: "The value of a literary work is continuously produced and re-produced by the very acts of implicit and explicit evaluation that are frequently invoked as 'reflecting' its value and therefore as being evidence of it. In other words, what are commonly taken to be the *signs* of literary value are, in effect, also its *springs*. The endurance of a classic canonical author such as Homer, then owes not to the alleged transcultural or universal value of his works but, on the contrary, to the continuity of their circulation in a particular culture" (34). I think we must parse this as saying that Homer has had enduring value in our culture because Homer has had enduring value in our culture: what we thought were reasons for valuing him were in fact values already built into our reading habits. In the effort to undercut any attempt to characterize that value independently of its cultural contingencies we have all those contingencies simply swallowed up in meta-claim that is nothing but a classical vicious circle. There is no way to use this claim to include or exclude any subsequent arguments, and no way to refute it because every claim would be evidence of the continuity that she sees shaping our valuations. Yet Smith's passage does do a good deal of rhetorical work: by eliding the different or competing concerns which drive the circulation of values and which can certainly be compared, contrasted, resisted, etc., for reasons that we attribute to the text, she seriously reduces what can enter our discourse about the functions Homer's text has performed and can perform, perhaps for reasons that testify to the containing force of that Greek intelligence.

Both difficulties stem, I suspect, from Smith's specific model of human evaluative agency: "It follows from the conception of value outlined here that evaluations are not discrete acts or episodes punctuating experience but indistinguishable from the very processes of acting and experiencing themselves. ... For a responsive creature, to exist is to evaluate. We are always calculating how things 'figure' for us, always pricing them so to speak, in relation to the total economy of our personal universe. Throughout our lives, we perform a continuous succession of rapid-fire cost-benefit analyses. ..." (23). One can hardly disagree. But is this enough for a theoretical framework in which to make decisions about important matters? This seems to me to say that all a theory of value can do is point to the fact that we are always valuing. The important question, though, is not when we evaluate but how. And that entails breaking those decisions down into their components and positing structures that do or should influence the ways in which we make these choices. However within Smith's framework it seems that theory can do nothing but demystify more reified models of value and make clear what contingencies it is that underly our competing interests. There is no need for theory to worry about how we connect those processes of valuation to continuities of character and no need to create a structure explaining what is at stake in the various calculi that we allow to shape our judgment. That may suffice for an account of how markets work. It cannot even address those second-order domains where traditionally what we choose is inseparable from how we represent our choices. These are the domains for which canons are instrumental in supplying moral vocabularies for assessing the various qualities, so Smith's terms simply do not address the kinds of functions which must enter the choices we make about what in our past makes claims upon our present.

Reading 'Nasty' Great Books

Lilian R. Furst

The *New York Times* of 1 January 1989 recounts an amusing little story. At the end of a course on Great Books, the students were given a final examination that consisted of just two questions. The first was: "Which work read this semester did you dislike most?" and the second: "To what deficiencies in your intellect and character do you attribute this dislike?"

Whether this anecdote is true is immaterial. It serves well to reveal a certain mentality towards that cornerstone of American Liberal Arts education, the canon of the Great Books. On the one hand, pressures are increasing to expand a canon that is perceived as having hitherto been both limited and tendentious through the inclusion of minority and Third World texts. On the other hand, however, there is a persistent and deep-seated reluctance to scrutinize the canon in any basic way, such as, for instance, confronting a response of "dislike." The orthodox belief has been, as illustrated in those exam questions, that a failure to like the accepted canon could only be attributed to a deficiency in education. The implicit underlying assumption is that once Great Books have been adequately explained and properly grasped, they will *ipso facto* become likable. The better, i.e., more closely and discerningly one is able to read a text, the more one will see its depths and subtleties. To dislike the canon is therefore taken automatically as a sign of boorishness, without much inquiry into what is subsumed into the idea of an adequate explanation or a proper grasp, let alone a discerning reading.

Yet a pronounced negative approach is as valid a starting-point for critical exploration as a positive one, although it goes against the normative expectations for a work hallowed by the privilege of the canon. "Dislike" as a category comprises an ethical as well as an aesthetic criterion. The canon, indeed, has traditionally rested on the postulate of the supremacy of the aesthetic. To supersede such a supposition is out of the question for it is precisely the aesthetic qualities of a text that make it worth re-reading, in contrast to yesterday's local newspaper. But the presence of the ethical factor must also be acknowledged, parallel to our recognition of the import of the social, the cultural, and the political. All these diverse elements coalesce into our system of values, which in turn creates the context for our readings/misreadings and for the formation of the canon. In his recent book, *The Ethics of Reading*, J. Hillis Miller has argued that "there is a necessary ethical moment in the act of reading as such, a moment neither cognitive, nor political, nor social, nor interpersonal, but properly and independently ethical" (1). To heed this ethical moment offers one avenue of renewed inquiry into the canon.

The nature of the ethical moment is open to speculation. Miller delineates one possible approach in his question: "Does the ethical act of the protagonist inside the book correspond to the ethical acts the reading of the book generates outside the book?" (2). This is perhaps rather a simplistic formula for a complex relationship, as Miller himself seems to concede in the tentativeness of his proposal. His alternative model, while equally hypothetical, leaves greater leeway for sophisticated development: "there are analogies among all four of these ethical moments, that of the author, the narrator, the character, and the reader, teacher, critic, though what is the basis of these analogies, what *logos* controls them, remains to be interrogated" (9).

The analysis of these analogies may help towards a more precise understanding of apparently deviant reactions to the canon. This is what I propose to consider in relation to Flaubert's *Madame Bovary* and Thomas Mann's *Death in Venice*. I choose these as paradigmatic texts because they feature so frequently in Great Books courses, and tend to elicit the objection: "I hate this book! it's so nasty." These are not merely the complaints of mediocre undergraduates who find the reading hard going. Similar comments have come from highly literate and sensitive readers, though evidently in more refined terms. Matthew Arnold, for instance, excoriated *Madame Bovary* as a "work of petrified feeling" over which hangs an atmosphere of bitterness and impotence (Arnold 203). Nor are these strictures moral in the narrow sense of the word. In that respect there has been a radical change since 1857 when Flaubert was indicted for "offenses à la morale publique et à la religion," and also since 1911 when homosexuality and pedophilia were unmentionable topics. These moralistic concerns are no longer the crux of the issue nor the root of that instinctive repugnance that grows in some readers' minds and breeds a dislike of these Great Books.

A study of the ethical moment suggests that readers' alienation stems not from their ignorance or idiosyncratic prejudices, but rather from the narrator's posture vis-à-vis his protagonists and, by extension, us as readers. There is a correlation between the narrator's tactics and readers' responses, although it may comprise opposition alongside and even within identification when readers' growing need to dissociate themselves from the narrating voice causes a disjuncture between narrator and readers. So ultimately readers are stranded in a conflicted position, where they are able to admire the aesthetic brilliance of the artifact's construction, but remain nonetheless deeply troubled by its ethical implications, notably in regard to the narrator's role.

The unresolved tension between aesthetics and ethics is thematically central to *Death in Venice* as to *Madame Bovary*. In admittedly very different ways, the action of both pivots on the emergence of a dissonance between them. This is particularly obvious in *Death in Venice* because of its overt preoccupation with the interaction of the two spheres. Gustave von Aschenbach has fashioned a personal and professional ethic out of aesthetics, and at the beginning of the *Novelle* he appears to have succeeded in so doing. In his classically lucid prose he has shown a whole generation "the possibility of ethical determination beyond the deepest insight" ("die Möglichkeit sittlicher Entschlossenheit jenseits der tiefsten Erkenntnis" – 194). He conceives life as an assertion of willpower, as a "despite" ("als ein Trotzdem" – 198), a heroic thrust beyond ambivalence and irony to "dignity of spirit" ("Würde des Geistes" – 203). The phrase "ethical determination" ("moralische Entschlossenheit" – 202) is repeated in the delineation of his personality, and again linked to a state "beyond knowledge, beyond dissolving and inhibiting insight" ("jenseits des Wissens, der auflösenden und hemmenden Erkenntnis" – 202). He is a "moralist of achievement" ("Moralist der Leistung" – 200), who has attained a highly respected social and artistic position.

The precariousness of his ethic is implicit from the outset. What is most crucial in his system is also what is most dangerous: his cult of beauty of form. It is dangerous because the aesthetic lies outside the bounds of the ethical; as an expression of discipline (as in Aschenbach's polished writing) it may be ethical, but it is decidedly non- and even anti-ethical in its drive to autonomy and in its indifference to normative limitations. The plot of *Death in Venice* represents the enactment of this dualism. In a well delineated irony of situation Aschenbach is betrayed by his own creed.

Whether he has knowledge of his self-betrayal is another, more intricate problem. One of the skills that he acquires in the course of his rigorous self-training is that of repressing, denying, and thwarting his innermost wishes. So he goes first to Pola before admitting to himself that it is Venice that is the destination of his longing. Similarly, he makes a pretense, albeit a rather feeble one, of leaving Venice. As he becomes increasingly entranced by Tadzio, he wearies of the struggle to maintain the façade he had painstakingly constructed over the years. To claim that he is a willing accomplice to his own destruction is an overstatement. He simply lets go. The justification that his moralistic ego gives to his rebellious id is an essentially aesthetic one: he is continuing to pursue the cult of beauty, as he always had done, though in a different guise. Ethics are divorced from aesthetics, and the latter is shown to have a dual potential for self-destruction as well as for self-creation.

Emma Bovary is equally enthralled by the lure of the aesthetic, although her drama is played out in the nineteenth-century woman's domestic context. Her ethical obligations are, without doubt, to her husband, her child, and the welfare of her household. But the role of angel in the house appeals to her only intermittently, when she has a specially bad conscience and makes amends by preparing a favorite dessert for Charles. Otherwise she lets her daughter run around with holes in her stockings, and feels unable to love her because she sees her as ugly ("laide" – 122). Her shortcomings as wife and mother are underscored, though not without strong satirical undercurrent, through the contrast with Mme. Homais, "the best wife in Normandy" ("la meilleure épouse de Normandie" – 101), who is totally devoted to her family, and totally devoid of either intelligence or sexuality.

Emma's fascination with the aesthetic becomes apparent in her adolescence in her behavior at the convent, where self-indulgent sentimentality captivates her rather than the altruistic devotion she is supposed to be learning. Her taste is formed – and perverted – by the figures and rhetoric of cheap romance, just as Aschenbach finds his model in Greek culture. The tawdriness of Emma's concept of beauty is a comment on the world in which she lives insofar as it offers her no loftier ideals of aspiration. She tries to satisfy her longings by the daintiness of her appearance, spending immense sums on lemons to whiten her skin, and buying scarves and baubles from Lheureux (whose name means "the happy") to the point of bankruptcy. Her lover's self-presentation is in marked contrast to her husband's growing sloppiness. With Leon she immediately notices his well-manicured nails, which match her own. The motif of nails recurs when Rodolphe calculates Charles's dirty nails and three-day beard among the factors likely to make Emma an easy prey to his advances.

This fundamental struggle between the claims of the ethical and aesthetic represents the main analogy between the characters and readers. The narrator's shifting signals have the effect of trapping readers in their own version of the dilemma between aesthetics and ethics that lies at the core of both these texts. The aesthetics of narration raise the issue of the ethics of the narrator's handling of the characters and, beyond that, the implications of this narrative situation for readers. To document this thesis requires an analysis of the delicate and changing relationship between the narrator and readers.

At the opening of both *Madame Bovary* and *Death in Venice* the narrating voice extends to readers an offer of friendship. This intriguing notion of friendship as a means of envisaging the alliance between narrator and readers has recently been put forward by Wayne Booth in his latest book *The Company We Keep: An Ethics of Fiction*. Booth maintains that: "Considered under the friendship metaphor, the implied authors of *all* stories, fictional or historical, elevated or vulgar, welcoming or hospitable on the surface, purport to offer friendships" (174). These friendships may vary in a number of ways: in the quantity of the invitations, in the degree of intimacy, in the intensity of the engagement they expect, in the distance or familiarity they project, in the kinds of activities they invite, in the level of responsibility they offer, i.e., reciprocity or domination between author and reader, and, I would add, in the response they seek to elicit from readers, i.e., trust, skepticism, playfulness. Booth's concept of friendship is another, more vivid and personal denotation of the narrative contract that binds narrator to readers and enables the fiction. At the same time, through the use of the term "friendship," it introduces into the narrator/readers relationship notions such as loyalty and mutual respect that are intrinsic to an ethics of reading.

In both *Madame Bovary* and *Death in Venice* a supposition of friendly solidarity with the reader is established through the use of the first person plural in the opening paragraph. In *Madame Bovary* it is the enigmatic "we" ("nous") that is the initial word of the text and that recurs through the first chapter, but only once again later near the end of the novel: "We were in class when the headmaster came in, followed by a *new* boy" ("Nous étions à l'étude, quand le Proviseur entra, suivi d'un *nouveau*" – 3). The silent spectators of Charles's arrival in the classroom could be his schoolfellows already seated there. In addition, however, that "we" can also incorporate implied observers/readers being solicited, as it were, to enter the realm of the fiction by looking at Charles with both his schoolfellows and the narrator. The indeterminate "we" is tantamount to a tacit invitation to readers to participate in the narrator's point of view. This shared perspective on Charles forms the basis of the friendly accord between narrator and readers in the opening sections of *Madame Bovary*. Similarly, the first sentence of *Death in Venice* contains a reference to "our continent" ("unserem Kontinent" – 185). That usage is no more casual than Flaubert's "we." Its design is to encourage readers to identify with the narrator's angle of vision as "we" step over the threshold of the fiction, and to stand by this side as we become acquainted with its configuration. The rhetorical questions that Aschenbach addresses to himself in the course of his walk about the sources of his sudden desire to travel serve to stimulate the entente between the narrator and readers. For while Aschenbach gives one answer, the possibility of others is hinted through the suggestiveness of the phrasing. Within the surface text articulated by Aschenbach there is a sub-text common to the narrating voice and readers.

The solidarity fostered by the first person plural also projects a measure of stability. The narrator in both instances seeks to fashion a positive self-image of himself in readers' minds. His voice inspires credibility because it is authoritative, not least on account of the control it is able to exercise. The narrator's power is substantiated through his thorough knowledge of the attendant circumstances as the pre-history of Charles in *Madame Bovary* and of Aschenbach in *Death in Venice* is unfolded in comfortable detail. The undercurrent of irony towards Charles and the innuendoes in regard to Aschenbach are sufficient to adumbrate the narrator as someone who has aesthetic and ethical standards. However, he does not emerge as a fictional persona with a distinctive personality. Flaubert's own characterization of his role in relation to his fiction in his letter of 18 March 1857 is largely apposite to most of *Death in Venice* too: that he wanted "to be in his work like God in his creation, invisible and omnipotent, everywhere felt and nowhere seen" ("être dans son oeuvre comme

Dieu dans sa création, invisible et tout-puissant; qu'on le sente partout, mais qu'on ne le voie pas" – *Oeuvres complètes*, xiv, 164). Both narrators keep an essentially low profile, in contrast to the self-dramatization typical of the self-advertising gamesman style of narrator. From the opening signals in *Madame Bovary* and *Death in Venice* readers are, therefore, led to the assumption that they are dealing with a fairly direct narration and a knowing, probably trustworthy narrator.

These assumptions are further encouraged by the way in which both narratives support readers' confidence in their ability to construct the text. Aesthetically *Madame Bovary* and *Death in Venice* are quite transparent. The plot of *Death in Venice* is the enactment of an inversion as Aschenbach undergoes the metamorphosis from the public persona he presented to the world at the outset to the other self of the end. A series of doubles – the tempter at the cemetery, the sinister gondolier, the cosmetized old dandy – function as alter egos to map the stages of this reversal. The ready intelligibility of the text is assured by the use of such immediately comprehensible symbols as the decaying city, Venice, sinking into the ocean, or Tadzio's less than perfect teeth, the visible indicator that he, too, is vitally flawed. The intertextual echoes of Platen and Gustav Mahler, as well as the extensive citations from the *Phaidros*, also facilitate reading by locating the narration in its cultural context. In *Madame Bovary* a similar function is performed by the expansive account (37-42) of Emma's artistic experience during her formative years and her response to it. The impact of romance as a model for her conduct could hardly be spelled out with greater force and clarity. Likewise, the significance of the reiterated motif of the wedding bouquet stands in little need of explanation. The intricate sub-text boosts readers' faith in both their own reading skills and the narrator's willingness to act as a reliable guide. Through our growing friendly engagement with him, we are imperceptibly drawn into complicity with him.

The narrative situation grows considerably more complicated with the increasing manipulation of indirect discourse as a mode of narration. The immediate access to the character's own thought processes and speech patterns intensifies readers' capacity to identify with them, and through the temporary empathy creates a greater receptivity to their predicaments. Emma's boredom in Tostes, her disillusionment with marriage, her contempt for Charles, her disdain for the vulgarity of her environment are all perceived through her eyes and expressed in her words. The effect of indirect discourse could be compared to an x-ray of the recesses of her mind in contrast to a picture of its surface given in third-person narration. Aschenbach's far more complex mind, too, is portrayed from within as he engages in various strategies of self-justification. His strong and, to him, surprising urge to get away from his disciplined life, his decision to head for the south, and his captivation under the dual spell of Venice and Tadzio are all conveyed to readers through his ratiocinations. So in the indirect discourse the narrator assumes the guise of the characters' intimate confidant through his familiarity with their thoughts and his ability to (re)produce them. After instituting himself as the readers' friend, he goes on to project himself as the characters' friend, and therefore acts as a mediator who enables readers vicariously to enter into the characters' lives. The illusion is thereby created of a triangular understanding between the narrator, the character, and readers.

But the symbiosis of this partnership is disturbed by the constant intervention of irony. It is not only latent in the alternation between direct and indirect discourse; it is also implicit within the indirect discourse as a scuttling of the very words being uttered. In *Madame Bovary* the insistent repetition of the same cliches, linguistic and ideological, points to the shoddiness of Emma's aspirations even as she cherishes them. In *Death in Venice* evasive understatement has the same effect. Aschenbach's dismissive surmise: "It was the urge to travel, nothing more" ("Es war Reiselust, nichts weiter" – 189) has a decidedly ironic edge. While he is endeavoring to reassure himself about the innocuousness of his desires, the narrator is, by the insinuation of under/overstatement, inviting readers to do the opposite, precisely to suspect that there is a great deal more here than Aschenbach is willing to concede to himself. The irony simultaneously conceals and reveals Aschenbach's self-deception. Its mainspring lies in the narrator's ulterior knowledge of the characters' mentality. It is at their expense for it casts doubt on their motivations and exposes their ideals as questionable. To the extent that readers grasp the ironies and assent to the narrator's vision, the bond between them and him is strengthened in a collusive complicity. Through our querying, skeptical withdrawal from the characters we are pulled closer towards the narrator.

Yet at the same time, paradoxically, we begin to harbor reservations about his methods. After posing as the character's friend, he emerges more and more as a sly fox of an ironist who bites with a considerable venom of malice. So the detachment, which is a product of irony, itself ironically initiates readers' distancing not just from the figures but from the narrator himself as well. The superciliousness of a voice that undercuts his characters while expecting to maintain readers' friendship arouses a certain self-protective recoil. It is important to distinguish this narrative situation from that in satiric fictions where the narrator has a good heart beneath his snarling surface, and addresses readers with what amounts to a friendly offer: "'I would like to give you something for your own good – a nasty medicine that may cure you'" (Booth 174). The therapeutic aspect of that kind of nastiness is operative too in such works as Zola's *L'Assommoir* or Virginia Woolf's *To The Lighthouse*, which students tend to reject as "depressing" because they overlook the authentic compassion held out to the characters. This is not the case in either *Madame Bovary* or *Death in Venice* where the hostility embedded in the irony triggers readers' negative responses. Though we may not particularly like the characters, we come to like the narrator even less for the snide way he treats them.

In *Death in Venice* it is possible to pinpoint exactly where and how the colloquy between narrator, protagonist, and readers undergoes a mutation. In the lengthy closing section the narrator switches roles by setting himself wholly apart from Aschenbach through a series of comments that record overt censure of him. He refers to him as "the confused man" ("der Verwirrte" – 275), "the spellbound man" ("der Betörte" – 277), "the much afflicted one" ("der Heimgesuchte" – 297), and "the ensorcered man" ("der Berückte" – 300). He goes on with pointed cruelty to gloat over Aschenbach's degradation as he portrays the "Master" ("Meister" – 302) sitting on the beach, his hair colored, his face made up, his eyes avidly following Tadzio's every movement. The note of contempt is unmistakable as Aschenbach's decline is described, detail by detail, each one evoking the contrast with his former high-principled respected persona. The deterioration of the former Aschenbach into the present self-parody is, aesthetically, a masterpiece of imagination. As readers we marvel at the artfulness of this *Novelle*: it is a superbly crafted, highly organized, and, what is more, economical piece of writing.

Ethically, however, it is dubious. The narrator's duplicity towards the protagonist is disconcerting as he shifts from his earlier position of somewhat ironical but basically friendly understanding into unconcealed aggression. T.J. Reed, in his study *Thomas Mann: The Uses of Tradition*, argues persuasively (162 ff.) that Mann's concept of the plot underwent a sea change in the course of its development. His original intention was to portray Aschenbach favorably in the light of Plato and Plutarch; he had

excerpted all the passages that are positive about love. The matter proved
flexible, and eventually the negative came to prevail with the result that
the *Novelle* turned in a different direction while retaining its structural outline. "Precisely this negative reworking of what was at first a positive conception," Reed maintains (167), "would account perfectly for the strange
mixture *Der Tod in Venedig* actually is, of enthusiasm and criticism, classical beauty and penetration, elevation and sordidness." But Reed simpli-
fies the issue when he envisages the *Novelle* as "a story whose overt intention is to pass a moral judgement" (162) so that the "increasing use of
adjectival nouns as judgements – *der Verwirrte, der Betörte* – are (*sic*) also a
simple and economical way for the narrator to establish his position as a
moralist" (163).

To typecast the narrator as a moralist is to flatten the narrative by
opting for a single denotative reading that abolishes its essential ambivalences. The narrator is very much implicated in that slipperiness. His con-
demnatory castigation of Aschenbach towards the end is in stark contrast
to the sympathetic understanding he shows at the opening. It is as if he
had carefully set the figure up expressly in order to put him down and in.
The friend whom the narrator gave out to be proves to be an enemy. For
this reason the negative value judgments on Aschenbach, which prompt
readers to scorn and reject him, end by backfiring. Readers' sense of anger
is directed not at the reviled character but at the narrator as his treachery
is unmasked. Because he betrays his created persona, for whom he has
feigned friendship, he forfeits the trust we as readers have invested in him.

In *Madame Bovary* readers face a similar dilemma, though it is less visible because the narrator is so adept at keeping up appearances. Nevertheless, the hostility against Emma becomes increasingly palpable, reaching its climax in the deathbed scene, which contains the same destructive
pleasure in portraying her at her nadir as the last glimpse of Aschenbach
on the beach. Here too the contrast is made between her earlier self and
her present state. To emphasize the ugliness of her dying it is set off
against the fantasies of ethereal fading she had brought from her reading
of romance. The horror of the situation is even greater than in *Death in
Venice* because Emma asks for a mirror and sees her own disfigurement,
where Aschenbach never consciously confronts what he has become. The
big tears that roll down her cheeks as she catches sight of her hideousness
are in counterpoint to her raucous, frenetic laughter as she hears the blind
man's song outside. As in *Death in Venice* the recurrent details are orches-

trated with utmost finesse to form a pattern of signification for readers. The aesthetic mastery is undeniable. But the orgiastic delight in excess affords a clue to the underlying violence, even though the Flaubertian narrator is too conscious of his art to admit the overt judgmental statements that Mann allows. Through the widespread use of the imperfect tense, the normative tense in French for both indirect discourse and for continuous past narration, the narrator of *Madame Bovary* is able so unobtrusively to slip in and out of the persona's consciousness that it becomes virtually impossible to delineate precisely between the voices. This technique attains its maximum effectiveness in the deathbed scene. John Porter Houston has shown, in his book *Fictional Technique in France 1802-1927* (66 ff.), that even the most searchingly meticulous stylistic analysis cannot disentangle the priest's liturgical formulae as he administers the extreme unction from the suggestive, erotically colored phrases of Emma's confused consciousness. It is indeed this aesthetic brilliance of *Madame Bovary* that makes it so difficult to analyze readers' reservations. The narrator's antagonism to the character is more insidious, more insinuating, and more resistant to diagnosis than in *Death in Venice*, yet just as reductive. It goes far beyond the want of compassion of which Flaubert has often been accused. The narrator's attitude towards the protagonist in both texts must be designated as full of guile.

It is because of this ethical violation of the narrative contract established at the outset that readers retreat from the complicity into which the narrator has endeavored to draw them. His betrayal of the character is, by a metonymic transference, experienced as a betrayal by readers too. His record of duplicity in dealing with the characters reveals his essential untrustworthiness. His mode of narration amounts to an act of transgression that activates in readers precisely the kind of revulsion he has sought to elicit against the figures. This ultimate unintentional irony of reader response stems from resentment at what is perceived as the narrator's deceitfulness. So readers refuse to assent to his manoeuvers or to submit to his manipulation. The bad faith apparent in the narrator's presentation of his characters contains a potential threat to readers also. The analogy that Hillis Miller posits between the narrator, the character, and the reader turns out to be one of misgivings. The ill-will generated within the fiction extends beyond it into readers' indistinct sense of aversion.

In Booth's terminology of friendship, readers' reactions could be described as a mixture of grief and anger: grief at the loss of the friendship offered by the narrator, and anger at his behavior towards the characters. In effect, readers feel duped as well as offended by a narrator who has cast them into the position of inferiors and has presumed on the power of his rhetoric not only to carry them along, but also to take them in – or, at least, into complicity. Like the listeners in Michel's account of his life in Gide's *L'Immoraliste*, readers are expected to become "almost accomplices" ("presque complices") because of "not knowing where to disapprove" ("ne savoir où la désapprouver" – 184). Such a posture on the narrator's part is predicated on a certain lack of respect for readers, analogous to his contempt for the fictional world. The hurt to the reader contingent on this kind of narrative situation can be brought more sharply into focus through comparison with narrators such as those of Jane Austen or Henry James, who treat readers as equals and endow them with an independent intelligence. These narratorial voices maintain a pact of generosity with readers, whereas those in *Madame Bovary* and *Death in Venice* are tainted with meanness.

In construing these texts, readers are playing out a dual drama. On a diegetic level they are engaged in the movements of Emma's and Aschenbach's desires. The indirect discourse, by positioning readers within the protagonists' minds, encourages identification. The intimacy elicits perhaps sympathy, perhaps pity for the pathos of the situation, eventually horror at the self-destructiveness that is the outcome of their self-deception. This participation in the realm of the fiction is, however, partnered by another sort of involvement of readers on the narrational level. This is where readers take an active role to the point of emancipating themselves from the narrator's guidance. In antithesis to the characters, who are totally in his power, readers have the privilege of reflection. They can distance themselves not merely from the characters but from the narrator too, subjecting him to scrutiny of his tactics and motives. His anger at the fictional world is in turn played out by readers as an only partially conscious animosity against the narrator, which explodes in the disparagement of "I hate this book! it's so nasty." Despite the naïvety of their phraseology, these readers have rightly experienced the treacherous undertow of this mode of narration.

The result is often an impasse. These readers may become convinced of the extraordinary subtleties of the work in question: the profusion of interlocking detail, the virtuosity in the management of viewpoint, the vivid specificity with which an entire world is evoked. Intellectually they may arrive at an understanding of the aesthetic brilliance of such works, which justifies their continued inclusion in the canon of Great Books. Emotionally they feel differing degrees of engagement with the character, depending on such extraneous factors as their own level of maturity, the breadth of their horizon, their gender, and their life expectations. But ethically they shudder in revulsion against a transgression of the narrative contract of friendship because it connotes a deeper infraction of basic human bonds.

Works Cited

Arnold, Matthew. "Count Leo Tolstoy." *The Works of Matthew Arnold*. London: Macmillan, 1903: iv, 198-214.

Booth, Wayne C. *The Company We Keep. An Ethics of Fiction*. Berkeley, Los Angeles, and London: University of California Press, 1988.

Flaubert, Gustave. *Madame Bovary*. Ed. by Edouard Maynial. Paris: Garnier, 1947.

Flaubert, Gustave. *Correspondance. Oeuvres complètes*. Paris: Conard, 1926-27.

Gide, Andre. *L'Immoraliste*. Paris: Mercure de France, 1902.

Houston, John Porter. *Fictional Technique in France, 1802-1927*. Baton Rouge, Louisiana: Louisiana State University Press, 1972.

Mann, Thomas. *Der Tod in Venedig. Meistererzählungen*. Zurich: Manesse, 1945: 183-308.

Reed, T.J. *Thomas Mann: The Uses of Tradition*. Oxford: Clarendon Press, 1974.

Marginality: Stickball, Narcissus, and the Demands of Faith

Michael G. Cooke

To take up the question of marginality is to be reminded how far we have moved from the world of Guillaume de Lorris and the *Roman de la Rose*. For we are rather ill-at-ease about the concept of the central garden, and we treat the border ranks of any putative garden as the truly challenging and worthy part of the landscape. Come to think of it, Guillaume may have been susceptible to a similar conviction. He spends a lot of time and a lot of fine poetry on extraterritorial goings-on.

Even if he is not of our party without realizing it, Guillaume does point to one prominent feature of marginality: its being beset with the thickets of misdirection, frustration, contradiction, and denial. Just on the practical level, it proves a task to keep the forces of marginality *marginal*. It is not the right to be marginal that one sees defended, or the respect due to the marginal as such, or the distinctive and non-cooptable virtues of being marginal. To the contrary, it is the right of the marginal to be central that is clamored for. The marginal resents the center, and also its own seeming eccentricity. Happy about itself it may in some sense be, but its idea of happiness is bound up with getting to, and getting to be the center.

Jane Marcus describes one form of this uneasy centripetality in language that oddly conflates a Darwinian "survival of the fittest" with what resembles a bare, or barren garden:

> The language of current theoretical writing is a thicket of brambles; the reader must aggressively fight her way into it, emerging shaken and scratched. Those survivors in the central clearing congratulate themselves on being there. Everyone on the other side of the bushes is a coward or an intellectual weakling. Bleeding and exhausted from their struggle, they invent a new hierarchy, with theorists at the top, vying to be scientists and philosophers. ("Feminist Issues in Literary Scholarship." *TSWL* 3, 1984, 86-87)

But this kind of centripetality raises a deeper conceptual issue. The binary of margin versus center displays itself as a stable field of inquiry, even as it camouflages the dangerous hollow of determining: margin or center *of what*? What Yeats might see as the "anarchy" of a dissolving center is the pre-resolution of a lovely new order for Blake in *The Marriage of Heaven and Hell*. Eliot's "cruellest month" is for Chaucer the source of "swich licour" and "vertu" as all life, sensual and sacred, testifies to. Where is the consistency, let alone the center in all of this?

The matter of marginality is also undermined by its own implied synecdoche. A relationship of part to whole is in force as soon as marginality is invoked, and as with all synecdoche, two effects occur: a part of the part is repressed, and the variety or complexity of the whole is denied.

The hackneyed example, "all hands on deck," cogently makes the case. The sailor is reduced to the hands the situation calls for, in that brain and will and stamina must work to foster the function of the hands, and the hands themselves set aside the ability to caress, play the piano, do card tricks, or clasp for prayer. And just as part of the part is repressed in synecdoche, so is the whole effectively focussed down or rather confined to some momentary function and call. Fighting a storm or feting an admiral, not writing a poem or berating the system will be demanded of the sailors, as singular agents more than versatile entities, on deck.

To do justice to synecdoche, and to marginality, we should recognize two sorts of consistency here: the simple, or material; and the complex, or conceptual. A slice of apple or orange stands in simple consistency with the rest of the fruit, but it makes no synecdoche for it. A seed is no more a synecdoche than a slice, but only a stage of growth. By contrast a hand enjoys a complex consistency with a body, a person, partly (a) because it cannot be separated in actuality (as opposed to rhetoric) and still have any but a ghoulish or a medical function, and more essentially (b) because it combines integrally in the being with elements strikingly different from itself: heart, spleen, nervous system, brain, glands, immune system. ... In other words, synecdoche confesses, as between part and whole, the very difference it suppresses for the sake of the occasion.

Does marginality do the same? Does it even pretend to do so? It is necessary to come back to the fact that there is no acknowledged occasion, no agreement as to where the center is, or what it is the center of. Allan Bloom feels as beleaguered as Amiri Baraka, and Elaine Showalter as beleaguered as they. All of them are vying for the same space, though starting from different premises on non-convergent paths. It is this space race to a desire rather than a destination that the issue of marginality seems to me to announce. And the race is occurring in a welter of conflicting forces, involving hierarchy, democracy, and the byplay of our century's arrested irony.

Now hierarchy may seem a reactionary throwback where marginality is at issue; it is what the marginalizer strives to consolidate, the marginalized to undo. But perhaps the essential difference between the two resides in the fact that the marginalizer clings to the form – the objects presently at the supposed center of things – and forgets the principle behind the form, whereas the marginalized contend against the form and forego the creative possibilities of the principle.

In so doing, both parties act as though hierarchy were generated by the marginalizer, or could be extirpated by the marginalized. But hierarchy runs deeper in the order of things. As Virgil Nemoianu has noted in his cogent study, *A Theory of the Secondary*, there exists a radical human leaning toward "the principal or the main," and a "decisive priority" goes to "what is central over what is marginal." In even broader terms, Nemoianu sees "human culture" as "single-minded and exclusionary," with features as varied and complex as "power, ... creativity, ... economic interest and ideological vision" taking "monolithic shapes and [fostering] streamlined uniformities. ..."

We need not look far to find that hierarchy prevails even where much more modest and casual matters are afoot than those Nemoianu cites. For a passion of excellence comes into play whether we are casting aspersions or bronze statues, and so playing the dozens no less than sculpture soon develops a hierarchy. The fact is that hierarchy always woos us with promises of a stable medium for and a stable supply of excellence.

To deliver on that promise is another matter, of course. But a game of stickball on a New York street makes it plain that hierarchy, or the faith that a stable center subsists and the fluctuating margin can be held in check, has a natural stand in the human scheme. It will also demonstrate how to escape enslavement to any form or set that hierarchy might at any given moment take.

Picture, then, the picking of sides for a Friday afternoon stickball game, in the lap of tradition and the teeth of traffic. Some people hang out of windows, some hover excitedly against buildings or on stoops. Oh, they would love to play, but they know they haven't a prayer. Some rigor of selection, even in this idle scene, is going to apply, and indeed the non-pickees, the marginalized in a manner of speaking, endorse this. A mother here or a father there has been known to mutter about their offspring never getting into the game, in the spirit of equality, but those very offspring plead with them to cut some slack, in the spirit of the game, the spirit of the community of excellence the window-watcher and the window-threatener share.

But suddenly the new kid, the roly-poly one with the lisp and the sly sense of humor, is approaching the group of aspirants from whom the captains are culling today's aggregations. Does Sidney Greenstreet or Oprah Winfrey-of-old plan to play Fred Astaire? Still and all, some curiosity is aroused. What if the kid can play? Suppose it is more than a case of sacrilegious self-ignorance and social miscalculation? The following Friday the kid is picked last, and put last in the batting order. And lo, when she gets the lumber in her hands, for the one turn at the plate she has been guaranteed, the ball is jumping off her bat and whipping off walls and under cars, and she is happily fleet of foot, if also a little short of breath. So now who cares what she looks like? The hierarchy is elastic in principle, though lazy and rheumatic in operation. And even in operation it needs newcomers. Yesterday's stars go off to college, to work, or maybe to mediocrity as new needs, new forces come to bear. The capacity to accommodate the new is the measure of validity for any principle, just as the view is measured by its survival of the amplification into principle.

This is all easier said than done, since the principle tends to insist on its present, guaranteed settlement (the new kid looks like a slob), and the new tends to insist on its sole self (the same to you; who needs you, anyway?). When Diane Arbus declares: "It's what I've never seen before that I recognize," or when Conrad in connection with "Amy Foster" identifies imagination with the ability to see beauty in what is strange, they point unerringly to the irreconcilable symmetry between principle and innovation, and the chafing synergy between the marginalizer and the marginalized.

Let me confess, as I seek to show how our age worsens this state of paradox into something akin to war, that I find the terms self and other used with an astonishing confidence as to their clarity and value. The self knows its terms, and its difference from the other. Even when we talk of a self that changes existentially, we seem to think of a series of clear points, rather than a slowly streaming, uncertainly synthesizing set of manifestations which operate reciprocally as part of a system-in-the-making with the environment. As regards the marginalizer and the marginalized then: each knows itself, each knows what the other is about, whether monolithically or choppily. But we are warned by Nietzsche against such self-centeredness:

> Thinking of oneself gives little happiness. If, however, one feels much happiness in this, it is because at bottom one is not thinking of oneself but of one's ideal. That is far, and only the swift reach it and are delighted. (*The Portable Nietzsche* 50)

The problem of the distant and elusive self is only compounded when the ideal of the self is a democratic one, and especially when, as now, the democratic ideal has led to a veritable Orphic scatter, with all parts singing the same song of defiant self-aspiration. Here is a synecdoche of all parts and no whole, save as the parts might convince themselves they are whole.

In the field of letters alone, the question of marginality has resounded around works by women and works by blacks, with increasing fragmentation of each category into special subsets. Thus we come to find among what were originally feminists special groups of womanists, of African American feminists and Third World feminists, materialist feminists and liberal feminists and psychoanalytic feminists, and anthropological feminists, etc.

Marginality also figures in consideration of native American work and people, and Chicano and Puerto Rican work and people (unaccountably lumped together), and Asian-American work and people. I have heard claims made for Eastern Europeans, on the grounds that (a) the majority of them have an inheritance of prejudice and exclusion under the system of serfdom, and (b) their prowess and cultural contribution in the field of letters receives inadequate recognition, even if members of their group (again too readily treated as homogeneous) do not suffer prejudice and exclusion on the sidewalk.

Indeed, in his lamentations concerning American youth and education and culture, Allan "the latter-day" Bloom all but claims marginality for the canon. I only wonder if the multitudes coming to swim give proof that the water is healthy. Behind the quarrel over marginality in the world of letters there is indisputably something of great courage and beauty moving, marshalling our sense of justice, of history, of self, of intellectual positiveness (as distant from mental customs), and of the integrity of democracy in the Western cultural vein. But all this is beset by a radical uncertainty that I have tried to formulate in the phrase: margin and center of what?

Furthermore, all this is set in a social context of unusual conformation. We appear to have a democracy without a *demos*, a sense of groups without a concern for common cause or common ground. The upshot is the creation of a kind of collective narcissism, where the society is the canopied stream and the separate groups multiply the mythical figure bent toward the stream without recognizing it as any more than an image-bearer for themselves; and on the whole a quite unsatisfactory image-bearer.

It is surprising how little severity we bring to the consideration of Narcissus, or at least the sense of helplessness we feel before him and his little myth. The whole episode is swathed in silken veils of pathos and beauty. The pathos of that drowning. The beauty of the flower poor Narcissus turns into. It seems a very generous metamorphosis that turns a soft and narrow-visioned youth into one of the first heartening signs of spring, full of lovable air and the authority of light, and the reemergence of color, the reappearance of human flesh from dark winter clothes. Who would not settle for a dispensation in which, for the sin of being prettily inane, like Narcissus, one would not drown and be done with, but turn into a symbol of resurrection and cherished beauty?

But it becomes necessary to ask: Is Narcissus marginalized by the circumambient reality, or does he marginalize and even dematerialize it? Is there some clash between personal democratic needs, in Narcissus, and democratic values, in the ampler framework of mortal experience? If indeed Narcissus is being pushed aside, by whom is this done, and with what efficacy?

In *Permanence and Change: An Anatomy of Purpose* Kenneth Burke notes that "to think through a matter is to trace an ever-widening circle of relationships," and points to a "search for wholes from which parts derive their meaning" (3rd ed., Berkeley University of California Press, 1984, 230). I would myself contend that wholes also derive their meaning from parts, in an incessant evolutionary negotiation. But Burke makes it hard to avoid the question whether the impasse of marginality as we now experience it, the impasse of conspiracy versus indifferentism, of vulnerability versus mustiness, energy versus randomness can be gotten past.

I remember once persuading a group of high school teachers who did not want to read Blake at all, but were holding out for Ntozake Shange, that our group should do both writers and indeed in terms of a close comparison. And so we took on *For Colored Girls* side by side with *A Vision of the Daughters of Albion*, canvassing questions like the roots and motives of authority, the play of compassion, opportunism and legitimacy, the manifestation of power in women, and the arrestedness of the male condition. It was agreed at last that Blake was well worth reading, and probably gave more to dwell on and sort out but that Shange was much more immediately compelling. It was also agreed that Blake had made the reading of Shange more reflective, i.e., saved her from pure relevance, while in turn Shange had made the reading of Blake livelier, i.e., saved him from mere importance.

That group of teachers saw Blake as part of the canon, and Shange as out on the margin, but to me Blake seemed more in danger of being marginalized than Shange, and it occurred to me that Milton, whom we treat as *very* canonical, expected to be marginalized: "fit audience find, though few." And John Donne was worse than marginalized. He was all but consigned to oblivion until T.S. Eliot and friends retrieved him for what has proven a short-lived glory. He is receding again into ordinariness, and none can say he will not again be forgotten, or at least returned to the coterie status with which he began.

Shakespeare seems immortal, or Dante, but obviously we marginalize particular works of theirs as even the most punctilious of us marginalizes parts of all works much longer than the sonnet (otherwise our comments would collapse into heavy-footed incoherence). With Shakespeare, two further comments will be of use. First, people used to rewrite parts of his plays to bring them up to snuff in the eighteenth century, and it was not until the romantic period that Lamb and Coleridge helped to "canonize" the Bard of Avon. Second, Shakespeare holds up by changing all the time. As criticism shifts its emphasis other writers rise or fall, but Shakespeare has the unique ability to meet each generation cogently on its own ground. Even so, the glossary gets longer and longer for a Shakespeare play. Will he be marginalized by sheer linguistic change, when the Oxford plot to marginalize him falls flat perennially? Or is he perhaps already marginalized in the academy? As Lawrence Levine has shown, up to the late nineteenth century Shakespeare remained part of the popular theater in the United States, and thereafter "ascended" to the narrower legitimate theater, from which he has been silently assumed into the specialized academic circuit. Higher is less, here, and certainly other than the center.

What indeed of material that refuses to be marginalized, even if like Emily Dickinson it strives to make itself so ("I would as soon go naked in public as give my poems" to the world)? Let me turn for a moment to what used to be called race music, and specifically rhythm and blues. This music was created by blacks for blacks. Slowly it has come to cross over the red sea of prejudice into the liberality of the gold and platinum record.

Is the larger culture also crossing its own Red Sea, or is R&B being bleached of its true character? What does it mean when you hear a ghetto blaster delivering a rap number that is being matched breath for breath by someone who as he rocks by you turns out to be white? Perhaps Ralph Ellison and Toni Morrison represent the equivalent in the world of letters. They tell decidedly Afro-American stories, and the real problem is not lack of acceptance at large but rather such thorough "recognition" that some readers in college courses don't realize these great writers, so fully centralized, are black.

Rhythm and blues of course differ from Ellison and Morrison in the extent of its reach into the culture. The literary artifact has a limited scope, indeed its scope is now so limited as to raise the issue whether the marginality of this text or that group in the literary domain is not small beer beside the fact that marginality is befalling the literally enterprise itself. In this light, marginality serves as a hothouse *topos*, rather than an urgent social and moral issue that would properly link the academic egghead to the nourishment of the culture.

Let us recall how Matthew Arnold, noticing that religion was being in a manner marginalized, proposed literature in its place, to order and inspire the culture. Clearly now the scene has been shifting again and literature, as opposed to reading in literate quarters, seems itself isolated. Producers of literature like Ngugi wa Thiong'o recognize and fear this development. In *Writers in Politics* Ngugi contends that "literature and writers cannot be exempted from the battlefield of major social issues (London: Heinemann & Co., 1981, 72)"; and he says, in his Lotus Prize speech, that writers must struggle against "forces that exploit, oppress, humiliate and dwarf the creative spirit of man." Ngugi sounds like Matthew Arnold and a long line of figures going back to Sir Philip Sidney when he argues that "Literature has often given us more and sharper insights into the moving spirit of the era than all the historical and political documents treating the same moments in a society's development" (*Writers in Politics* 73). But any line of centripetal function or even ambition for literature unravels with the private imagination of Stevens, the private irony of Eliot, the private mysticism of Lawrence, the private traditionalism of Yeats, the private sodality of Williams, the private cosmogony of Joyce. And does the genuine absence of hierarchy among these writers tell us they are clustered at the heart of the culture, or scattered on the margins?

In point of fact our general or habitual sense of literature goes back to the dizzying conviction that the epic poem embodies the highest expression of the human mind (we think theoretical physics does that now). But this conviction was being undermined even as Arnold strove to exalt it as the true bearer of cultural value. For Darwin with *The Origin of Species* was radically changing what we talk about and hold urgently if not always happily near. Darwin did more than render moot the principles of religion that Arnold saw losing their centrality. Quite apart from the validity of his postulates concerning material evolution, he gave an irreversible drive to a new cultural taste for high-powered theorizing. This was no frivolous craving for what Wordsworth calls outrageous stimulation. To the contrary, it was a daring to communicate with the profoundest reaches of understanding and implied value, a revision of child's play into ultimate truth *and* consequences. In short, I think Darwin is the origin of the marginalization of literature and the canonization of abstractive theory. He was more novel than the novel, and more potent, in that he could combine a great story, a great concept or myth, and a great store of useful information. How could mere "literature" compete? And so, even within the sphere of literature we find theory magnetizing the attention at the expense of the material the theory is supposed to be about.

Perhaps this is what Pater was foreseeing when in his essay on "Style" he came out with the opinion that expository prose, with its vast range and swiftness of response, would be the wave of the future. If Arnold with his ideal of poetry seems misguided today, Pater with his conception of prose must seem downright deluded. Todorov's *Poetics of Prose* devotes itself to fiction, and Thoreau and Emerson are esteemed as transcendentalists of American romantics, not as prose writers, though Hawthorne is lauded as both American romantic and novelist.

But if we consider the culture of the literate world, and not just that of academe, Pater's point looks a lot more telling. Anthropology, medicine, biology, politics, history, physics all have a powerful hold on the literate imagination; the "non-fiction aisle" in a bookstore provides the setting for a budding romance *in a popular song*. Not to have a way or a will for dealing with prose academically is not to prevent prose from coming into its own culturally. The heir-apparent is still the heir-apparent when incognito among the servants. Or to put it another way, a redefinition of the circle does as much as a change of position for establishing effective centrality or marginality.

On what basis, then, might the circle be redefined? It will be opportune here to acknowledge that to ask "margin and center *of what*?" is not necessarily a hopeless poser. We have been contesting fixed positions in an environment replete with incertitude. Who would have expected, a decade or two ago, that rhyme and stanzaic patterns would be on the upswing again, or that the epistolary novel would be once more looming on the norizon? Will we, when the authoritarian and the opportunistic dust settles, think *The Satanic Verses* another triumph for Rushdie, or a sign of his tilting into prolixity and ad-lib self-indulgence? On the other hand, might *The Satanic Verses* signal the revitalization of satire in our conscious concerns, to match the fact that it flourishes, along with our modernist intricacies, in Anglophone African literature, in the Caribbean, and in Australia?

If we are not attacking/defending fixed positions, margin and center come to be seen as positions in a ceaseless and elaborate negotiation not only among texts and among critical minds within the field of literacy, but a negotiation also with time, which one romantic poet calls both destroyer and preserver, and another at once corrector, beautifier, and (not unimportantly) avenger.

Let us fairly recognize that the dimensions and shape of whatever the marginal pertains to do not remain constant. The universe was expanding before we realized it; it is becoming to it to be always becoming, and thus surprising as well as inevitable. As much holds good for the universe of literature. It is a kind of open, slow kaleidoscope, with pieces added and subtracted, and the pattern of margin and center changing, and even the plunging hand changing in angle and force. Activity may be rapid, but change comes slow, in the sense that when a friend says: "I'm going upstairs a minute to change into a sweat suit," we know it is a mild locution; we expect the same friend and not a sweat suit on its own, via metamorphosis, to come back down.

The position, or as Robert Hariman would put it, the *status* of the material in relation to margin and center is intrinsically a shifting one, as soon as time, invisible but ineluctable, enters into the structure of evaluation. In "Status, Marginality, and Rhetorical Theory" (*Quarterly Journal of Speech* 72, 1986, 38-54), Hariman notes that "status may be compared to theatrical scrim: a cloth that can appear solid or translucent depending on how it is illuminated. Thus [since] sociality is the foundation of thinking, one must accept this reversibility as a condition of one's thought" (43). In place of 'reversibility' I would favor the term 'versatility', and would add that 'versatility' is not just the necessary condition and basic strength of thought, but also, as thinkers from Ecclesiastes to Vico and Nietzsche have observed, the way of things and their relationship to one another. It is not change that threatens and offends, only incoherence. It is not constancy that offends and threatens, but petrifaction. At bottom, though, our quarrel lies with the fact that knowledge forestalls knowledge. Earned and established views for *both parties to a debate* make straw men of each other. We suffer from an agitating if unacknowledged ignorance of a field we long to master, to wit, the future, and the bitter fission over fusion now shows what to expect when, as Conrad says in the Preface to *The Nigger of the "Narcissus,"* "the changing system of successive generations discards ideas, questions facts, demolishes theories."

In the "sociality" of literature, is there a possibility of living with the shifting chiaroscuro that we happen or choose to see as a solid state of black and white, propaganda and silence, arrogance and relegation, a formal "elitist, socially effective art on one hand and a popular, widespread but socially vilified art on the other" (Gottner Abendroth, *Feminist Aesthetic*, ed. Ecker. Boston: Beacon, 1986, 83)? For surely something needs to be done as we face a crisis of definition and a crisis of confidence in our profession. I imagine that Chief Nanga's list of "great writers" in Achebe's *A Man of the People* might produce, instead of scorn for his pretentiousness, hope of a new find and rescue from injustice. Chief Nanga, Achebe tells us, "prophesied that before long our great country would produce great writers like Shakespeare, Dickens, Jane Austen, Bernard Shaw and – raising his eyes off the script – Michael West and Dudley Stamp" (62). Of course we know that he prophesied aright: Flora Nwapa and Elechi Amadi join Achebe and Soyinka and J.P. Clark as Nigeria's topflight literary names, and Ayi Kwei Armah and Ama Ata Aidoo from neighboring Ghana must also be cited, along with Ngugi wa Thiong'o from Kenya. But that is beside the point: *he judged execrably.* I wonder, though, if we have not put ourselves in a position to run off to the library, clucking with guilt and sympathy, to set things right for the wickedly neglected Michael West and Dudley Stamp. Marginality leads us around by the nose, such is our crisis of confidence.

We may be driven in all this by more than an honorable fear of omission. We are prone to a longing for a particular result both in the social spirit of what we call 'control', and in the sly messianic spirit of what Nietzsche calls the "ideal." But we still must face the reality of two forces that introduce uncertainty into our result. The first is the sheer economy of attention, the second is the imperative of curiosity. For economy of attention, the impossibility and, as Luria indicates in "The Man who Couldn't Forget," unhealthfulness of holding everything in the front of awareness, will fall short of "our result," and the imperative of curiosity, which busily seeks what it may devour, will simply rush beyond it. Economy and curiosity may coincide, but they do not abide (with) each other.

The thing that needs observing, though, is that on the institutional/ social level the story of the last hundred years of American education, and the last forty of English education, is a story of expansion and innovation with an energy now visibly multiplying in impact. The quarrel over marginality is occurring at a time of great propitiousness, not of conservatism at all. It is not being pushed or held aside that makes for difficulty, but indifference of admission into an indifferent scheme.

The real problem arising hereupon is not the congestion of the channels of attention. It is the impasse of value *within,* as well as across our collective narcissisms, since even within there is such an insistence on serving the *already me* that the possibility of surprise and of enlargement is shut off. For the gratification of an echo we surrender the challenge of a vision, preferring to cuddle crooning with *The Color Purple* than to grapple groaning with *Meridian.* The problem across our collective narcissisms is only a sterner version of that within; one person's echo is another's *yech.*

With everyone in effect playing discrete stickball on the same street, are we witnessing a new order of equality *and dissatisfaction,* or is the hierarchy of nature somehow at play? Certainly a welter of debates is afoot, umpires as it were making judgments that apply to one another's games. That very welter may be our most favorable sign. As Gaston Bachelard observes in *The Poetics of Space,* "all values must remain vulnerable, and those that do not are dead" (trans. by Maria Jolas, Boston, Beacon Press,

1964, 59). What we are fighting, I would contend, is the form, not the principle, of hierarchy and the instrument we need is not a bludgeon. The concept of a floating hierarchy steadily debating its terms and dimensions, naturally revising the status of its elements: this seems true to our experience as a discipline that has come from marginality vis-à-vis classics to centrality and back again to marginality vis-à-vis culture. It has also a virtue for the future, by giving us a place in the larger debate which alone can have real meaning at this juncture. The concept of a floating hierarchy makes us no promise, because it makes no promises. The promise must arise within our labors in the creative domain and the arguments we mount and maintain on their behalf in the critical enterprise.

The solution to the issue of marginality lies not in the mere multiplying of names, Chief Nanga or no. Nor does it lie in vigilance, with its poignant assumption that we can see all and sort it all fast enough to foster the good and forestall the bad. What Marx and Hegel at least left to vast historical process we would manage with our own little gifts: the bringing of time to a point where it suits us, and stopping it there. Narcissus plays stickball, only to call the game at the point of his own heroism.

It is a significant advance, of course, that we say no to essentialism and grant the influence of time. But it would appear that we are falling into a kind of sequential essentialism, the casuisitry of discrete periods. Beyond this, then, lies the possibility of granting the inventiveness of time, or its ability to surprise (and even displease) us with what it makes and what it takes away. To know this about time, and about thought, is to go beyond the vanity of vigilance and the blockade of archaeologically settling knowledge. One alternative would be a relationship of faith in time, and in our own capacity to cope with its relentless abundance. We would teach not answers and rules, but powers and capacities, not safeguarding but the capacity for surprise. Thus we would not have to feel ashamed or slighted because other people do not yet recognize Alice Walker's *Meridian* or the Australian Louis Nowra's *The Golden Age* as major works in our century. We would teach the importance of alertness to marginality and still see that the whole change of attitude toward silence and exile in our century, starting with Joyce's comment on "silence, exile, and cunning," makes marginality a pre-atavistic concept. We would even conceivably wonder why we dote on narratology but do not love stories, and wonder why the subject of magic is making a comeback in the teeth of our passion for analysis and theory (there is a striking kinship between Louis Nowra's *The*

Anxiety of Beauty and Robertson Davies's *World of Wonders*, suggesting for historicists a possible concern with time as spirit and not just as things and gestures.)

I do not mean that there wouldn't be explicit or "latent scenes of unresolved canonical, i.e., social warfare" to use Louis Renza's phrase for what sounds like "Dover Beach" relived ("Exploding Canons," *Contemporary Literature*, 28.2, 259). There is always room for malice and ineptitude of judgment, and for fleeting fascinations and dogged aversions. I *do* mean that we would see the desire for a "noncanonical theory of value and evaluation" (Barbara Herrnstein Smith, in *Canons*, ed. Robert von Hallberg, University of Chicago Press, 1984, 11) as a defiance of the play of time and mind by which we are identified. Instead of that sneakily rigidist position, we would see the canon not as theological but as intrinsically neological, as an evolving manifestation more than a monolithic form. The strain between any present manifestation and any future one is the strain between knowledge that seeks to control and knowledge that consents to discover, or faith.

If the supposed center is the matter of the day, the danger arises that the margin will be a distorted mirror-image of it, or, worse, a kind of forever unavailable anti-matter. The movement of time and mind may be invisible, but it is going on apart from our vigilance. When the center is a stickball game of seemingly inviolate narcissism, an improbable figure of faith, a roly-poly figure of another character is always slouching toward the scene, not only to play the game but also probably to revise it, by lisping in numbers that get between the lines and change the bottom line. For, paradoxically, to submit ourselves to being in the uncertainty of time is certainly to be never left out and always on time and on the gyroscopically shifting target implicated in its own floating hierarchy.

Creative Intuition, Great Books, and Freedom of Intellect

Robert Royal

Nietzsche – one of the bad boys of Great Books lists – once remarked: "Every idea has its autobiography." This provides an explanation, if not an excuse, for the facile linkage of vast concepts such as Creative Intuition, Great Books, and Freedom of the Intellect in the title of this essay. During the controversy at Stanford in 1988 over required readings in Western Culture, I happened to be reading Jacques Maritain's *Creative Intuition in Art and Poetry*. Before beginning his philosophical analysis of intuition in that work, Maritain distinguishes the characteristics of Indian and Chinese art on the one hand from those of the art of the West on the other.[1] He draws these distinctions generously, but sharply, based on categories he accepted as a self-conscious and self-critical inhabitant of the West. His concern is not so much to judge value as to analyze difference; such an aim takes intellectual clarity as an overriding virtue whether one is dealing with one's own culture or another. Maritain's powerful and magnanimous *method* could not differ more from the very weak and condescending arguments about some presumably generic need to study non-Western culture that were then issuing from Palo Alto. But beyond Maritain's methodological superiority, his effort to apply high standards of rationality to world art suggests the deep connection of the controversy over the canon to maintaining – or perhaps achieving again – a vibrant, high, and free common culture.

But before we examine that subject, a little further autobiography. I feel honor bound to confess at the outset my own prejudices, if that is what they are. Like most of us who worry over these questions, as an undergraduate, I attended a prestigious university, one of those described by Allan Bloom in the *Closing of the American Mind*. My not-so-*alma mater*, however, goes Bloom's typical institution one better; it is so open and tolerant that it prides itself on having no requirements at all. A student must only complete a certain number of courses to graduate and must work out with a faculty member something called a "concentration" (a post-modern term, it seems, for a "major"). Academic life without canons or even much in the way of educational authority is for me, therefore, a vivid memory. And contrary to the usual rhetoric about the freedom and sense of intellectual excitement such a system is supposed to create, most adolescents – even very bright adolescents – are not as delighted with the radical "openness" of this "curriculum" as administrators and professors think. For many of them, it is a source of profound anxiety. In fact, the very etymology of "curriculum" ("lap of a racing track") shows the antithesis between most ancient and some modern concepts of education. Running around a track may be many things, but "openness" is not the first word that comes to mind.

All the university's promotional material touts this "New Curriculum" (even though it is now over fifteen years old) for its "flexibility" as well. Now for a student of the classical philosophy of education, this term "flexibility" may not immediately inspire awe. Plato and Aristotle seem to have thought it not worth mentioning. In fact, most theories of education until the last few decades would have thought mere flexibility good only in so far as it permitted better approaches to well-defined and dynamically pursued disciplines. The idea that flexibility in and of itself could be grounds for choosing a school had to wait for the lucid tranquillity of the Vietnam War era to raise its shining banner on the campuses.

To be fair to the university in question, which shall go unnamed, the reputation for flexibility has made it one of the two or three most popular colleges in the country. Some of us who continue to work with our brains, however, reflect occasionally on what good and harm all this flexibility did us. A recent poll of alumni found that in spite of all the huffing and puffing in university materials and the applause from guidance counselors' offices around the country, about half of the university's graduates say they liked their four years because of the flexibility, and about the same number say they didn't like their four years because of the flexibility.

People who wanted to learn at this institution (leaving the merely idle aside for some future sociological study) fell into two large categories. The first knew little, but were constantly being told they were the best and the brightest. They left the ivied halls happy and still mostly ignorant – some the kind of feminists who make stern criticisms of Western Civilization, but seem to know nothing much of anything that happened in the West prior to the 1950s, let alone philosophical and literary works that belong to other modes of thinking. These groups of students, along with the engineers, pre-med students, and all those others whose primary interests lay elsewhere, probably make up the bulk of those who remember being flexible with pleasure.

The other large group seriously wanted an education, and finding none available in any systematic way, went about picking up odds and ends and reading into interconnected subjects with the passion, but also the unavoidable eccentricity, of the autodidact. These people found great books – the present writer certainly did – but they tend to order them in personal, idiosyncratic ways that make discourse about them, even with one another, very difficult. As a result, for the most part we did our reading and conversed little with one another. Perhaps it would have been too painful to find that there was so little commmunity of thought even among the few people trying to do some thinking.

Having been through this experience, I am probably in a better position than most people to appreciate the value of Great Books courses and courses in Western Civilization (the terms will be used interchangeably for the remainder of this essay even though there are great differences between the two). But it is necessary to keep in mind some principles that Maritain would have introduced into this debate. Let's begin by way of what the medieval Schoolmen called *remotion*; let us make clear what mere lists of the monuments of Western culture are *not*.

First, while Great Books nourish our ethical and social roots, they are not salvation from our current cultural crisis.[2] To say that they can resolve the tensions and incoherences of our moral, social, political, and philosophical predicament is to argue that some secular canon, like the canon of Scripture, is an all-sufficient guide. *Sola scriptura* is a bad principle in either realm.

Some advocates of Great Books give the opposite impression – that passionate reading of crucial texts alone will give us the guidance we need to get through the dark wood of contemporary life. The wisest refutation of this view is Saul Bellow's novel *Herzog*. The character who gives his name to the book writes brilliant intellectual analyses of great Western books – as well as desperate letters to their authors – but his own life is far more troubled than that of the average person. Commenting on this novel, Bellow rightly identifies *the* modern problem as first of the soul rather than the intellect.

To finish with *Herzog*, I meant the novel to show how little strength
"higher education" had to offer a troubled man. In the end he is aware
that he has had *no* education in the conduct of life (at the university
who was there to teach him how to deal with his erotic needs, with
women, with family matters?) and he returns, in the language of games,
to square one – or as I put it to myself while writing the book, to some
primal point of balance. Herzog's confusion is barbarous. Well, what
else can it be? But there is a point at which, assisted by his comic sense,
he is able to hold fast. In the greatest confusion there is still an open
channel to the soul. It may be difficult to find because by midlife it is
overgrown, and some of the wildest thickets that surround it grow out
of what we describe as our education. But the channel is always there,
and it is our business to keep it open, to have access to the deepest part
of ourselves – to that part of us which is conscious of a higher consciousness, by means of which we make final judgments and put everything together. The independence of this consciousness, which has the
strength to be immune to the noise of history and the distractions of
our immediate surroundings, is what the life struggle is all about. The
soul has to find and hold its ground against hostile forces, sometimes
embodied in ideas which frequently deny its very existence, and which
indeed often seem to be trying to annul it altogether.[3]

Though some may be embarassed by the blunt use of the term "soul" in
this context, there is no easier way to refer to the ultimate issues that confront us as human beings. Human flourishing, Aristotle's *eudaimonia*, is
the end of all our activities and keeping clearly in mind that the needs of
the "soul" come first gives us, perhaps, an Archimedean point from which
to judge great books independent of all ideology.

A second preliminary point on Great Books follows from the first,
even though it is a contradiction of one of the main strands of Western
high culture. *Contra* some Great Books proponents, the unexamined life *is*
worth living. Such a life may be virtuous and valuable without the Socratic
exetasis entering into the question, especially when education is likely to
lead to the wild thickets that Bellow mentions. We all know simple people
who are wise and good without being learned, *per modum inclinationis*.
Contemporary America and most nations at most times through history
generally depend on this repository of simple virtue for their basic functioning. Unless Great Books programs make it clear that they have the
philosophical breadth to account for this, they tend to discredit themselves
as elitist studies with arrogant and unwarranted claims.

Third, to return to the ecclesial parallel for a moment, we should be clear that there is no list of *the* Great Books, because there cannot be. My colleague, Edwin Delattre, the president-emeritus of the Great Books school St. John's College at Annapolis and Santa Fe, rightly changed the materials on those campuses during his tenure in office to indicate that Great Books, not *the* Great Books were read there. One might, perhaps, go still further and say there *should* not be such a list. The canon of Scripture is defined by proper authority at a given moment. The landmarks of human history, intelligence, and creativity cannot be defined once and for all. They are either open to new arrivals and discovery of lost or overlooked eminences – in short, to active intelligence – or they are a series of fossils. Intellectual authority plays a crucial role in defining what is worthy of study and the question of authority must be examined later. But it appears, to say the least, doubtful that a mere list, absent some serious prior intellectual analysis, can either preserve the best from the past or properly credit what is deserving in the present.

All the misconceptions and exaggerated hopes about Great Books are understandable reactions to the cultural chaos in which we find ourselves. In current conditions, what could be more desireable than a manageable set of readings that define what an educated person should know? In many cases, such programs probably do a good job, though personal experience suggests that many people who have been through these programs, or teach in them, show a good deal of narrow sectarian spirit and far less catholic intellectual tastes than might be expected. This is a problem that does not even take us to the main questions of intellectual depth and power – the tough questions of sheer competence, both for teachers and students. Perhaps these phenomena of rigidity are only to be expected as the reaction to the excessive flexibility of other educational institutions.

In this regard, one of the most striking aspects of Jacques Maritain's reflections on the products of creative intelligence is precisely his catholicity and willingness to study less-than-great books. *Creative Intuition in Art and Poetry*, for example, overwhelms with philosophical and esthetic insight. But even more important is how much more "modern," in the best sense, Maritain is than most of those who prescribe Great Books for the ills of current culture – even thirty-five years after Maritain was writing. Perhaps this is because he is so confident of certain truths that he finds them simultaneously anti-modern and ultra-modern,[4] i.e., timeless. Maritain illustrates his arguments with passages from and reflections on Apollinaire, Cocteau, Gide, the Surrealists, Rouault, Chagall, Debussy, Hart Crane, Eliot, and Baudelaire among others. His lively appreciation of true poetic intuition, that profound freedom of the intellect, leads him to understand sympathetically what is alive and unique in modern works that most Great Books advocates would think beneath their notice.

Maritain does not. He rejects the kind of prudish classicism that he calls *misoneism*.[5] Instead, he carries out the classical mission of rational understanding in trying to account for why, under modern philosophical and social conditions, modern works are what they are. In so doing, he explains the non-representational aspect of more purely "poetic" modern work from a rare philosophical and psychological depth. These works have *their* rationale, and their rationale is modern. As he puts it, "it is difficult for a modern poet not to be the child of modern man."[6] This method is a good corrective to the kind of Great Books program that eschews all discussion of context for fear of historicism or relativism.[7]

In any case, Maritain never commits the sectarian's error of dismissing work simply because it is not comparable to the greatest of the past. Even less great contemporary work is important to us because it gives us the sense of living creation that past work usually cannot. Maritain beautifully presents the case for the greatness of Dante's *Divina Commedia*, for example. Dante was not only one of the greatest poets who ever lived but he had the advantage of innocent self-assurance and the luck of a solid culture behind him. Maritain defends modern writers who lack these advantages, "it would be nonsense to require from modern poets a 'greatness,' an objective intellectuality and universality of theme comparable to those in Dante."[8] Modern poetry for us gathers together all those bits and fragments of contemporary life into poetic intuition that hints at more *for us* at times than do the abstractly "Great" works. So the border between great and merely good is permeable, giving us opportunity to seek lucidly the relationship that obtains between them, over and above the pleasure and exaltation they provide us.

The reverse side of this intellectual generosity is that there are transcendently great works that must be actively appropriated if we are to make contact with the fullest range of human life we can appreciate. And for this need, study of Great Books is crucial. The curriculum of a very fine school based on a modified *paideia* program defines this part of its curriculum as the "Habitual Vision of Greatness,"[9] a striking way of putting it.

Creative or poetic intuition has direct and essential links to this full range. As Maritain sees it, the poetic and the mystical are somewhat akin in that they are authentic human dimensions that regularly pass outside of our everyday experience without losing touch with the regulations of intelligence. For him, true poetry and mysticism are never mere flights of the spirit that make their own laws as they go. Rather, he associates both with what he calls the human preconscious. Adopting an Aristotelian psychology, he seems to think that poetic intuition is linked in various ways with the more usual function of the agent intellect in transforming the phantasms derived from the senses into intelligible material for the possible intellect. The difference in poetic intuition is that the human faculty does not merely grasp the object as material for discursive reason. Instead, by a kind of connaturality, it *creates* an object that trails its roots in God's larger creation and shows its affinities with Being Himself.[10] How this occurs is not entirely open to our discursive mind; but that it does occur we are sure, as anyone who has ever really "gotten" a poem can attest. Perhaps, the best way to convey this point is to quote a poet, as Maritain does. In "Maid Quiet," Yeats says, "The winds that awakened the stars / Are blowing through my blood." *That's* poetic connaturality.

At first sight, this may merely seem of interest to esthetics and that part of the Great Books course that deals with poetry or art. But this view is a mistake, as Maritain shows. We might recall here a sentence from Saint Thomas that Maritain quotes frequently: "*Ex divina pulchritudine esse omnium derivatur.*"[11] As he elaborates this formula in *Creative Intuition in Art and Poetry*:

> a kind of poetic intuition can come into play everywhere – in science, philosophy, big business, revolution, religion, sanctity, or imposture – when the mind of man attains to a certain depth or mastery in the power of discovering new horizons and taking great risks.
>
> There is poetry involved in the work of all great mathematicians. Secret poetic intuition was at work in the primary philosophical insights of Heraclitus and Plato, Aristotle and Thomas Aquinas, Plotinus, Spinoza, or Hegel; without the help of poetry Aristotle could not have extracted from experience the diamond of his fundamental definitions; in the background of all the ideological violence of Thomas Hobbes there was something which poetry had taught him, his awareness that he was the twin brother of Fear. Poetry helped Francis of Assisi, and Columbus, and Napoleon, and Cagliostro.[12]

This passage confirms an important insight that the truly great thing in these diverse figures, before the more humble application of discursive tools, is this larger human insight that makes great the work not only of a Homer, or Dante, or Shakespeare, but of a Newton, Einstein, or – Cagliostro. Prudence, the virtue of art, and science all have a deep and common root in this view.

If our students are not taught that it is this greatness of conception, some sort of light flooding things from the pre-conscious or agent intellect or some other source, they may be tempted to think that the figures we hope they will familiarize themselves with are merely "clever" thinkers, or, still worse, convenient political props for the Western system.

It is no accident that the radicals who chant, "Hey, hey, ho, ho Western culture's gotta go" at Stanford have put themselves in the same position as the Soviet cultural bureaucracy (at least as that bureaucracy existed prior to Gorbachev). Whenever the free play of intellect – a freedom, that is not mere license but a freedom of connaturality with reality – is subordinated to a political orthodoxy, the human prospect narrows. This should not come as any surprise to us, even if the political vision claims to be humane and broad. Politics by nature is only a part of human life, but precisely the part we are most tempted to substitute for still larger things, which occupy only a tenuous hold on the modern world.

Sectarianism afflicts both teachers and students of *"the"* Great Books, but that problem pales in comparison with the recent threat to the freedom of intellect reflected in the politicization of the teaching process. The advocates of this politicization argue that the choice of what to study has been politically determined already: we just are not yet conscious of it. This is a minor charge, one that should be kept in mind to make us wary of unintentional blindness, but it entirely misses the main point of education. Education is not simply an indoctrination in correct political views. The radicals themselves are always decrying that. But in fact the free play of intellect, that unpredictable arrival of poetic intuition in a really well-wrought work, is constantly now being submitted to political tests.

Our vision of truly great books must remain open to the arrival of new masterpieces. But the current plea for virtual abandonment of all we have come to regard as great shows, by the very form of its argument, how feeble the alternatives are on the one hand, and how strong the Western tradition is on the other. Writing a blank intellectual check to non-Western cultures, without specification of what work is worth studying, is condescension of the worst sort. We do not insist that students simply study some work from Britain, or Germany, or France, as a sop to those who think these nations important. We read Shakespeare, Montaigne, and Goethe, and would want to read them in whatever parts of the globe they had written.

The current weakness of many Western intellectuals in the defense of the West has two causes, one legitimate and one not. A legitimate reason for wanting to look beyond Western culture is that there may be some major strands of the human experience that the West does not include. In fact, though, these elements are far fewer than most people think because what goes by the name "Western" is not even a full representative of the West – only a modern ghost of the riches actually within Western traditions. Hutchins and Adler mentioned this in the introduction to their series of Great Books.[13] The desire to break the stranglehold on what passes for *the* Western Tradition is not only just, it is devoutly to be wished.

Another stream plays into this one, however. There are many who want to go outside Western traditions because they think them, as they say, deeply racist, sexist, imperialist, and so forth. Admittedly, the West has shown all these unfortunate tendencies at times throughout its long history. The irony, however, is that these terms have been developed *in the West*, because we are concerned to answer the legitimate questions that they raise. This fact lies beyond the horizon for most of our cultural radicals. Around the time that the controversy was raging at Stanford, for example, an Indian scientist wrote to a Washington magazine to say, "Nearly all the knowledge of the past glories of these non-Western cultures – in which their intelligentsia take such great pride – is the result of Western scholarship. These cultures, for all their greatness, have little history and no archeology. So they owe a great debt to Western culture."[14] This debt is so great, in fact, that it induces great resentment – something that we should understand, but reject sympathetically as an impediment to the free play of thought.

One of my colleagues once gave a speech in which he mentioned that he and his daughter have put their desks next to one another at home under a bust of Aristotle so that they can study together. A woman in the audience rose after his presentation to express her puzzlement that he would have anything to do with Aristotle since he regarded women as inferior and thought some people slaves by nature. My friend replied, as is quite true, that the remedies for these blind spots may be extracted from

Aristotle himself, and that it would be a shame if so much intellectual trea-
sure were discarded because of some errors.

However well understood this may be among most scholars, we should
not underestimate how pervasive a more simplistic radical view has become among students. Put bluntly, this view holds that cultural figures who
are not politically "correct" are to be dismissed wholesale. I once gave a
lecture to a group of university students about Great Books, and a young
woman confidently informed me after my presentation that the Bible,
Plato, Aristotle, the Romans, the Father of the Church, Aquinas, and
many other major Western figures right up to the present were hopelessly
"sexist." "I've already looked into them," she said with finality. Whatever
legitimate political interests may lie behind challenges to current lists of
Great Books, their result is often – this anecdote could be easily multiplied
– precisely a closing off of thought rather than an opening up of a wider
dialogue.

Great Books or Western Civilization programs leave themselves open
to these ignorant attacks if they try to present themselves as what they are
not: as some sort of ideal intellectual order. If, instead, some of the figures
just mentioned are presented as moments of great human intuition involved in the ongoing human task of better understanding human life and
contributing to human flourishing – that enjoying Shakespeare does not
mean you cannot enjoy some non-Western dramatist of equal power and
depth – mere honesty will lead most students to see the obvious.

The question of the significance of non-Western figures needs further
clarification. Anyone familiar with philosophical, historical, and literary
works in their several original languages will know from experience that to
read Great Books in English translations and to think you are "getting
them" is a chimera. To take a crucial example, the Greek term *eudaimonia* is not exactly the same as *felicitas*, and neither is what we call loosely
happiness. Those of us who are not classicists but who still dip occasionally
into classical scholarship are probably surprised at how little most of us
see when we read the text of Homer or Virgil. The worlds they represent
need varied exposition and hard study at the original languages, no easy
task. Otherwise we are simply using our great forebears as mirrors for our
ignorant selves. And these works are supposedly accessible to us as parts
of our Western tradition.

Without doubt highly important works exist in other cultures, Confucius or the *Bhagavad-Gita* come immediately to mind. But the quick insis-

tence in academic debates on the importance of non-Western works, without specification of what we are talking about, is likely to be far less intellectually respectable than even a superficial reading of a Great Western book in translation. Are the advocates of these additions interested in them because they are great human achievements, or just because they are non-Western? As William James might have put it in his much understood phrase, what is the cash-value of these non-Western works? Even if this question can be answered, how are students really to understand these works without large chunks of time being devoted to linguistic, historical, and cultural matters? Or are we going to be content to colonize further non-Western mentalities by sentimental but slovenly intellectual approaches? We already have plenty of difficulty teaching works drawing on concepts within our own general culture.

We should be wary of a second problem of translation also. It is the very core of modern cosmopolitanism to believe that all works are transparent to the modern eye. There is great reason to doubt this. Many works, the Bible most definitely among them, require strenuous and long habituation before we even begin to understand them adequately. In *Whose Justice? Which Rationality?*, Alasdair MacIntyre puts the case forcefully:

> The type of translation characteristic of modernity generates in turn its own misunderstanding of tradition. The original locus of that misunderstanding is the kind of introductory Great Books or Humanities course, so often taught in liberal arts colleges, in which, in abstraction from historical context and with all sense of the complexities of linguistic particularity removed by translation, a student moves in rapid succession through Homer, Sophocles, two dialogues of Plato, Virgil, Augustine, the *Inferno*, Machiavelli, *Hamlet*. ... If one fails to recognize that what this provides is not and cannot be a re-introduction to the culture of past traditions but is a tour through what is in effect a museum of texts, each rendered contextless and therefore other than its original by being placed on a cultural pedestal, then it is natural enough to suppose that, were we to achieve consensus as to a set of such texts, the reading of them would reintegrate modern students into what is thought of as *our* tradition, that unfortunate fictitious amalgam sometimes known as "the Judeo-Christian tradition" and sometimes as "Western values." The writings of self-proclaimed contemporary conservatives ... turn out to be one more stage in modernity's cultural deformation of our relationship to the past.[15]

Whether he is right about the original locus of the problem – that part of his argument is historically doubtful – MacIntyre develops a very interesting idea of tradition that may help in these reflections. Modern cosmopolitan culture thinks of itself as a neutral observer of all particular traditions, says MacIntyre. In fact, however, it has turned into one more tradition, and a tradition with so many internal problems and self-contradictions that we are justified in looking upon it with a cold eye. There are competing main traditions, at least in the West: those deriving from Aristotle, Augustine, Aquinas, and Hume. We might want to add to MacIntyre's list Kant as well. MacIntyre ultimately favors the blend of Aristotle and Augustine carried out by Aquinas, but his view of this blend is different from the usual Thomism.

As he views St. Thomas, Thomist thinking is an open-ended advancing tradition that establishes itself on a broad ground of reality and seeks to incorporate new material and the solutions of new problems. The good Thomist will not only internalize Thomas's views, he will move them forward in ways that Aquinas could not have foreseen, but would have approved. The very idea of a "tradition" – a handing down of wisdom and knowledge – requires this dynamic. A culture is the incarnation of such a tradition. Culture provides us with a starting point for thinking without which progress is not possible both for lack of a place to stand and for the infinite complexities that would overwhelm any inquiry we think we can undertake *de novo*. As G.K. Chesterton put this, "culture is the mental thrift of our forefathers."

Recognizing that we can only make intellectual progress as part of some tradition is anathema to the modern paideia, though it is practiced by all those who belong to the modernist tradition. The principle value of great books is, arguably, that they help us to locate ourselves among the traditions. Many of us have had the experience of reading some great text that suddenly explains where basic beliefs we have long held took their origin. Granted, most undergraduates will leave such a program with little idea of what it all means. Some will, alas, think they understand everything on this brief acquaintance. But those who learn what large task really lies ahead will be worth the failures of the program.

This leads to another serious modern problem: how do we deal with the mass of secondary materials that have now proliferated around every subject? Each person knows and can know only a small part of even his own field. What does this mean for the organic nature of culture?

The work of the chemist turned philosopher Michael Polanyi is very useful here.[16] Polanyi did fine work, not only on epistemology, but on the idea of tradition, the scientific tradition in his case. When a discipline is in good condition, as science is in our time, the vast network of individual researchers and writers organizes itself into a self-criticizing mechanism that resolves small-scale problems. As regards the grand scale, Polanyi's vision is similar to Maritain's in that he sees the big advances in science as not merely the result of logical increments, but also as the effect of scientific intuitions that take a great step beyond the available evidence without being mere fantasy. Einstein, Heisenberg, and other great figures of twentieth-century science all had intuitions of theoretical truths long before data could be obtained to confirm or falsify these truths.

The difference between natural science and what we may broadly call culture, however, is that modern culture is not in good condition. As Aristotle noted long ago, questions of culture and ethics by their very nature differ from natural science in a way that calls for a different method of procedure. Failure to recognize this has led to theories like deconstruction, which assert that because a text is unknowable in its totality in the way we know something in natural science, it is unknowable period. In some ways, this is merely a reflection of the situation in which many professors find themselves: they are constantly inundated with a flood of contradictory readings of texts and events. It's no wonder that their characteristic *déformation professionelle* is to regard them all as plausible without possibility of rational choice among them.

As MacIntyre has shown, such a predicament underscores the need for developing a tradition – or traditions – of rationality that will preserve us from the perturbations of mere logic. Great Books advocates who would seek to save the situation by throwing our secondary materials entirely – a recommendation unfortunately embedded in the original Great Books program – are profoundly misguided. Most of us would probably not have benefitted from not reading secondary materials, in fact, we would for the most part have been crippled by this limitation. One of the tasks of modern teaching is to show students what is and is not important among the secondary material. To revert to the ecclesiastical metaphor, we need to have an idea of who are the best expositors and theologians of the developing secular canon if we do not wish to be cultural fundamentalists.

The best reason for seeking to avoid this fate is that as in religion there is *no* good reason for such a narrow conception of human culture. We may forgive its advocates who are reacting to what they quite rightly see as cultural chaos. But as in religion, the answer to chaos is not fundamentalism. The answer to chaos and fundamentalism alike is today, as it has always been, catholicity, in the sense of universality, supported by legitimate authority. In this, the Great Books will be helpful to us, but not if we sin against the light.

And as in ecclesiastical matters we must at some point confront the question of authority. On this question, Yves Simon, a friend of Jacques Maritain, provides some useful hints, particularly in his *General Theory of Authority*. He says in that work that "when the issue is one of action, not of truth, the person in authority has the character of a leader; but when the issue is one of truth, not of action, the person in authority has the character of a witness."[17] This distinguishes between two functions, both of which the university educator must possess, because he is involved both in the action of teaching and learning, as well as in the pursuit of truth.

These functions have been ill served by a false conception of teachers and students as merely and equally pursuing truth. As Simon says elsewhere of the relationship of liberty and authority,[18] both are necessary and only the virtue of prudence can correctly determine the way they should combine in given circumstances. Unfortunately many of those called to authority in modern higher education have virtually abdicated, refusing either to lead or to witness. An administrator at my *alma mater*, admittedly an extreme case, explained a couple of years ago why there are no requirements at the university: "We admit highly intelligent and very motivated students to this institution. The least we can do for them when they arrive here is to get out of their way." If this is true, why bother to send students to such institutions at all? Though this is an extreme form of an attitude present in higher education today, as an unintentionally pure sample, it probably shows better than anything else the root of the problem.

That administrator, and thousands like him not carried away by their own emotion to make explicit the principle, think universities and their faculties have no responsibility to *lead* in Simon's sense. They do not see learning as an action that may be performed better or worse in which an experienced leader might serve a function other than that of a "resource person" for neophytes. Such educators make themselves into mere technical facilitators, or less, not leaders in an ongoing tradition.

One of the odd things about teaching that allows such a confusion to occur is that it lies on the borderline between action and truth. The action of teaching calls for educational leadership. We have always tacitly acknowledged as much by creating institutions that require certain types and levels of performances, by empowering teachers to evaluate student achievement. The authority of truth, Simon's witnessing, is the essential element in education, but only after students have been *led* to the essential *foci* of significant action – the perennial human questions reflected in the wisdom of the race.

Some people denounce the cowardice of current educators for their failure to lead and to witness. This is too judgmental. Most educators have simply been misled, like much of the rest of the society, into believing that authority is in and of itself evil, that we are all pretty much on a plane of equality, and any privileging of some persons or some ideas over others sets us inexorably on the road to totalitarianism. On this view, authority must be authoritarian.

This is almost the precise opposite of the truth. The petrification of intellectual life for political reasons, a danger more likely to come from broad anti-Western forces today than from the tradition itself, is a tyranny already in place in some institutions and threatening others. At Stanford, a coalition of black, Hispanic, and Asian students were reported to have called the Western culture course "a year-long class in racism." The irony here, of course, is that it is only in Western or Western-style terms that African tribalism, Asian caste systems, and Western slavery may even be rejected under the rubric of "racism." But even worse in this respect is the uninformed and presumptuous reduction of the immense and polyvalent fruit of Western history, matching the achievements of any known human culture, to a paltry political category.

Only a properly constituted authority may begin to address this youthful presumption and ignorance. Great Books programs try to correct prejudice of this sort by teaching, in Mortimer Adler's unfortunate formula, what it means to be a "truly educated person." This is a modest goal, but the somewhat priggish tone of the phrase may put off the very people who need teaching most. Instead, we might approach the problem by quoting the authority of a non-Westerner, Confucius (in Pound's high-modernist translation), on his path to wisdom:

1. He said: At fifteen, I wanted to learn.
2. At thirty, I had a foundation.
3. At forty, a certitude.

4. At fifty, knew the orders of heaven.
5. At sixty was ready to listen to them.
6. At seventy could follow my own heart's desire without overstepping
    the t-square.[19]

The Chinaman's geniality and self-deprecating humor not only give us a
better idea of the lifetime task of learning, it reminds us that the ultimate
end of education is not merely to have the right political views nor to
become a "truly educated person." The "soul" is relentless. And whether
we conceive of it in traditional theological terms or in Bellow's more
sinewy fashion, there is some sense in which it is useful to affirm, even at
the risk of appearing simple-minded, that Great Books are important so
that ultimately the soul may come to know – and *listen to* – the orders of
"heaven."

Notes

The original, and somewhat different version of this essay was presented at the 1988
meeting of the American Maritain Association at the University of Notre Dame.

1. Jacques Maritain, *Creative Intuition in Art and Poetry* (New York: Pantheon Books,
    1953), pp. 10-21.

2. In his study *Education at the Crossroads* (New Haven: Yale University Press, 1943),
    Jacques Maritain suggests that the reading of great authors is the usual path of
    acquiring natual morality (p. 68). But he rightly observes later that already in the
    1940s, "The normal way ... does not suffice in the face of tremendous degradation
    of ethical reason which is observable today," (p. 94).

3. Allan Bloom, *The Closing of the American Mind* (New York: Simon and Schuster,
    1987), pp. 16 and 17.

4. Jacques Maritain, *Antimoderne*, in *Oeuvres Complètes*, vol. II (Fribourg: Editions
    Universitaires Fribourg Suisse, 1987), p. 928.

5. *Ibid., loc. cit.*

6. Maritain, *Creative Intuition*, p. 355.

7. Cf. Maritain, *Education at the Crossroads*, p. 71, "the great books should be accom-
    panied by enlightenment about their historical context and by counsel on the sub-
    ject matter."

8. Maritain, *Creative Intuition*, p. 399.

9. See brochure of the Trinity School, South Greenlawn Avenue, South Bend,
    Indiana.

10. Maritain, *Creative Intuition*, chapter IV.

11. Jacques Maritain, *Art and Scholastisism* (Notre Dame: University of Notre Dame Press, 1962), p. 31. The citation is from Aquinas' *Commentary* on *De Divinis Nominibus*, Cap. 4; lect. 5.

12. Maritain, *Creative Intuition*, pp. 238-39.

13. Robert Maynard Hutchins, ed., *Great Books of the Western World*, vol. I, *The Great Conversation* (Chicago: Encyclopedeia Britannica, 1952), chapter IX, "East and West," particularly pp. 70-71.

14. *Insight*, April 11, 1988, p. 4.

15. Alasdair MacIntyre, *Whose Justice? Which Rationality?* (Notre Dame: University of Notre Dame Press, 1988), pp. 385-86.

16. See Michael Polanyi, *Personal Knowledge: Towards a Post-Critical Philosophy* (Chicago: University of Chicago Press, 1962).

17. Yves Simon, *A General Theory of Authority* (Notre Dame: University of Notre Dame Press, 1962), p. 84.

18. Yves Simon, *Nature and Functions of Authority* (Milwaukee: Marquette University Press, 1948), p. 5.

19. Ezra Pound, *Confucius: The Great Digest, The Unwobbling Pivot, The Analects* (New York: New Directions, 1928), p. 198.

Perplexing Lessons:
Is There a Core Tradition in the Humanities?*

Roger Shattuck

The eighth chapter of *Life on the Mississippi* reads like a parable on education. Mark Twain gave it a cleverly appropriate title, "Perplexing Lessons." Urged on by Mr. Bixby, an experienced river boat pilot, the narrator and cub pilot has "managed to pack my head full of islands, towns, bars, 'points,' and bends." One day when the boy has learned most of the names, Mr. Bixby turns on him.

> 'What is the shape of Walnut Bend?'
> He might as well have asked me my grandmother's opinion of protoplasm.
> By and by he said, –
> 'My boy, you've got to know the shape of the river perfectly. It is all there is left to steer by on a very dark night. ... You learn it with such absolute certainty that you can always steer by the shape that's in your head, and never mind the one that's before your eyes.'

With no time to adjust to his new task, the cub pilot learns a further factor: that the river's shape keeps changing.

> Two things seemed pretty apparent to me. One was, that in order to be a pilot a man had got to know; and the other was, that he must learn it all over again in a different way every twenty-four hours.

How much comment belongs here? The classroom teacher might have a hard time with this secular American version of *Pilgrim's Progress*. How far need a teacher go to pick out the name writ large over the whole book: The River of Life? Mark Twain is content to keep the reader laughing at

---

* This paper was delivered at the annual meeting of the American Council of Learned Societies in May 1988.

Twain's bedraggled self as a boy. For those of us cogitating about cores and traditions in the humanities, Mark Twain has provided a vivid metaphor for education itself. To gain initiation into a culture, you have to know the shape of things, not the names only. We shall come back to Mr. Bixby in the wheelhouse sputtering at his inept pupil.

All of us are concerned with these cultural rites of passage not only because we may be professional educators, but primarily because we are citizens and parents. I envision the challenge that faces us in education as a two-headed dragon demanding daily human sacrifice to keep it placated and to prevent it from devouring the city. One awful head stands for the tens of millions of young minds all over the country waiting to receive nourishment, an almost sensible hunger for some form of knowledge that will make life possible and worth living. The second head rearing up with gaping jaws represents the other side of the same situation. It symbolizes the nearly one thousand hours each student and each teacher must spend in a classroom every year, time occupied by the long battle between boredom and alertness.

These two insatiable mouths must be fed. Enormous obstacles stand in our way. For two centuries now, well meaning and convinced educationalists have been telling us to allow children to follow their natural proclivities. The great defender of childhood as the period of natural freedom, Jean-Jacques Rousseau, invented a term that should have opened our eyes long ago to his program. "The first education must be purely negative" (*Emile*, Book II). He means that we should withhold any systematic or formal education, including reading, until the age of twelve. We have practiced negative education so effectively that today many students are admitted to college still unschooled and have to educate themselves six years too late, when their memories are slowing down, their doubts increasing. Rousseau devised the negative education theory for a very special, highly tractable, and imaginary pupil with a full-time tutor and other privileges. Carried on by progressive schools, the misbegotten scheme of negative education intersects another present danger – not a theory but a mood. For thirty years we have been living through a series of searing national traumas. Three major assassinations and the crises of Vietnam, Watergate, and the Iran-Contra affair may have left us disenchanted with the still fragile progress we have made toward true democracy and equal justice. Is it worth trying to maintain a rigorous universal education in an open, pluralistic society?

I shall not answer for others. Response must come primarily as a declaration of personal faith in chosen ideals. What I can insist on is a principle that operates as inexorably in a society as it does in physics. *Nature abhors a vacuum*. If we do not provide adequate knowledge to fill those hungry minds and empty schoolroom hours, something else will. That something else may well be deadening and corrupting – estrangement, anomie, idle vandalism, drugs, crime, suicide. These things cannot be said too often. In schools more than anywhere else, we can make an effort to establish the principle of equal opportunity by leveling everyone upward as far as possible. Family upbringing and college education quite properly tend to increase inequalities. Free public schools constitute our only major institution serving both individuals and the national interest.

Yet think for a moment. No authoritative document sets out what high school students should know. Powerful legal suits challenge school boards for doing their duty. Can we blame state boards of education for wobbling? One readily available reference is the booklet, *Academic Preparation for College: What Students Need to Know and Be Able to Do*, published by the College Board (1983). In science and mathematics, the booklet describes fairly well-defined content requirements. In the humanities (English, the arts, and foreign languages) the emphasis falls entirely on what I call "empty skills" – to read, to write, to analyze, to describe, to evaluate. To what specifics or content are these skills to be applied?

Silence. Not a single work of art or literature is mentioned. One could surmise that basic academic competencies can be acquired by working with any materials at all. Still, someone will decide on substance; too often the buck is passed down to the individual teacher, who must fill all roles – planner, helper, taskmaster, and final judge. We are here to reflect on the question, "Is there a core tradition in the humanities?" Our answers should do something to help put substance back into the humanities – and do so for the majority of students, not exclusively for the college-bound who read the College Board booklet.

The core of the humanities, as I envision it, is shaped less like the proverbial onion than like a simplified orange with three large sections or segments fitted closely together. My analysis leans inevitably towards a definition of culture, a term we have had in English in its general sense for barely a hundred years.

1. Official rituals and ceremonies and celebrations; monuments like the Statue of Liberty; the flag; the national anthem; the pledge of alle-

giance. These elements are mostly associated with some form of public enactment.

2. A loose, shared store of stories (legendary and history); folklore (including proverbs); ideas and concepts; historical and presumed facts. This common knowledge may remain unwritten and orally transmitted.

3. A collection of concrete, lasting works (images, buildings, music, writings in poetry and prose) considered significant or revealed or great or beautiful.

All I ask of this schematic division is to help us deal with questions of content in education. Segment two, the common fund of lore and knowledge, corresponds to all the names cub pilot Mark Twain learned – and did well to learn – in order to begin to know the river. Segment three, the lasting works and particularly books used in schools, provide Mr. Bixby's "shape of the river" – never beheld all at once, endlessly changing, yet a shape held in the mind to refer to under the most difficult conditions. Reading is the principal activity that allows us to move between these two segments, a kind of two-way membrane or circuitry that makes the connections between an amorphous mass of materials and a collection of recognized forms. Reading gains pertinence when it mediates between our available cultural knowledge and another realm loosely called literature.

Schools are concerned with all three segments of the humanistic orange. Fortunately I am not going to have to talk about the whole fruit. Recently my colleague E.D. Hirsch at the University of Virginia published a book called *Cultural Literacy*. This intelligent synthesis of history of education, developmental psychology, and recent research on perception, memory, and reading eloquently reaffirms the principles of universal education in a democratic society. He diagnoses our national illness as a condition based on misguided educational theory after Rousseau and on a faulty conception of pluralism that dismisses a common culture. What Hirsch establishes persuasively is a truism we should not have to be shown again.

But we do. Unless you know enough – enough facts and names and ideas – you cannot read. Decoding words and sentences will not produce meaning unless the reader knows the variety of items to which the passage refers. Then Hirsch has the imagination and the courage to go a step further. He answers the sassy question that may follow: So who is to decide what every American needs to know? He takes the dare himself. In sixty pages and about 5,000 entries he and two collaborators list the items you probably have to be able to recognize and identify in order to read and understand a newspaper.

Of course, such a list makes addictive reading, something between a quiz program and a collective psychoanalysis. Any citizen, reasonable or bigoted, can find fault with the entries. Most directly and importantly the list represents a challenge to all the rest of us educators who have evaded the task of defining what we expect students to know. Hirsch's book is a wonderful reciprocating engine: in order to read, you have to know a lot about the world as our culture conceives it; in order to acquire that knowledge, you have to read writing that will expand your mind. Here, to help in that process, is the best existing approximation of what you have to know and what our schools should aim to teach as a minimum. A list will not do the job; a list will help set the sights. If we put our minds to it many more citizens could really read. No Utopia here, rather a concise and exciting contribution.

Hirsch calls his list "the *extensive* curriculum," by which he means the basics of generally held information. Such basics will make available to everyone who masters them the elements of the culture through which we communicate with one another, particularly in writing. He hopes and I hope that more of these basics can be conveyed to students by revising our readers, by modifying our current approach to reading as a mere skill, and by making sure that all students, not just those from middle-class homes, learn the facts and ideas essential to understanding prose on the level of newspapers. Hirsch does not address except in passing the matter of the *intensive* curriculum – what specific books Johnny and Jenny should read in order to learn and apply these enhanced reading abilities of full literacy. Hirsch is perfectly right to proceed one step at a time. He already has an undeclared war on his hands with what I shall call – naturally – vested educational interests. Still, someone will have to talk and finally decide about the intensive curriculum; we shall talk about it here and now.

Hirsch, then, to my great satisfaction and with my vigorous support, has demonstrated the crucial role of section two in my three-section humanities orange. He has picked up the challenge of collecting what Mark Twain refers to as the names of the places and features along the river. You have to know them in order to talk with others about the river. As a cub pilot soon learned, however, the names do not give you the river's shape. That shape, elusive, mysterious, frequently changing in detail belongs to section three, around which I wish to build the center piece of my sermon.

Any discussion of a humanistic core, of how to recognize a classic or a masterpiece, of what makes up a canon, rests on three tacit presuppositions. Perhaps there are more. We assume a profound continuity in human life; to track and to measure that continuity we turn first of all to the immense palace-archive of history, which sits at the heart of the humanities. We expect to find continuity both in the macro realm of culture – mores, institutions, artifacts – and in the micro realm of human character, of human nature.

Here, I can do no better than produce two of my favorite quotations. Ortega y Gasset saw very deep. "Man has no nature. What he has is history." Emerson had passed that way earlier and left his unmistakable markings. "Properly speaking, there is no such thing as history. There is only biography." Whatever its precise form – history, biography, literature, the arts – a belief in the continuity of the human over many millenia lies behind any discussion of a tradition in the humanities.

Second, within the continuity of perception and imagination we have developed a limited number of versions of human greatness. These ideals – warriors, saints, martyrs, explorers, prophets, chiefs, sages, artists – provide several scales of human eminence, qualities to admire and perhaps to emulate. I cannot think of a culture, I cannot imagine a culture, without its slowly constructed versions of greatness.

Third, human beings long ago came to believe that continuity and greatness are effectively conveyed and celebrated in lasting artifacts or masterworks. Greek theater, Medieval stained glass windows, modern Islamic festivals for reciting the Qur'an serve the purpose of broadcasting cultural traditions to a large audience. As that cultural function has become increasingly concentrated for developed societies in organized public schools, school systems have universally found that the most practical and economic instrument of acculturation is the printed book. No other teaching aid even begins to rival it. The world has three great faiths that speak of themselves as the religions of the book. In its schools at least, the United States remains, and should remain for the foreseeable future, a culture of the book.

These presuppositions – human continuity, greatness, and recognition of them in masterworks – often remain undiscussed. Yet they belong to my definition of the humanities – indeed to my deepest sense of humanity. I shall proceed to how, as a teacher of a course in masterworks of Western literature since 1650, I deal with the tasks of selecting books out of the vast number put forward by tradition and by available anthologies. A classic that stands up through years of teaching will display a series of what I used to see as polarities. I now consider them to be complementaries. A classic will make its historical moment vivid and important; it will also have other features that make it remain contemporary. In other words, it is at the same time a period piece and forever young. In my course I would cite Molière to illustrate the point; Shakespeare does so even better.

A masterwork displays aspects that allow us to perceive in it a strong element of simplicity and clarity. It also awes us by the mystery and complexity it contains. We may well find it both reassuring and scary. Tolstoy's *The Death of Ivan Ilyich* will serve as an example. A masterwork will create the sense of confronting concrete, individual situations and character, which at the same time reach toward the domain of the general, the universal. In her best poems, Emily Dickinson's literary persona becomes a very concrete universal.

My three suppositions and my rules of thumb for recognizing masterworks brings me to a far more important point about a core tradition in the humanities. A discussion like the present essay would never have occurred in Europe before the eighteenth century, nor would it occur in most Islamic countries today. For those societies, the core has been revealed from on high and creates a center around which most aspects of life find an appointed place. For us, perhaps because some of us have lost our faith, certainly because of our hard-won "wall of separation" between church and state in public schools, the core cannot be presented as revealed. I would go so far as to say that in this open, pluralist society, the core is not even given. We have traditions and institutions and conventions. But they must answer to many pressures, political and commercial and religious. It seems more accurate to say that the past constantly *offers* a core tradition in humanities, an offer each of us plays some role in refusing or accepting. Can one say that each generation comes to a decision about these traditions? But what is a generation? School principals and school boards and college professors wrestle with these decisions in terms of curriculum and requirements. As long as the people involved are acting on the basis of actual reading on their part and careful reflection about cultural literacy and the shape of the river, these debates can be exciting and fruitful. The "intensive" curriculum of books read in class should not be handed down from on high by a minister of education to all schools in the nation, as happens in most parts of the world for reasons of national unity. There are less implacable ways of establishing a core, especially for a system like ours that must incorporate into its curriculum such essentials as healthy skepticism, verification of asserted facts, scrutiny of logical argument, minority views, and "critical thinking."

Teachers and professors all over the country should be spurring one another on to select the knowledge students need most in order to face a citizen's responsibilities – not just empty skills – and the books they should not leave school without having read. Choices will vary; a few brash committees will seek concensus. The federal government may wish to favor selected programs. States may decide to establish lists of works from which school districts may choose. Publishers will play a major, yet unpredictable, role. Blue-ribbon panels may make useful recommendations.

All this swirl of seeking and dissent will contribute to the improvement of education at all levels as long as one principle stands. Even in our pluralistic society the humanities have a core the way the river has a shape. The very process of discovering and gradually modifying that shape lends meaning and excitement to the intellectual life of a community. The most stimulating discussions I have had with my colleagues have dealt with specific content of curriculum change and how to define the knowledge we would require of all students and why. The answers may not satisfy everyone, but without those questions seriously pressed we resign ourselves to an invasion of empty skills and a confusing dispersion of minds. The Greeks, of course, already had a word for this state of things in which one learns primarily from the search, from the debate itself. A heuristic exchange of this kind will help us prevent education from becoming empty, the way it tends to be now, or rigid, the way some would like to see it. Established lists and recently published surveys demonstrate that a good deal of agreement already exists among educated citizens about the shape of our river. My own informal soundings on this subject over the past twenty years tell me that even a randomly-picked group of intelligent and educated people will agree on a handful of books that everyone should read at some point, in some form. Then the going becomes very slow. Mark Twain seems to point at these dilemmas with his title, "Perplexing Lessons."

It is time for a few specifics. If we are going to pick school books not entirely by reading level and word frequency, but by culturally useful content and effective writing, then the whole category of biography and autobiography falls beautifully into place. One of the most eloquently written and humanly valuable personal accounts available to us already fills many classroom shelves. Helen Keller's *The Story of My Life* makes the essential revelation that what we too easily think of as a given, the very condition of being human, is not given but learned. Deprived of the two senses we rely on most, living by touch alone, this magnificent woman can help us learn courage and imagination and appreciation of the simplest acts of living. Every detail provokes reflection. Only late in her childhood under a teacher of genius did Keller learn not to register on her face, as though through a window or on a screen, all her inner feelings. She discovered how to write fine English without ever hearing the language.

Another modern autobiography has been almost entirely forgotten by school programs. After a colorful early life as barnstormer, army pilot, and mail carrier, Charles Lindbergh helped design the single-engine, high-wing, almost windowless monoplane in which he had to fight sleep for hours and navigate alone and without radio from New Jersey to Paris. The book he wrote himself the same year, at age twenty-five, about his youth and that historic flight, rivals Plutarch in its depiction of small qualities of character that add up to greatness. The book is called simply *We*.

Allow me to pick up another example perhaps too close to home, I would like to think that in a book for high schools it took me five years to write, *The Forbidden Experiment*, I learned something from Keller and Lindbergh. For the story of the Wild Boy of Aveyron – not necessarily in my version – deserves its place, in my estimate, among these stories and in the core we are seeking and constituting.

I am not going to propose an exhaustive list of a core curriculum of even a short list. Rather, I advocate the heuristic goal of arguing over and drawing up such lists without neglecting modest candidates like Sherlock Holmes, folktales and fairy tales, the great religious works of the Greeks, the Jews, and the Christians, along with biography and autobiography.

Two prickly problems raise their heads immediately before we even begin to outline a core. First the question of timing. Is there an optimum moment to read *Hamlet*? When should we read *Huckleberry Finn*, the *Republic, Candide*? Should there be a national agreement on which works will be kept for college students? Which could be read in primary school –

perhaps in a simplified version? And there is the second problem already. Should we tolerate or even encourage the rewriting and adaptation of significant works in the humanities? *Don Quixote? War and Peace* for the schools? I once read and remembered large parts of *Moby Dick* in such a version. There is no categorical answer to any of these questions. My own experience tells me that skillful editorial work or even a complete retelling (like the Lambs's *Tales from Shakespeare*) can serve a valuable function in schools and in homes. But edited and truncated versions must be prepared with enormous skill and devotion.

Everything I have said up to now will come to nothing unless we adopt in our schools and maintain in colleges a coherent set of examinations on the subjects taught, on the content of books read. I shall have to summarize here an argument I set out at greater length in another place ("Helping Teachers Do What They Cannot Do Alone," *The Virginia Assembly*, Institute of Government, University of Virginia, 1984). Our present high school diplomas certify very little – mostly perseverance. Probably on a voluntary basis to start, our high schools should offer a state diploma based on a defined curriculum and on examinations in five basic subjects (English, history and geography, mathematics, science, foreign language). The New York State Regents examinations and the International Baccalaureate program adopted by a number of public high schools, demonstrate the feasibility of such a scheme.

Objections will come tumbling out from all sides. Standardized examinations lead to teaching to the test. Some teachers will feel that their autonomy is being invaded. But the advantages outweigh the criticisms, I believe. Only outside examinations will establish anything resembling quality control. Grades given by classroom teachers make an unreliable guide to what their students have learned. State certification based on examinations will give genuine integrity to the high school diploma, help employers choose workers, and begin to break the pro-higher education prejudice, which implies that in order to be adequately educated you have to go to college. The reinstitution of meaningful, earned high school diplomas will help every aspect of our society. Furthermore, classroom teachers could benefit enormously from the coach-player relationship that develops in athletics and dramatics. An outside examination provides a kind of performance in preparation for which everyone can work together without the adversary relationship that may set in between a student and the teacher who awards the final grade.

I began by comparing the core tradition in the humanities to the shape of Mark Twain's elusive and shifting Mississippi. I shall close with a second analogy. It reveals another aspect of our cultural survival. Almost immediately after fertilization, the human embryo sets aside a few cells that are sheltered from the rest of the organism and from the environment. These cells retain a special ability to divide by meiosis into haploid cells needed for sexual reproduction. Our gonads represent the most stable element in the body and are usually able to pass on unchanged to the next generation the genetic material we were born with. Except for radiation and a few diseases, the life we live does not affect our gonads. They guard the status quo; they change very slowly by mutation (usually rejected) or by other processes we do not understand.

A core tradition in the humanities, the three aspects of it that we expect schools to convey to all children, operates on the essentially conservative principle of gonads. A dynamic culture needs a steady center. After we have been to school, we may decide to test the center or challenge it or revise it in the give and take of democratic process. First, we should know where the center lies. It is not idealism, but deep skepticism about meliorism and about the witless inflation or our needs and desires that leads me to this analogy. Unless we teach in our schools a fairly steady sense of our humanistic traditions, of what has been called our civil religion, I envision a run-away culture seeking all extremes at once.

Jorge Luis Borges and the Canon of English Literature

Rosa E.M.D. Penna

Jorge Luis Borges was connected to English literature in many ways; he taught it first at the Universidad de Buenos Aires (the National University), from 1956 until 1964, when he was dismissed on turning sixty-five. Later he was appointed emeritus and taught again for two or three years, but not in the regular courses.

The story about his teaching at the Universidad Católica Argentina in Buenos Aires is a different one. The fact that Borges taught there is ignored by all the chronologies published so far. He was professor of English literature from March 1970 until December 1974, when he left for reasons unknown to me. Strangely he refers to this period as lasting for a year (*Borges en diálogo* 33).

In order to put together these notes centered on Borges and English literature I have borne in mind Borges's own words and opinions but I have preferred to use such material as can be found among the many occasions in which Borges put down his own thoughts on the subject, and also those scraps he scattered so lavishly in conversation with different people: María Esther Vázquez, Professor Burgin, Osvaldo Ferrari, and many others.

If one is patient enough to go over all these sources, one will certainly find a kind of coherence: certain statements come to be repeated again and again, they reappear in endless variation.

Taking as starting point the syllabus Borges agreed to teach at the Universidad Católica and which he used for five years with little alterations,[1] I have sorted out some of Borges's opinions on English literature, which he really loved, and which should be considered when studying or reading his poems or his fiction.

Evidently Borges thought of himself as a teacher: he has written a strange epilogue to his *Obras completas* (1143), in the third person, as a

note to be published in a nonexistent future encyclopedia in the year 2074.
There we read:

> He was professor at the universities of Buenos Aires, Texas, and
> Harvard with no other official degree except from a vague Genevan
> high school which critics are still investigating. He was Doctor Honoris
> Causa from Cuyo and Oxford. A tradition repeats that in exams he
> never asked a question and that he invited students to choose and con-
> sider any aspect of the subject whatsoever. He did not ask for dates,
> since he himself ignored them. He abominated bibliography which
> leads the student away from the sources.[2]

It is interesting to compare this passage with what Borges says in his conversations with Professor Burgin about exams and how literature should
be taught (*Conversations with J.L.B.* 122-25).

There is a quite perfect document on Borges by Borges in English,
published in the *New Yorker* in September 1970. There we read that for
Borges the memories of his father were connected to English literature:
"Though he was very proud of his English ancestry, he used to joke about
it, saying with feigned perplexity, 'After all, what are the English? just a
pack of German agricultural labourers.' His idols were Shelley, Keats and
Swinburne." And then he adds "When I recite poetry in English now, my
mother tells me I take on his very voice." (41)

Borges's ancestors came form Northumberland and the Midlands. He
used to say that fact linked him to a Saxon and perhaps a Danish past. In
his book of poems *El otro, el mismo*, there are several poems which refer
to Saxon poets or to the Anglo-Saxon world, e.g., "A un poeta sajón,"
"Composición escrita en un ejemplar de la Gesta de Beowulf," "Hengist
cyning," "Al iniciar el estudio de la gramática anglosajona", "Un sajón."

He used to start his teaching of English literature with Anglo-Saxon
poetry: *Beowulf*, the elegies, and the Christian poems. He knew "The
Dream of the Rood" by heart in Anglo-Saxon. This was in the seventies
and by then he had been giving Anglo-Saxon literature and language all
his attention and love for a number of years. Borges tells in one source
how it all started back in the year 1957, but he retold it differently on different occasions. As he also used to say, remembrances may be false.
Once a group of girl students from the Universidad de Buenos Aires, who
had passed their exams, went to see Borges and as he remembers it:

I said "I have a strange idea. Now that you have passed, now that I have fulfilled my duty as a teacher, wouldn't it be interesting to study a language and a literature we hardly know?" "Which is the language and which the literature?" they asked me. "Well, naturally, the English language and the English literature," I told them. "Let's begin to study them now when we are free from the frivolity of exams. Let's begin at the origins." (Borges, "La ceguera" 2)[3]

In the "Autobiographical Notes" Borges says: "I had always thought of English literature as the richest in the world; the discovery now of a secret chamber at the very threshold of that literature came to me as an additional gift." (93)

He referred repeatedly to the pleasure he felt when he began to study the Anglo-Saxon language, and how he learned the two runes for the "th": "I could not see these letters but I made them draw them very big on a board, and now I have an exact image of them" ("La ceguera" 2). The words in the new language "seemed like a talisman" (2) and they turned out to be one of the gifts blindness had brought to him:

The fact is I had achieved what I wanted, i.e., I had replaced the visible world by something different, by an aural world. I had replaced it by that world of the Anglo-Saxon language. ... blindness was not a despair for me, ... it was the beginning of something new. ("La ceguera" 2)

When recalling his first trip to England,[4] he used to say that on a winter day in a small Saxon church near Litchfield where he went to Dr. Johnson's birthplace, he did as he had promised long before in Buenos Aires, when he had no hope of ever travelling to England; he recited the "Our Father" in Old English: "And I made resound after ten centuries, in that small forgotten church the 'Faether ure, thu aert on hoevenum / sie thin nama gehalgot.' I think that I did it to give God a small surprise" (M.E. Vázquez, *Borges: imágenes* 71).

Borges was really fascinated by the metaphors in Anglo-Saxon poetry. This was a subject he always took up in his lectures and he has left an essay on the *kenningar*, written as far back as 1932:

An epigram in the Greek Anthology declares "I want to be the night to look at you with a million eyes." Chesterton defines the night as a monster made of eyes.[5] Both examples equal eyes and stars, but the first expresses the anxiety, the tenderness, the exaltation, and the second the terror. Our imagination accepts both. The *kenningar* instead are or seem the result of a mental process that looks for eventual likenesses. They do not correspond to any emotion. They originate in a laborious combinatory play, not in a sudden perception of intimate affinities. Mere logic may justify them, not feeling. (*Nueva antología personal* 301)[6]

The names of English authors and works that appear more frequently in Borges's writings coincide with his choices when lecturing on English literature:[7] Chaucer, Langland, Francis Bacon, Christopher Marlowe, Shakespeare.

There are not many allusions to Shakespeare. A prose piece entitled originally in English "Everything and Nothing" (*Obras completas* 803-4) centers on him.[8] In his classes Borges invariably commented on *Hamlet*, *Macbeth*, and the *Sonnets*.

From Donne he used to choose passages from *Biathanatos* and the "Hymn to God, my God in my Sickness" – both texts led him to speak on death and suicide. After Donne his syllabus included Milton, Johnson, and Boswell, three favorite subjects.

Milton attracted him mainly as the author of *Samson Agonistes* and because of his doctrines on creation which connected him to some medieval cabbalistic writers (Vázquez, *Borges: imágenes* 158-59). Borges spoke of the identification of character with author in the case of Samson:

> Milton, already blind, betrayed as he thought by his wife, could identify himself with Samson and write this drama which conforms strictly to the three classical unities. ... It has beautiful metaphors of an Oriental kind like the one, for example, when Dalila appears and the chorus asks "But who is this? What thing of sea or land?" and compares her to a stately ship. Images of a Biblical kind. And then that line where Samson deploring his condition says: "Eyeless in Gaza at the mill, with the slaves." (Vázquez, *Borges: imágenes* 157)

Milton's blindness had a special appeal for Borges. He thought of himself as connected to Milton through the fact of blindness, the same as he was connected to Paul Groussac, a literary critic from the beginning of the century and once director of the National Library in Argentina. When Borges spoke on the subject of blindness he also remembered Joyce, Homer, and his own father who became blind.

There are three poems, at least, by Borges written on Milton *and* blindness, and the three of them are sonnets: "Una rosa y Milton" (*El otro, el mismo* 115), and two entitled in English "On his blindness" so that we must remember Milton when we read them (*Obras completas* 1099; *Los conjurados* 59).[9]

When lecturing on English literature, after Milton Borges used to speak on Dr. Johnson and Boswell, and immediately after that on the Romantic poets. James Macpherson usually started the list. *Fingal*, Borges commented, had been read by Napoleon in an Italian version, and by Goethe: "It may not be an authentic reconstruction of a Celtic epic; but there is no doubt that it is the first romantic poem in European literature" (*Obras en colaboración* 830).

Blake, Wordsworth, Coleridge, Keats, and Lord Byron were the poets on whom he commented, choosing a short poem which could be read out loud in class, or a fragment from a longer work. For example, from William Wordsworth he invariably chose a long fragment from *The Prelude* (Book V: 'Books') where there is a vision in a dream which includes an Arab on horseback who is also Don Quixote and a stone which is also a book – notice how Borges's own work is reflected in a choice of texts like this one. The subject of dreams and their connection to poetic creation is like a thread which can easily be followed from Caedmon to Wordsworth to Coleridge to De Quincey and Stevenson.[10]

On Coleridge, Borges has left at least two prose writings, "La flor de Coleridge" and "El sueño de Coleridge" (*Otras inquisiciones* 19-30). "Kubla Kahn" fascinated him maybe because of its relation to creation in dreams.[11] He referred to John Keats as "the highest lyrical poet in England" (*Obras en colaboración* 833) and spoke of the enduring quality of two of his poems "Ode to a Nightingale" and "Ode on a Grecian Urn."[12]

Thomas De Quincey was another favorite author. He was almost conjured up in a poem "A cierta sombra, 1940" (*Elogio* 65-66) to come and help save England from the German and the Italian:

> Vuelve a soñar, De Quincey.
> Teje para baluarte de tu isla
> Redes de pesadillas.
> Que por sus laberintos de tiempo
> Erren sin fin los que odian.[13]

In another place Borges says: "Visions of the Orient haunted him; in dreams he believed himself to be the idol and the pyramid. His delicate and intricate paragraphs open up as cathedrals of music" (*Obras en colaboración* 833).

Lines from Tennyson's and Browning's poetry had a place in Borges's prodigious memory. He often quoted Tennyson's line "Far on the ringing plains of windy Troy" as an example of the untranslatable in poetry, though he himself gave it in Spanish as "Lejos en las resonantes llanuras de la ventosa Troya" (*Obras en colaboración* 841).

Robert Browning is an author few teachers would choose to include in a short course on English literature, but Borges always included him. And he has also left numerous references to him in his works. He used to say: "He differed from Tennyson because he sought, like his Anglo-Saxon ancestors, the music of hardness, not sweetness" (*Obras en colaboración* 841).

The way Browning and his England were mingled in Borges's mind with himself and his Buenos Aires can best be seen in a very strange short passage to be found in one of his lesser known books, the long essay on a minor Argentine poet, Evaristo Carriego, written in 1930:

> I write these recovered facts and with apparent arbitrariness I am haunted by the thankful line from *Home Thoughts* "Here and here did England help me" which Browning wrote, thinking on an abnegation on the sea and on the stately ship ... on which Nelson fell, and which repeated by me, translating as well the name of the homeland, because for Browning the name of his England was not the less immediate – it serves as symbol of nights alone, enraptured and eternal walks alongside the infinitude of the suburbs. Because Buenos Aires is deep and never amid disillusion or grief have I abandoned myself to its streets without receiving an unexpected consolation, grasping irreality, guitars from the deep end of a patio, the friction of lives. "Here and here did England help me." Here and here did Buenos Aires help me. That reason is one of the reasons why I decided to compose this first chapter. (*Ficcionario* 34)

Borges used to comment on the plan Browning had of using a purely Germanic English; he recited the first lines of the *Odyssey* in Browning's translation, "Tell me, oh Muse of the Shifty, the man who wandered afar, after the Holy Burg, Troy-town, he had wasted with war," and added "which suggests less the Mediterranean than the Northern Sea" (*Obras en colaboración* 844).[14]

Among the nineteenth-century prose writers and novelists, Borges's favorite authors were Carlyle, Dickens, Conrad, Kipling, Stevenson, and Henry James. Although when he taught at the Universidad Católica in Buenos Aires the last names included in the program were Shaw and Chesterton, he has written on Oscar Wilde, W.B. Yeats, James Joyce, and Virginia Woolf.[15]

In 1925 he wrote a poem entitled "Manuscrito hallado en un libro de Joseph Conrad." Two of Borges's themes, personal identity and time appear in it. On the other hand, Conrad's themes, treason and fidelity, appear quite often in Borges's fiction, as is the case with "La otra muerte" (in *The Aleph*), originally called "La redención," where a heroic posthumous action that tries to redeem an act of cowardice brings to the mind *Lord Jim*.[16]

Robert L. Stevenson was for Borges "one of my favourite authors" (Burgin, *Conversations* 124). He comments:

> One of his first books, *New Arabian Nights*, anticipates the vision of a fantastic London and it was rediscovered much later by his fervent biographer Chesterton. ... Like Kipling, the circumstance of having written books for children has perhaps diminished his fame. *Treasure Island* has made us forget the essay writer, the novelist and the poet. (*Obras en colaboración* 845)[17]

Dickens, Browning, Stevenson, and Shaw are united in another favorite author who was mentioned more than any other, I think, always with love and admiration, Gilbert K. Chesterton. In Argentina, Chesterton was very popular in the 1940s and 1950s. When he died in 1936, Borges wrote a long essay on him, published in the literary periodical *Sur* (reprinted in *Ficcionario* 117-22). Since that date Borges has spoken about him innumerable times. Their names will be linked by a strange coincidence: Borges died on the same day as Chesterton, fifty years later. Borges's long critical essay *Evaristo Carriego* – a literary biography that tells us more about Borges than about Carriego – is modelled on Chesterton's book on Stevenson. And when teaching Chaucer, although Borges did not usually recommend any bibliography on the authors, he always mentioned Chesterton's book on Chaucer, "an excellent book about him."

In *Introducción a la literatura inglesa*, Borges wrote: "The most famous of his novels *The Man Who Was Thursday*, has as a subtitle *A Nightmare*. He could have been an Edgar Allen Poe or a Kafka: he preferred – we should thank him – to be Chesterton" (*Obras en colaboración* 851).

When Borges discussed the detective story, one of his favorite subjects, Chesterton was always commented on. For instance, there is a documented occasion, June 1978, at the Universidad de Belgrano:

> Chesterton said that there were no better written detective stories than those of Poe, but Chesterton – it seems to me – is superior to Poe. Poe wrote purely fantastic stories. ... And besides stories including reasoning like those five detective stories. But Chesterton did something different, he wrote stories which are at the same time fantastic stories and that finally have a solution including detection. (*Borges, oral* 78)

That day Borges continued the lecture retelling Chesterton's *The Invisible Man*, one of the texts he really liked. And he was also very fond of two of Chesterton's metaphors (see note 5).[18]

I would like to end this article referring to Borges as a reader and a reader of English literature. It is a natural outcome of what has here been said. He taught English and American literature because he had read a number of authors and because he loved them. He himself made the point clear in essays, in some poems and in his conversations, in Spanish and in English, in Argentina and in different parts of the world. For example, in a conversation with Osvaldo Ferrari he said:

> In several continents I have diffused the love for Stevenson, the love for Shaw, the love for Chesterton, the love for Mark Twain, the love for Emerson; and, well, maybe it is not the essential part of what has been called my work – to have diffused this love. Well, also to have taught. (*Borges en diálogo* 207-8)

In his book *Elogio de la sombra*, there is a page entitled "Una oración" ("A Prayer") written in July 1969. He says this is a personal prayer, not an inherited one like the "Our Father," which "my mouth has pronounced and will pronounce, thousands of times and in both the languages which are intimate to me" (143). In this prayer Borges says:

I want to be remembered less as a poet than as a friend; let someone repeat a cadence by Dunbar or by Frost or from the man who saw at midnight the tree that bleeds, the Cross, and may he think that he heard it first from my lips. The rest does not matter to me; (143-44)

And let us finish with two lines from "Un lector" ("A Reader") in the same book: "Que otros se jacten de las páginas que han escrito; / a mi me enorgullecen las que he leído" ("Let others boast of the pages they have written; / I am proud of those I have read.") (151).[19]

Notes

1. See Appendix I for a copy of the syllabus used at the Universidad Católica Argentina in 1974.

2. I have tried to give only quotations from published sources, using my own translations into English from the Spanish originals, including lines from poems. The titles of poems are cited in Spanish.

3. For a revised version of this lecture, published in a book, see Borges, *Siete noches*. This episode is also remembered with slight variations in Borges, "Autobiographical Notes," 93; in M.E. Vázquez, *Borges: imágenes* 151, and in M.E. Vázquez, *Borges, sus dias* 169-70.

4. The love for English literature included the love for England and vice versa. In March 1962, he wrote: "Those of us who love England do it with a personal love, as if it were a human being, not an eternal form. There is something unexplainable and something intimate in the idea of England, something that shows through the austere lines by Wordsworth, in the straight and careful typography of certain books and in the spectacle of the sea in any place in the planet" (*Páginas* 225). Later he composed a poem, "A cierta isla" (*La Cifra* 89-90), which we give in Appendix II.

5. Borges was very fond of two passages from Chesterton's poetry, which are both examples of metaphors and which he often quoted. They are: "And Marble like solid moonlight/And gold like a frozen fire," from *The Ballad of the White Horse* (Book III, stanza 21, lines 10-11) and lines 27-30 from the poem "A Second Childhood." See for example Barnstone, 165.

6. See Burgin 12 for a commentary on Borges's writings on the kennings.

7. It is interesting and rewarding to have a look at Balderston's compilation.

8.   In 1984, in conversation with Osvaldo Ferrari, Borges referred to this writing on
     Shakespeare (*Borges en diálogo* 64-68). He linked Shakespeare to the problem of
     identity in a "maker" who has created many characters. Besides he refers it to his
     own identity problem in "Borges and I." See also in his *Historia de la noche* (119-20
     and 143) the poem "The Thing I Am," thus originally entitled. And the prologue to
     an edition of *Macbeth* in *Prologós* 142-47.

9.   The sonnet in *Obras completas* is preceded by two other sonnets with a common
     title "El ciego" (1098). We should note that Borges admired Milton as a sonnetist
     though he also wrote of him as an epic poet: see, e.g., Vázquez, *Borges: imágenes*
     157, and *Obras completas* 264-65.

10. For nightmares and dreams connected to Coleridge, Wordsworth, and De Quincey
     see Borges, *Siete noches* 44-53.

11. See also Burgin, 129. In his *Introducción a la literatura inglesa* (in *Obras en colabo-
     ración*) Borges also describes how "Kubla Kahn" was conceived: "Coleridge
     dreamed a triple dream, musical, verbal, and visual. ... He knew (like one knows in
     dreams) that music built the palace" (832).

12. There is an essay on the "Ode to a Nightingale" in *Otras inquisiciones* ("El ruiseñor
     de Keats" 149-53) and a poem entitled "John Keats" in *Obras completas* 1095.

13. In English: Dream again, De Quincey. / Weave for a bulwart in your island / nets of
     nightmares. / That through its time labyrinths / may wander endlessly those who
     hate.

14. See Burgin 57, for Borges's comments on *The Ring and the Book*, which he really
     did introduce to a lot of readers in Argentina. In the foreword to *El otro, el mismo*,
     Borges speaks of the influence of Browning's dramatic monologues on one of his
     poems "Poema Conjetural" (10).

15. Borges used to review books for a weekly magazine *El Hogar* (Buenos Aires) at the
     beginning of his literary career, from 1936 to 1939. These texts have been gathered
     in *Textos cautivos*. Besides Borges has written introductions to different editions of
     English authors in translation, e.g., to the works of Thomas Carlyle, Wilkie Collins,
     Henry James, and Lewis Carroll.

16. On Conrad see Borges, *Ficcionario* 436-37; *Obras en colaboración* 849; Burgin 55;
     and Borges and Ferrari, *Libro* 48-55.

17. See *Borges en diálogo* 85-86, and Barnstone 119.

18. It would take a lot of space to comment on Chesterton as seen by Borges. It is a
     subject that deserves an independent essay, if it has not been already written.

19. See also Barnstone 118: "I always thought of paradise as a library."

Works Cited

Balderston, Daniel, compiler. *The Literary Universe of J.L. Borges: An Index to references and allusions to Persons, Titles and Places in his Writings*. New York: Greenwood Press, 1986.

Barnstone, Willis, ed. *Borges at Eighty*. Bloomington: Indiana University Press, 1982.

Borges, Jorge Luis. *Elogio de la sombra*. Buenos Aires: Emecé, 1969.

Borges, Jorge Luis. *El otro, el mismo*. Buenos Aires: Emecé, 1969.

Borges, Jorge Luis. *Ficcionario: una antología de sus textos*. Ed. by Emir Rodríguez Monegal. México: Fondo de Cultura Económica, 1985.

Borges, Jorge Luis. *Historia de la noche*. Buenos Aires: Emecé, 1977.

Borges, Jorge Luis. "La ceguera." *La opinión* [Buenos Aires]. 31 August 1977, III: 1-3.

Borges, Jorge Luis. *La cifra*. Buenos Aires: Emecé, 1986.

Borges, Jorge Luis. *Los conjurados*. Madrid: Alianza, 1985.

Borges, Jorge Luis. *Nueva antología personal*. Buenos Aires: Emecé, 1968.

Borges, Jorge Luis. *Obras completas*. Buenos Aires: Emecé, 1974.

Borges, Jorge Luis. *Obras en colaboración*. Buenos Aires: Emecé, 1979.

Borges, Jorge Luis. *Otras inquisiciones*. Buenos Aires: Emecé, 1960.

Borges, Jorge Luis. *Páginas de Jorge L. Borges seleccionadas por el autor*. Buenos Aires: Celtia, 1982.

Borges, Jorge Luis. *Prólogos: con un prólogo de prólogos*. Buenos Aires: Torres Agüero, 1975.

Borges, Jorge Luis. *Siete noches*. México: Fondo de Cultura Económica, 1980.

Borges, Jorge Luis. *Textos cautivos: ensayos y reseñas en "El Hogar" (1936-39)*. Ed. by E. Sacerío Garí and E. Rodríguez Monegal. Buenos Aires: Tusquets, 1986.

Borges, Jorge Luis and Norman Thomas di Giovanni. "Autobiographical Notes." *The New Yorker*, 19 September 1970, 40-99.

Borges, Jorge Luis and Osvaldo Ferrari. *Borges en diálogo: conversaciones de J.L. Borges con Osvaldo Ferrari*. Barcelona: Grijalbo, 1985.

Borges, Jorge Luis and Osvaldo Ferrari. *Libro de diálogos*. Buenos Aires: Sudamericana, 1986.

Borges, Jorge Luis and Martín Müller. *Borges, oral*. Buenos Aires: Emecé/Editorial de Belgrano, 1979.

Burgin, Richard. *Conversations with Jorge L. Borges*. New York: Rinehart and Winston, 1968.

Vázquez, María Esther. *Borges: imágenes, memorias, diálogos*. Caracas: Monte Avila, 1977.

Vázquez, María Esther. *Borges, sus días y su tiempo*. Buenos Aires: Javier Vergara, 1984.

Appendix I

Universidad Católica Argentina
Facultad de Letras
Programa de Literatura Inglesa
Curso 1974

1. Caracteres generales. La raza, el idioma, el individualismo. Elementos de la poesía germánica: acento, aliteración, metáfora. Poesía épica y elegíaca de los sajones. La Gesta de *Beowulf. El sueño de la cruz.*

2. La Conquista Normanda. El siglo XIV: Chaucer; las visiones alegóricas de W. Langland. Los poemas aliterativos: *Sir Gawain y el caballero verde.*

3. William Shakespeare y su época.
   – Hipótesis relativas a F. Bacon y a Christopher Marlowe.
   – Las tragedias de Shakespeare: *Macbeth, Hamlet, Julio César.*
   – Las comedias: *Noche de epifanía.*
   – Las historias: *Richard II.*
   – Los *Sonetos* de Shakespeare. La evolución de la forma 'soneto' en Inglaterra.
   – Dos contemporáneos de Shakespeare: Christopher Marlowe y Ben Jonson.

4. Los poetas metafísicos o conceptistas: John Donne y Andrew Marvell.

5. Vida y obra de Milton: *El paraíso perdido, El paraíso recuperado. Samson agonistes.* Su teología secreta.

6. El siglo XVIII. Johnson y la biografía de Boswell.

7. El siglo XVIII. Orígenes del movimiento romántico. Las "traducciones" de Macpherson.

8. El romanticismo inglés. Los poetas de las escuela Laquista: William Wordsworth y S.T. Coleridge. Teorías y poesías. La segunda generación de románticos: Byron, Keats.

9. El siglo XIX y la novela. Charles Dickens. Robert Browning. Los Pre-Rafaelistas.

10. La obra de Henry James, de Robert L. Stevenson y R. Kipling. Dos amistosos adversarios: Chesterton y Shaw.

Buenos Aires, Marzo 1974.

Appendix II

A cierta isla

¿Cómo invocarte, delicada Inglaterra?
Es evidente que no debo ensayar
la pompa y el estrépito de la oda,
ajena a tu pudor.
No hablaré de tus mares, que son el Mar,
ni del imperio que te impuso, isla íntima,
el desafío de los otros.
Mencionaré en voz baja unos símbolos:
Alicia, que fue un sueño del Rey Rojo,
que fue un sueño de Carroll, hoy un sueño,
el sabor del té y de los dulces,
un laberinto en el jardín,
un reloj de sol,
un hombre que extraña (y que a nadie dice que extraña)
el Oriente y las soledades glaciales
que Coleridge no vio
y que cifró en palabras precisas,
el ruido de la lluvia, que no cambia,
la nieve en la mejilla,
la sombra de la estatua de Samuel Johnson,
el eco de un laúd que perdura
aunque ya nadie pueda oírlo,

(How to invoke you, delicate England? / It is evident I must not try / the pomp and din of the ode / unsuited to your coyness. / I shall not speak of your seas, which are the Sea, / nor of the empire which was imposed on you, intimate island / by the challenge of the others. / I shall mention in a low voice some symbols / – Alice, who was a dream of the Red King, / who was one of Carroll's dreams, today a dream, / the taste of tea and sweets, / a labyrinth in the garden, / a sundial, / a man who misses (and tells nobody that he misses) / the East and the glacial empty spaces / which Coleridge did not see / and ciphered in precise words, / the sound of the rain, which does not change, / the snow on the cheek, / the shadow of Samuel Johnson's statue, / the echo of a lute which remains / though nobody can

el cristal de un espejo que ha reflejado
la mirada ciega de Milton,
la constante vigilia de una brújula,
el libro de los Mártires,
la crónica de oscuras generaciones
en las últimas paginas de una Biblia,
el polvo bajo el mármol,
el sigilo del alba.
Aquí estamos los dos, isla secreta.
Nadie nos oye.
Entre los dos crepúsculos
compartiremos en silencio cosas queridas.

(*La cifra* 89-90)

---

*hear it now, / the crystal of a mirror which has reflected the blind look of Milton, /
the constant wake of a compass, / the Book of Martyrs, / the chronicle of obscure
generations / in the last pages of a Bible, / the dust under the marble, / the
concealment of the dawn. / Here we both are, secret island. / Nobody hears us. /
Between the two twilights / we shall share in silence beloved things.)*

(Translated into English by *Rosa E. Penna*)

The Teaching Anthology and
the Canon of American Literature:
Some Notes on Theory in Practice

Glen M. Johnson

The past two decades have brought a shift in usage of the term "canon" by American scholars. Once used primarily to refer to the body of works by a single major author, "canon" increasingly has come to denote those works *considered to be* "literature," works for that reason preserved, taught, written about, and surrounded by the scholarly and critical activities that constitute literature as a field of study. The shift toward primacy of the latter definition has occurred for the most part without the term's losing its definite article, so that while it seems obvious that there are different canons,[1] discussions of literature characteristically refer to "*the* canon." Further, the question with regard to the canon of an author's works is one of authenticity, a question open to controversy but discussable within bounds that are fairly well defined. In the wider sense of "the canon," however, discussions evoke issues fundamental to the term in its scriptural analogy: the *rule* – how does one define "literature"? – and the *authority* – who does the defining?

A number of trends have combined to make "the canon" an issue. The most visible has been the rise of feminist scholarship and the interest in "minority" voices of all kinds. In the United States, feminist scholarship has for the most part pursued an agenda of affirmative action, the "opening" of the canon to more authors and a wider variety of expression. Poststructuralist literary theory, a European import that has moved unevenly into the American academy, with its attack on "logocentrism" has called into question anyone's ability to appropriate a text and deal with it through interpretive norms; on the face of it "deconstruction" makes impossible a canon and perhaps "literature" as well. Although the debate over poststructuralism has focused mainly on Derrida and de Man, the most influential European may have been Michel Foucault. Foucault's discussion of authority in discursive practice[2] – always, to his mind, a manifestation of power, and always repressive – has proved useful to American critics of a variety of persuasions. The mixture of theory, sociology, and politics academic and otherwise congealed in the 1980s in the work of the "new Americanists," who have brought a vigorous ideological critique to the works not just of the major American authors but of the mid-century critics like F.O. Matthiessen who canonized them.[3]

My purpose in the present article is not to generalize further about this rich, sometimes confused and often confusing mixture of trends and approaches, but rather to investigate how its effects are visible within a specific venue, the teaching anthology of American literature. My particular focus is the *Norton Anthology of American Literature*, which has appeared in three editions since 1979, in the context of competing anthologies and various other canon-ratifying documents of our recent past. My approach is analytical and descriptive – a close reading of what the anthologies say or reveal about themselves. The possible conclusions from this procedure are limited, but should reveal something about both theoretical trends and the practical job of teaching literature in an interesting time. In particular, I hope to contribute to the growing interest in institutions of literary study,[4] and in so doing partly to fill the vacuum in which much theoretical discussion of canon formation has taken place. Although "the compiling of anthologies" gets mentioned as an important factor in canonizing, studies of the actual compilations have been rare.[5] Equally rare has been acknowledgement, even by the compilers, of the practicalities of anthologies: how much will fit and how to organize it, how rival claims are mediated, how (or whether) to suggest thematic focuses or to label continuities large or small, how much (or whether) to anticipate specific uses of the volumes in classrooms – even whether anthologies are advisable at all. One result of the lack of reference to such practicalities is that discussions of "the canon," especially in the form of regrets for what has been excluded, are vulnerable to what Werner Sollors has seen generally in the new literary history, an "unrealistic combination of pluralist faith and the idea of limitless space."[6]

The teaching anthology is one obvious place where the academic world intersects with the marketplace. This is true in several senses. The American literature survey is on many campuses the main, last, or only course through which a large portion of students encounters literature.

The anthology may be the means by which the canon reaches the broadest segment of the rising educated class. For professionals of literature, current and apprentice, the anthology is an intersection: it ratifies whatever consensus exists about the canon; it perpetuates that consensus in the act of presenting it and preserves the consensus through assuring that the works are accessible; and it is a forum for changing the consensus through additions, deletions, or changes in format. The dynamics are indeed those of the market. Like any product in a competitive market, an anthology addresses demand that has been to a great extent defined by previous entries of the type. On the other hand, a new product cannot establish itself without presenting distinctive features. That dynamic assures a balance, perhaps even a productive tension, between tradition and innovation.

These generalizations are clarified by a preliminary look at the self-presentation of the *Norton Anthology*.[7] The dust jacket of the first edition featured vitae of the six editors: their distinguished educations (four Harvard Ph.D.s), affiliations (mostly research universities), and scholarly activities including the prominence of two in activities of the Center for Editions of American Authors. "Name" editors have long been a feature of anthologies. Foucault's authorities of delimitation, whatever else they may be, are a selling point within the network that they epitomize. The prestige value of an anthology's editors presumably resides in the promise that the book is in touch with recent scholarship and critical thinking. But while the *Norton*'s cover features its star editors, the inside "Acknowledgements" thank "many critics, advisors, and friends" of the anthology, a list that by the third edition had grown to more than one hundred names with a wide range of affiliations and interests. John Benedict, a vice president of W.W. Norton, clarified how these advisors were used for the third edition. "In cooperation with the academic editors, I devise a questionnaire with some general questions about how the earlier edition fitted real courses, and also a table of contents on which boxes are provided for teachers to 'vote.'" The questionnaire went to about 150 teachers nominated by Norton's traveling representatives.[8] All publishers presumably do market research, but the *Norton* has been distinctive in emphasizing the claim to reflect a "consensus," derived from polling, which will "supplement" the expertise of the distinguished editors (1979 preface, I, xxiii). Obviously, such a claim represents a movement away from earlier anthologists' reliance on inherent worth as a justification for their selections. I shall address criteria for inclusion below; the point for now is that a responding pressure exists within the top-down process by which anthologies codify a canon. The mechanism represented by market research is inherently more democratic than the pronouncements of prestigious editors. But it is not necessarily more pluralistic. In a time like the present, when professional elites tend to define themselves through innovation, a more democratic canon-forming procedure is likely to conserve a consensus.

The *Norton Anthology of American Literature* replaced on its publisher's list an earlier compilation, *The American Tradition in Literature*, which first appeared in 1956 and whose fourth edition (1974) bore the imprint of Grosset and Dunlap but was distributed by Norton.[9] The 1979 *Norton Anthology* presented itself as "entirely new," but it had the same design and format as the *American Tradition*, and indeed for a while was popularly called the "new Norton." One of its unacknowledged innovations has been the convention of naming anthologies of American literature after corporations. Macmillan's 1974 entry bore the generic title *Anthology of American Literature*, but the *Norton Anthology* has been followed by the *Harper American Literature* and the *Heath Anthology* of 1990. That melding of corporate and academic identities seems to validate Richard Ohmann's observation about culture as a core industry.[10]

Norton's anthologies are scholarly and conservative, known especially for their extensive annotations of historical and literary allusions. In the context of 1979, cultural or even methodological conservatism was inevitably political. The editors of the *Norton Anthology of American Literature* made a statement simply by acknowledging their "greatest debt" to M.H. Abrams, chief editor of Norton's market-dominating anthology of English literature, whose recent exchange with J. Hillis Miller at the 1976 MLA convention had made him perhaps the most eloquent opponent of poststructuralism and defender of textual determinacy, authorial intention, and critical objectivity.[11] Conservatism was signalled in other ways as well, notably the association of the anthology with the Center for Editions of American Authors. The CEAA began its career at a meeting of the "Committee on Priorities" of the MLA, called to decide which American authors were worth scholarly editions.[12] Its early years had seen Edmund Wilson's attack on the CEAA's first products, expensive to purchase and topheavy with editorial apparatus, and an attempt at the 1968 MLA convention to deny funds on the basis of the CEAA's inherent elitism.[13] Two of the new *Norton*'s editors, Ronald Gottesman and Hershel Parker, were mentioned by name in Wilson's pamphlet; Gottesman had responded on behalf of the

Howells edition that was a specific target of Wilson's wrath. The choice of Hershel Parker for the section of the *Norton* covering the American Renaissance was particularly significant, as he signalled by adopting the CEAA Thoreau edition's controversial title change of "Civil Disobedience" to "Resistance to Civil Government." The *Norton*'s preface thus stated a political position simply by claiming an unprecedented level of "scrupulous care" for texts that reflect "the intentions of the author." And indeed the anthology presented several works in newly edited texts, among them Franklin's *Autobiography* and Crane's *Red Badge of Courage*.

As is suggested by its scrupulous attention to textual authority, the 1979 *Norton Anthology* is a markedly consistent and coherent presentation. But it also reveals the kinds of compromises necessary – though not always acknowledged – in any *practical* effort of this kind. One example involves a perennial problem in American literature anthologies: where to put Walt Whitman and Emily Dickinson in a two-volume text. A variety of solutions has appeared over the years, including putting the same selections in both volumes or, with Whitman, printing early works in one and later works in the other. The *Norton* editors characteristically make an unambiguous decision: they put both Whitman and Dickinson into volume one. Their justification for doing so consists of two arguments: The new alignment of volumes makes more room for twentieth-century literature, and the switch was approved by "more than 75 per cent of the 1700 teachers we polled" (1979 preface, I, xxiii). These quantitative arguments omit any substantive discussion of what historical or literary context is most appropriate for the works of Whitman or Dickinson. Placing the two in volume one inevitably means seeing them in the context of the American Renaissance, rather than as what a heading of the *American Tradition* called them, "pioneers of a new poetry." The earlier historical context was consistent with the treatment of both poets in influential histories of American poetry by Roy Harvey Pearce and Hyatt Waggoner;[14] but the qualitative implications of the editors' decision are not noted in their justification for it, so that their eventual characterization of Dickinson (in the headnote to selections from her poems) as "a distinctively modern poet" falls into a vacuum.

Although the discussion of placement for Whitman and Dickinson seems to evade the question of historical context, it is consistent with a larger decision of the anthologists, to drop traditional period labels as well as any organization according to schools, influences, or other generalizing tags. The anthology is subdivided simply by large time "spans" (1620-1820, 1820-1865, 1865-1914, 1914-1945, 1945 on) with a further generic division (poetry, prose) in the last division only. Authors are organized chronologically by birthdates. Focusing on that decision reveals how the divergent theoretical positions of recent years may produce a no-win situation for anthologists. Both Barbara Herrnstein Smith and Werner Sollors argue, from quite different perspectives, against "preclassification" by cultural labels – Herrnstein Smith because "preevaluation" by category functions as "culturally certified" endorsement of certain qualities of works, Sollors because the wide range of "literary and cultural" influences on creativity is oversimplified by labels that emphasize a single consideration such as ethnicity.[15] On the other hand, Russell Reising castigates the *Norton* editors for "merely including" minority authors without adequately contextualizing them: "Sandwiched between 150 pages of Edgar Allan Poe and 300 pages of Thoreau, Frederick Douglass, 'represented' by ten pages, may well, like Ellison's hero, still remain invisible – separate *and* unequal."[16] Reising's statement performs a rhetorical shift the opposite of the *Norton* editors' in discussing Whitman and Dickinson: he phrases his objection in qualitative terms while indicating that it actually relates to allocation of space. In any case, these three theorists show that, given today's adversarial climate, any practical decision is open to attack from a range of theoretical positions. As for the actual motives of the *Norton* editors, in the overall context of their decisions, printing authors (and works) chronologically suggests a formalist position that connects them, via the text-editing institutions of the 1960s and 1970s, to the New Critical hegemony of mid-century.

Other features of the 1979 *Norton* also identify it in the formalist tradition. Most obvious is the printing of longer major works in their entirety, including Franklin's *Autobiography*, Hawthorne's *Scarlet Letter* (with the "Custom House" preface), Melville's *Billy Budd*, Whitman's *Song of Myself*, Clemens's *Huckleberry Finn*, Crane's *Red Badge of Courage*, Chopin's *The Awakening*, Pound's *Hugh Selwyn Mauberley*, Eliot's *The Waste Land*, Hart Crane's *The Bridge*, and novella-length works by Melville, James, Faulkner, and Bellow. The devotion to completeness extends to printing in full works one might expect to be condensed, like Mary Rowlandson's *Captivity* and Margaret Fuller's "The Great Lawsuit." On the other hand, it might be possible to extrapolate "minor" status on the basis of willingness by the editors to excerpt works by Cooper, Stowe, Howells, Henry

Adams, Steinbeck, and others. And it may be the principle of completeness, colliding with limitations of space, that explains the entire omission from the first *Norton* of drama. (That particular gap had been remedied by the third edition, which prints six plays in their entirety.)

"Copiousness" pairs with completeness among the *Norton*'s self-proclaimed virtues (1979 preface, I, xxiv). In part this means simply more literature: the 1979 volumes are larger by one-third than the last edition of the *American Tradition* distributed by Norton. But it also means fuller representation of major writers. The 1979 *Norton* prints ampler selections from the major nineteenth-century writers canonized in Floyd Stovall's *Eight American Authors: A Review of Research and Criticism* (1956),[17] and also gives them a larger proportion of the anthology. Copiousness of representation designates major status and implicitly responds to T.S. Eliot's criticism that anthologies provide only a shallow sampling of important writers.[18] Also relevant here are the *kinds* of materials printed. The *Norton* devotes significant amounts of space to primary materials of a sort rarely seen in anthologies previously: letters, journals, notebooks, and similar writings published not by their authors but by twentieth-century scholars. Indeed, it is the inclusion of such materials that accounts for the *Norton*'s relatively larger allotments of space to major writers: there are, for example, 125 pages of Emerson's journals and letters, and similar though shorter excerpts from letters, notebooks, and journals of Poe, Hawthorne, Thoreau, Whitman, Dickinson, and Henry James. The *American Tradition* printed virtually none of this kind of material; Macmillan's anthology still does not. Its presence in the *Norton* exemplifies the greater scholarly orientation of the anthology and testifies to the major status of the writers for whom such materials are included. Indeed, as critics of the CEAA charged, major status is something of a self-confirming circle. These scholarly materials are available largely through the efforts of the CEAA and similar undertakings; the CEAA began with a determination of which authors were major and thus worthy of that kind of scholarship; the scholarship, once completed, was attached to the canons of the authors and included in the canon of American literature, thus confirming the status of the authors and indeed increasing it both quantitatively (more space) and qualitatively (more *kinds* of writing).

I shall return below to questions of major status and criteria for inclusion. But it is appropriate at this point to ask whether recent teaching anthologies of American literature reflect a consensus, about which authors should be included and about relative allotments of printed space. If my hypothesis (stated above) about the conservative effect of market research is valid, then the broad agreements that characterized literary study at mid-century should have survived, to a significant extent, the innovating pressures of the 1970s and 1980s. Numbers alone suggest a significant level of agreement among various anthologies. Collating the first and third editions of the *Norton Anthology* with the earlier *American Tradition* (fourth edition) and the later *Harper American Literature* and Macmillan *Anthology of American Literature* (fourth edition) shows a total of about 275 authors represented.[19] The *American Tradition* has the lowest number (131), while the *Harper* has the largest (222). An apparently small proportion of the total writers appears in all five compilations: 84. But a closer look shows that these 84 "consensus" authors get the bulk of each anthology's total pages: over 85 per cent in the first *Norton*, 80 per cent in both the *American Tradition* and the Macmillan, more than two-thirds in the *Harper* and third *Norton*. Even more similarity is shown in allotments of space to the authors given major status by recent canon-ratifying guides to scholarship. For example, Stovall's *Eight American Authors* get at least 30 per cent of the space in every anthology, and close to 40 per cent in the first *Norton*. Adding to Stovall's eight the *Sixteen Modern American Authors* of Jackson Bryer's 1974 review of scholarship – a volume whose selections were based on a poll of academics[20] – one finds twenty-four major authors receiving between 40 and 50 per cent of the space, with the first-edition *Norton* again having the highest percentage. Another addition, the *Fifteen American Authors Before 1900* of Robert Rees's and Earl Harbert's 1971 bibliographical review,[21] provides thirty-nine major authors who are allotted no less than half the total pages of any of the anthologies under consideration, and more than 60 per cent of the *American Tradition*, the first *Norton*, and the most recent Macmillan *Anthology*. Finally, perhaps the most striking figure of consensus comes from looking at the five anthologies' treatment of the authors canonized by Matthiessen's *American Renaissance* (1941). Emerson, Thoreau, Hawthorne, Melville, and Whitman: these five get among them between 43 and 53 per cent of the space in each anthology's first volume. Indeed, the relative allotment of space is remarkably consistent among the *American Tradition* (45 per cent), third *Norton* (45 per cent), *Harper* (44 per cent), and Macmillan (42 per cent) anthologies; the first *Norton* gives these five authors over 53 per

cent of volume one's pages. After a half century, agreement on the importance of the American Renaissance (and on who constitutes it) holds firm.

A consensus seems clear: there *are* major writers due disproportionate
amounts of space in any anthology. Moreover, the consensus is nearly un-
animous on who these writers are: the ten most amply represented (strictly in space) in each anthology include Emerson, Thoreau, Hawthorne,
Melville, Whitman, Mark Twain, and Henry James. No doubt not coinci-
dentally, these are seven of the eight American authors in Stovall's bibliographical review of 1956; Stovall's eighth choice, Poe, is among the top
ten space-getters in each anthology but the Macmillan, where he is
eleventh. If one looks at poets only, allotments of space make Whitman,
Dickinson, and Eliot major figures, with Frost and Pound well represented
in all anthologies, Stevens and Williams ample in all but the *American
Tradition*, and Robert Lowell first among his contemporaries in the most
recent editions.

Differences among the anthologies currently in print are often more
apparent than real. For example, as noted above the *Norton* drops generalizing historical or topical labels for its sections, arguing that such labels
encourage readers to "prejudge." Nevertheless, the *Norton* like all other
anthologies offers historical introductions and biographical headnotes.
There the labels survive – "The Puritan Experiment," "The Quest for an
American Literary Destiny," "Regional Writing," "The Expatriates," and
so on – defining the importance of the authors selected. In terms of representation, relative allotments of space to major or second-level writers
reveal no fundamental canonical disagreements. It is true that James Feni-
more Cooper gets ten times as much space in the Macmillan *Anthology* as
in the third *Norton*, due to inclusion of *The Prairie* in full; the *Norton* somewhat downplays his importance, but hardly revises his canonical status: "It
now seems clear that no revolution in taste will lead to widespread admiration of Cooper as a literary artist, but he will always be a major source
for the student of ideas in America" (1979, I, 754). Cases where an author
is included in one anthology but not in others involve almost exclusively
writers given the smallest allotments of space. The presence in the *Norton*
of Elizabeth Ashbridge, Johnson Jones Hooper, Richard Harding Davis,
Jane Addams, Edgar Lee Masters, Ellen Glasgow, Elinor Wylie, Dorothy
Parker, and others seems attributable mainly to what marketing theorists
call marginal differentiation: competitive products must differ *somehow*.
With anthologies as with automobiles, marginal differentiations often are

emphasized in advertising. Thus the *Norton*'s preface gives a female head-count ("fifty women writers, of whom sixteen are new"). One can conclude without undue cynicism that in this regard the difference from competing anthologies is indeed "marginal." Addams, Wylie, and Parker do not make the *Norton* a feminist canon any more than Ring Lardner and Raymond Chandler make the Macmillan a macho one. On the other hand, marginal differentiation is not inherently without substance. It can be the market's mechanism for introducing important innovations. I shall discuss that more fully below, as I turn to the question of how anthologies change. To conclude this discussion of consensus: a number of explanations are possible for the high level of agreement among anthologies – inherent worth of the major authors, inertia of literary tradition, the repressive hegemony of professional authorities, a consensus reflected in polling for market research, the tendency of competition to produce a high degree of sameness in competing products. How convincing any of these explanations is depends to a great extent on one's prior assumptions about canon formation. But it is unmistakable that important horizons of consensus exist and that these have endured through the past busy generation.

What, then, has changed about the anthologies, and how does change occur in them? Prefaces to the anthologies show developments in the *rhetoric* of canon formation. Two examples involve the stated criteria for selecting included writers and the language used to describe those getting the largest blocks of space. Looking back to the first preface to *The American Tradition in Literature* (1956), one finds an unambiguous statement of a single criterion: "literary merit," say the editors, was the "final" consideration. Furthermore, "no author was introduced primarily for the purpose of illustrating literary or social history" – though the introductions and notes *would*, as appropriate, "emphasize the relations between the literary work and the general movements of American civilization." By the time of the first *Norton Anthology* two decades later, works were included for "high literary merit *and* because their presence is needed to make sense of ... literary history" [emphasis added]. History has been promoted as a criterion, though one notices that the conjunction is "and" rather than "or," and that "literary" is attached to both "merit" and "history." An even more insistent repetition of "literary" appears in a promotional brochure sent out to announce the appearance in 1987 of the *Harper American Literature*. There four criteria are listed: "literary merit"; "reflection of the range and depth of the author's literary accomplishments"; "significance in American literary and intellectual history"; and "'place' thematically and stylistically, and ... power to evoke the writer's literary values as well as the cultural context of the period."[22] History is now "intellectual" and "cultural" as well as literary – but the conjunction is still "and." Moreover, the repetition of "literary" seems almost compulsive in the *Harper* brochure, suggesting something of a conservative tension (or reassurance) in a promotion that emphasizes a "comprehensive reassessment." There has been a reassessment, the brochure seems to say, but it has not extended so far as to embrace the current questioning of "literary" as an intellectual category. Another interesting tension is seen in the *Harper* brochure's summary statement of purpose: "to create the most responsible, scholarly, diverse, and innovative collection ever assembled." The four adjectives neatly offer pairs of divergent assurances. Whether "diverse" and "innovative" are consistent with "responsible" and "scholarly" is not a matter that the brochure addresses.

Epithets for traditionally canonical authors show similar tensions and increasing rhetorical fastidiousness in the anthologies' prefaces. In 1956 the *American Tradition* could refer unapologetically to "the titans" who got and deserved the bulk of its space. The 1979 *Norton* more modestly referred to "major authors," but by the late 1980s even those terms seemed fraught with implication. The *Harper American Literature* puts "'major'" and "'minor'" between quotation marks and largely replaces "authors" with "writers" (or "voices" or "figures") – these alternate terms apparently being more generic. (The *Harper* editors use "author" primarily, but not exclusively, as a modifier, as in "author headnotes" and "an author's career.") This anthology also prefers "classic" as a term for traditionally major authors. A generation ago "classic" would have seemed more conservatively value-laden than "major," but it has recently been rehabilitated by Frank Kermode and given a new descriptive meaning, designating a work open to reinterpretation.[23] As with its listing of criteria, the *Harper American Literature* shows a certain inconsistency in employing terms connoting status; for example, while downplaying words like "author" and "major," it unaccountably lets "literary masters" slip in once without apparent irony. As for the most recent Macmillan anthology, its preface speaks of "individual authors" but "landmark" *works*, the latter adjective designating stature without carrying much evaluative or ideological force.

The prefaces of all anthologies after the *American Tradition* specifically acknowledge what the *Norton* calls a "major responsibility" to increase representation of women and minority writers. This is the most obvious response by these recent collections to pressures for innovation within the academy, but a certain ambiguity lurks in the acknowledgement. In each preface the statement of this responsibility to affirmative action is physically separated from the discussion of criteria for inclusion. Such apparent evidence of ambivalence is most suggestive in the latest Macmillan *Anthology*, which says that "some of the principles that informed previous editions ... had to be retained," whereas "we have added the principle of increasing the representation of women and minority authors in the American literary tradition." It seems unclear why, if these authors are in the "literary tradition," a new principle is needed to add them to the anthology. That logical anomaly is emphasized by the Macmillan editors' assurance that "writers such as Anne Bradstreet, Louisa May Alcott, Frederick Douglass, Kate Chopin, Zora Neale Hurston, Tillie Olsen, and Alice Walker are truly significant when measured by the standards generations of scholars have applied to Nathaniel Hawthorne, Herman Melville, Walt Whitman, Henry James, Stephen Crane, Robert Frost, Eugene O'Neill, and F. Scott Fitzgerald." The reader is left with the impression, not acknowledged or clarified by the textbook, that the principles behind the Macmillan's first three editions were either defective or unjustly applied. In any case, among recent anthologists, only the Macmillan's editors make this attempt to address just what standards of evaluation follow from the "responsibility" to increase representation by women and minorities. The other anthologies leave the relationship between "literary" criteria and cultural "responsibility" unaddressed.

One obvious question raised by these prefaces is to what extent rhetoric translates into practice. Has the announced commitment to writing by women and minority authors produced a substantial revision in the canon? Or is the representation token? My considered answer to both questions is negative, but the issues are not simple and considering them goes to the heart of how we think of "the canon" today. To begin with, however crude the *Norton* editors' prefatory head counts of women and black writers may appear, they evidence a commitment that appears genuine. One external evidence of this is the history of the editors themselves: ten years have brought the deaths of two of the original all-male team, and both have been replaced by women. The most significant replacement is Nina Baym after the death of Laurence B. Holland. Baym – now alphabetically *primus inter pares* on the *Norton* title page – had fired a feminist canon shot in her 1981 article, "Melodramas of Beset Manhood: How Theories of American Fiction Exclude Women Authors."[24] Her addition to the editors in Holland's place was particularly significant because it violated, at least on the surface, the *Norton*'s assignment to each historical section of a specialist in that era. Holland's responsibility was American literature from 1914 to 1945, whereas Baym's scholarship has been in the nineteenth century. Obviously the decision to include a distinguished *woman* editor overrode the earlier decision to specialize.

The last edition of *The American Tradition in Literature* distributed by W.W. Norton included twenty-three women authors and ten blacks. The "new *Norton*" of 1979 increased the figures to twenty-nine and fourteen; but by the third edition of 1989 there are fifty women and twenty-one blacks (now identified as "Afro-Americans"). A similar increase in emphasis is observable in terms of the proportion of the anthology's total pages: the *American Tradition* was slightly more than 6 per cent women and slightly less than 3 per cent black; the first *Norton* was 13 per cent women and somewhat more than 3 per cent black. The most recent *Norton* increases these proportions to 19 per cent and 6 per cent: in other words, the current edition devotes one-quarter of its space to women and Afro-American writers, a significant increase from less than 10 per cent in the *American Tradition* and about 16 per cent in the first *Norton*. Numbers alone can be misleading, but other evidences lead to the same conclusion. Whereas Emily Dickinson was the only "major" author in the *American Tradition* who was not both male and white, the third *Norton* gives major treatment – extensive selections or a long work – to Anne Bradstreet, Mary Rowlandson, Olaudah Equiano, Rebecca Harding Davis, Frederick Douglass, Edith Wharton, and Willa Cather. The represenation of Sarah Orne Jewett, Mary Wilkins Freeman, Gertrude Stein, Katherine Anne Porter, Zora Neale Hurston, and Flannery O'Connor now goes beyond the standard "minor" treatment of a single short story; it is no doubt significant that each of these writers gets more selections and more space than Ernest Hemingway.

Expansion of the *Norton Anthology* has been predominantly in terms of women and minority writers. That this fact reflects "political" pressures within the academy is not particularly noteworthy: "American literature" as a field arose largely in a "political" reaction against philology, whereas

"American studies" gained its impetus after World War II from a mixture of Cold War patriotism and resistance to New Critical formalism.[25] A more important consideration involves the tendency to add these writers in an expansion of the canon that is fundamentally horizontal. Instead of aggregating new voices within a cultural discourse, canon expanders have tended to proliferate separate but ostensibly equal categories based on such considerations as gender and ethnic identity. The hesitancy to characterize new writers in ways that might connote minor status has led anthologists largely to ignore scholarly work that expands the canon vertically. Nina Baym, for example, has studied women's sentimental fiction of the nineteenth century, and more recently David Reynolds has researched the genres of sensation literature "beneath" the American Renaissance.[26] The works studied by Baym, Reynolds, and others enrich our sense of the literary and cultural contexts of classic writers. But for the most part the anthologies have ignored the writers of such minor works. This is a change in canon formation from a generation ago, when anthologies incorporated the southwestern humorists and local color writers at least partly to enrich awareness of the accomplishments of such major realists as Mark Twain and Henry James.

Recent additions to anthologies have been justified primarily on the basis of cultural "responsibility," thus widening the *theoretical* gap between that claim and repeated assertions of "literary merit" as a criterion. Moving from the prefaces discussed above to author headnotes does not provide much clarification. Generalizations about a female writer's "depiction of the courageous response of women to frustration" or her "ideological world view," for example, are not usually coordinated with other generalities about the "scale" of her writings or relative "quality" among her various works.[27] The *Norton*'s headnote to Ellen Glasgow is atypical precisely because it offers a summary paragraph combining her social and moral "aims" and her "crusade against ... injustices" with attention to her "command of the traditional resources of her craft" – with these resources then enumerated.[28]

Teaching anthologies are obviously not suited to extended theoretical discussions. Nevertheless, their lack of clarity about literary criteria, during a time of significant development, seems a lost opportunity. Important efforts have been made over the past two decades to maintain or rehabilitate the notion of "literary merit" within, but not limited to, contemporary sociological or ideological concerns. One thinks of Charles Altieri's notion of a "cultural grammar" or E.D. Hirsch's "cultural literacy," Frank Kermode's redefinition of the classic, Wayne Booth's explorations of irony and ethics in fiction, or Richard Rorty's turning from philosophy to literature for its potent mixture of contingency, irony, and liberal solidarity.[29] Different as they are, these theorists are engaged in a project that is conservative in the most basic sense – as is the anthology by its very nature. My point is that the anthologies have not participated in a reintegration of principles to match their expansion of contents. Opponents of the "literary," ranging from deconstructionists to those who attack efforts like Hirsch's as nostalgic reaction,[30] have found in "the anthologies" targets that do not respond. The danger here is that "literary merit" will lose its meaning even while the anthologists' prefaces intone the phrase more and more.

Anthologists have been able to avoid addressing criteria in any substantive way because the physical make-up of their volumes has accommodated expansion. "Yes, but what would you leave out?" is a standard gambit in arguments about opening the canon. It is an obvious question, since "the canon" is selective by definition. And inert by its nature: As Alan C. Golding noted in studying two centuries of poetry anthologies, once an author has been anthologized he or she is rarely excluded altogether. In Barbara Herrnstein Smith's more cynical formulation, "nothing endures like endurance."[31] Anthologies do record the ebb and flow of reputations. Even during the limited time span studied here, one can trace a decline in the status of the Schoolroom Poets of the nineteenth century and of e.e. cummings and Allen Tate (among others) in the twentieth. Writers do disappear, as has happened to William Vaughn Moody and to Sidney Lanier in all but the Macmillan anthology. Still, while the Schoolroom Poets have lost major status, they are all still in every anthology under consideration. In other words, Golding's or Herrnstein Smith's generalizations are valid in the sense that expansion of the canon has not been at the expense of authors already represented. The anthologies have met their "responsibility" simply by growing larger.

The steady expansion in the size of the anthologies is striking. Whereas *The American Tradition in Literature*'s fourth edition occupied something over 3600 pages in two volumes, the first *Norton* was over 4950 pages. The third *Norton* is over 5200 – and that is in a larger format which allows between 10 and 20 per cent more matter per page. ("Song of Myself" and "The Beast in the Jungle" occupy 47 and 35 pages in the first *Norton*, 43 and 29 pages in the third.) The *Harper American Literature*, currently the largest entry in the market, packs 5300 pages into two volumes and provides a paperback *Huckleberry Finn* on the side. These anthologies provide an illustration of what Godfrey Hodgson has characterized as the "liberal consensus" that became America's secular faith at mid-century: if the pie isn't big enough to accommodate all the deserving, one simply makes a bigger pie.[32] The anthologies of American literature have opened up the canon by stuffing themselves fuller. The principle of "copiousness" (as the *Norton* preface puts it) widens the difference between what anthologies make available and what any teacher can use in the classroom. Depending again on one's assumptions, this is either a step toward anarchy or pluralism made manifest.

Anthologies have always been pluralist; that is a source of their value and a reason for their survival. But anthologies of American literature now seem to be approaching maximum reasonable size, defined (if in no other way) by limitations on the design of volumes and financial limitations on students' ability to purchase. (The two volumes of the third edition *Norton* retail for nearly $50.00.) It is possible that anthologies could go to more than two volumes – though one recent attempt at a four volume option was unsuccessful – or that they could abandon print altogether and put "on line" much larger quantities of material. Both these possibilities seem at present unlikely. We are left then with the sense that canon expansion, within the limited forum of the teaching anthology, is finite. The anthology as an institution and an artifact is approaching saturation; additional "openness" will require sooner or later that something give. So far that decision has not been faced by any published anthology.

Given the large areas of consensus among anthologies now and recently in print, talk about alternatives, "opening up," or radical restructuring exists in that convenient void where, as Werner Sollors notes, physical limitations do not exist. However, some indication of what happens when "radical" aspirations run up against realities of the marketplace is provided by the *Heath Anthology of American Literature*, in planning (at this writing) for almost a decade. The anthology's general editor, Paul Lauter, traces its "roots" to the radical 1960s: his "brief history" of the project evokes the "time of conflicts" surrounding the 1968 MLA convention and specifically the "lost motion" at that meeting to end support for the Center for Editions of American Authors. Twenty years later, the "on-going process" set in motion during those days promises to produce a new teaching anthology reflecting "a systematic and global overhaul of the canon."[33] The history of the *Heath Anthology* thus parallels that of the *Norton* despite the time span between their first editions; in a sense they developed from opposite sides of the CEAA controversy. The *Heath Anthology* appeared while the present article was in press; my observations below are based on Lauter's statements, promotional materials, and a preliminary table of contents.

One legacy of 1960s politics has been an attempt to make the *Heath Anthology* a communal effort. It began by collecting syllabi of innovative courses and has included an institute with fifty participants, the soliciting of suggestions from "the profession at large," and mailings of proposed tables of contents for evaluation by teachers of survey courses. One notes the similarity of this procedure to Norton's market research. But its more open nature produced what Lauter calls "an organizational nightmare." Perhaps for that reason the *Heath Anthology* has been announced with a structure of authority overtly more centralized than that of the *Norton*. Communal participation persists in the assigning of author introductions to over one hundred individuals; but the masthead identifies a fourteen-person editorial board (eight men, six women). There is a "general editor" and a "sponsoring editor" from the publishing house. *Heath* follows *Norton* in naming its anthology after the publisher – and indeed, its promotions go out under the letterhead of a corporate conglomerate: "D.C. Heath, A Raytheon Company." The role of the corporate sponsor is addressed briefly in a promotional newsletter, in terms of the academy's obligation to support a publisher willing to risk innovation: "Fact: this is the day of the corporate merger in the publishing field, and thus corporate rather than individualistic business practices dominate. Publishers must be profitable to be stable, and houses generally must reject projects that are not sure to attract enough customers. ... Publishers, editors, and managers at commerical houses are not awarded tenure and, thus, must rely on their customers – first, to tell them exactly what they and their colleagues want in print and, then, to support that effort financially when it is published."[34] The authority of delimitation involved here is, as Foucault or Ohmann might have predicted, corporate and professional as much as communal.

As Foucault also might have predicted, one inevitable function of authority for the *Heath* editors has been repressive. The focus of Lauter's "organizational nightmare" was the receipt of "interesting and persuasive" arguments about contents that, if accepted, would have produced an anthology of 20,000 pages, or four times any previous entry into the market. Someone – Lauter uses both "me" and "our editorial board" in his discussion – decided this was untenable, so "*the* major challenge" [my emphasis] became "to find some bases for cutting down." Early on, this anthology, designed overtly to counter exclusions in the canon, set about making exclusions of its own. What its editors found was that, however one talks of openness, a "canon" in any sense other than the purely theoretical is necessarily finite.

A cynical view would be that these editors simply wanted to replace others' exclusions with their own. Some support for this view is provided by a response to suggestions that the *Heath Anthology* include "even more minority constituencies (teenagers, the elderly, 'rednecks,' evangelicals, Canadians, etc.)": "We recognize the claims of these groups, and yet feel our primary mission in this edition of the text is to focus on including writers until now excluded primarily because of gender or race" (Spring 1989 *Newsletter* 2). This statement is of interest for its linking of teenagers and Canadians in an apparently limitless equivalence of "constituencies," as well as for the religiously tinged sense of "mission." But my main point is that canonical authority inevitably upholds the "claims" of certain constituencies – those currently in professional favor – and thereby represses the claims of others. Yet this repressive aspect of canon formation is rarely acknowledged, and in the *Heath Anthology*'s promotions one quickly comes upon the familiar rhetoric of liberal consensus: "This two-volume text, ... will offer not only a full selection of traditionally canonized writers but also the most comprehensive integration to date of literature produced by writers previously excluded for reasons of race, gender, political ideology, or ethnic background" (Paul A. Smith's letter accompanying 1988 *Newsletter*). The "liberal consensus" has been a bugaboo for the new Americanists. But we see here its continuing usefulness, if for no other reason than to evade an extended discussion of choices.

The present article was written without access to Paul Lauter's extended "To the Reader" discussion of the *Heath Anthology*'s principle of selection. However, the *Newsletter*, promotional materials, and a working table of contents suggest that the anthology will be open to "political" charges such as those levelled at Gilbert's and Gubar's *Norton Anthology of Literature by Women*:[35] Whittier, for example, is represented by abolitionist poetry but not by "Snowbound," and the anthology will include a segment from Doctorow's *Book of Daniel* but nothing at all by James

Merrill. Charges of bias are easy to make regarding any selection, and discussions about them usually argue to the converted. My concern here lies more with the practicalities of making selections. The list of contents for *Heath*'s anthology shows some results of attempting to open the canon to the excluded without excluding the traditional, and at the same time staying within the practical physical limitations of a teaching text.[36] In physical format and total pages, the *Heath Anthology* is to be about the same size as the *Harper* and third *Norton* anthologies, but it will include a significantly larger number of individual selections by a larger number of authors. The number of authors in the *Heath* tops 300, with about 270 separate author or section introductions. The *Harper* represents about 220 writers or equivalent segments, the third *Norton* 181, the current Macmillan *Anthology* 141, the first *Norton* 131, and the 1974 *American Tradition* 128. The ballooning of anthologies is strikingly apparent in these figures, and with the *Heath* the increase in separate items within the anthology goes beyond the incremental. Obviously some choices have been made.

The choices made by Lauter and the other *Heath* editors do not appear to challenge the distinction of "major" from other writers on the basis of allotted space. The preliminary table of contents for the *Heath Anthology* includes no pagination, but on the basis of the items listed it is clear that some writers get disproportionate representation – and that they are the same "major" writers distinguished by the competing anthologies. This is particularly the case before 1900, with Franklin, Poe, Emerson, Thoreau, Hawthorne, Melville, Whitman, Dickinson, Mark Twain, and Henry James all given extensive coverage, as are Douglass and Chopin, both previously so treated by the *Norton*. The one significant promotion in status may be Harriet Beecher Stowe, something of a cause célèbre among the new Americanists.[37] But beyond its retention of space for the traditional major writers, the *Heath Anthology* achieves a high degree of success in including the previously excluded: one finds, for example, a large group of "Pre-Revolutionary Women Writers" as well as "voices" like Chief Seattle and Sojourner Truth and categories like "Chinese Immigrant Poetry."

How has room been made for these many new voices? Two expedients are immediately apparent: more frequent excerpting of longer works and providing fewer selections from most writers included. Thus *Walden* is represented by four chapters, and many full-length works yield selections only, in the case of standard writers such as Cooper, Stowe, and Howells

as well as of formerly ignored "voices" like Harriet Wilson, Charlotte
Perkins Gilman, and Mary Antin. Although the phenomenon of fewer
selections per writer is general in the anthology, it is particularly striking
with twentieth-century poets. Thus while Frost, Stevens, and Williams
have thirty, nineteen, and twenty-two selections respectively in the latest
Norton, the figures in the *Heath* table of contents are seventeen, ten, and
fifteen. Beyond the Modernists the difference is even more striking.
Roethke, Bishop, Berryman, Lowell, Brooks, Levertov, and Rich – each is
represented in the *Heath* by fewer than half the number of selections provided by the *Norton*; Olson, Ammons, Merrill, Kinnell, O'Hara, James
Wright, and Merwyn are represented not at all. It is easy enough to see
"politics" in the suppression of this last group of previously canonical
writers – all white males, however else they differ – in favor of such poets
as Mari Evans, Sonia Sanchez, Bernice Zamora, and Roberta Hill White-
man. But equally important is the fact that the *Heath* anthology represents
the newly added group by a few short poems each. The *Norton Anthology*
consistently gives more generous representation to the writers it chooses
to include.

Excerpting and fewer selections are not inherently ideological decisions, since they are more likely forced by the practicalities of anthology
making. But such decisions have pedagogical implications, and these are
largely ignored by both sides of recent debates over canon formation. Two
implications are worth noting here. First, the providing of fewer selections
deemphasizes any notion of the "career author"[38] or the development of
an individual creative consciousness over time. In that regard, the construction of a survey course focused on a limited group of individual
authors becomes more difficult. Second, increased recourse to excerpts
from longer works makes formalist approaches virtually impossible.
Having *Walden* in the form of chapters two, eleven, seventeen, and
eighteen puts the overall shape of the book – the yearly or daily cycles, for
example, so carefully developed by Thoreau – beyond consideration by
teachers or students. Both these implications point to the aggrandizing of
content as the point of literature, and thus at least implicitly devalue those
considerations of "literary merit" which, consistently if vaguely, have characterized the making of previous anthologies. Obviously that is also the
effect of the increasing recourse – in the *Norton* with major authors, in the
Heath with minority voices – to diaries, letters, and similar private writings,
into which formal considerations presumably enter less than they do in

published works belonging to traditional "literary" genres. Whether these developments are salutary or otherwise is a complicated question; but they are occurring without much attention to the practical pedagogical implications of such choices.

The textbooks looked at above provide a limited sampling, and anthologies are only a part – though an important part – of the process of forming and maintaining a canon. While keeping those qualifications in mind, I will offer a series of generalizations that are suggested by examining twenty years of anthologies. To begin: anthologies depict "the canon" in its fundamental character of selectiveness. Developments within the academy over the past generation have called into question this selectiveness. But for the most part discussion has focused on the specific authors selected, not at all on the theoretical necessity of selectiveness, and on the criteria for selection mainly by indirection or through unexamined generalizations about "literary merit" and cultural "responsibility." The response of contemporary anthology makers to these various pressures has been to expand the size of their compilations without eliminating traditionally canonized authors or altering an established format with its implicit distinctions between major and minor authors. The process of expansion, while illustrating in action the pluralism that American culture has at its best embodied, is nevertheless a process with limits. The notion that almost every "voice" or constituency can be accommodated underlies much of the rhetoric of anthology prefaces. That belief in limitless accommodation may be untenable in logical terms – and indeed contradicts any possible definition of a canon – but it has proved workable, if only temporarily as a safety valve in a time of diverse and complex pressures on the institutions of literature. That workability seems to be declining as anthologies press against practical physical and economic limits to their internal expansion.

The belief in unlimited expansion has been to some extent evasive, in canon formation as in economics. Their ability to thicken volumes and widen pages has enabled the editors of existing anthologies largely to forego any substantive discussion of their criteria. In particular, the anthologies have contributed little to the effort – these days seemingly rearguard – to maintain or rehabilitate a notion of literary value. The insistent repetition of the word "literary" in prefaces and promotional materials seems increasingly defensive. Established, self-evident "literary" worth – a notion perhaps derived by analogy from the canon of scripture – is increasingly less acceptable as a prior assumption, even within the network of authority on "literature." The danger is that anthologies, vague about their criteria, will make the canon seem increasingly arbitrary even as they strive to be inceasingly accommodating.

Despite that qualm, my conclusion from this look at a generation of anthologies is sanguine. The past twenty years in the American academy have seen salutary change mingling with confusion; it has been a time of sincere pluralism and egregious faddishness. Amid all this the teaching anthologies have been true to their conserving function, but demonstrably open as well. The *Norton Anthology of American Literature* has introduced a new level of textual scrupulousness to the field, including respect for the formal integrity of longer works in several genres. Above all, it and competing anthologies have maintained a consensus about major authors – both as to the validity of major status and as to who deserves it – virtually unchanged. The ebb and flow of smaller reputations has been reflected, and many new voices have been given a forum. In the anthology as in the academy and the culture as a whole, a good proportion of these new voices has come from groups previously not well represented. The mixture of all these voices has not been so orderly as to allow for analogy to another kind of canon – the musical fugue – but it has not been cacophonous either. Some appearances to the contrary, the American profession seems to be conveying its inheritance, and enriching it as well.

Notes

1. See Alastair Fowler, *Kinds of Literature* (Cambridge: Harvard University Press, 1982), pp. 213-16, and *Canons*, ed. Robert von Hallberg (Chicago: University of Chicago Press, 1984).

2. *The Archaeology of Knowledge*, trans. A.M. Sheridan Smith (New York: Harper and Row, 1976), pp. 41ff.

3. See especially *Ideology and Classic American Literature*, ed. Sacvan Bercovitch and Myra Jehlen (Cambridge: Cambridge University Press, 1986). The term "New Americanists" comes from Frederick Crews, "Whose American Renaissance?", *New York Review of Books*, October 27, 1988, pp. 68-81.

4. Important works have been Gerald Graff, *Professing Literature: An Institutional History* (Chicago: University of Chicago Press, 1987); Kermit Vanderbilt, *American*

Literature and the Academy (Philadelphia: University of Pennsylvania Press, 1986); and Jonathan Culler, *Framing the Sign: Criticism and Its Institutions* (Norman: University of Oklahoma Press, 1988).

5. Barbara Herrnstein Smith, "Contingencies of Value," in *Canons*, p. 29. Exceptions have been Alan C. Golding, "A History of American Poetry Anthologies," in *Canons*, pp. 279-307; and Fowler's brief survey of Renaissance poetry in various anthologies, *Kinds of Literature*, pp. 230-34.

6. "A Critique of Pure Pluralism," in *Reconstructing American Literary History*, ed. Sacvan Bercovitch (Cambridge: Harvard University Press, 1986), p. 255.

7. The *Norton Anthology of American Literature*, ed. Ronald Gottesman, Laurence B. Holland, David Kalstone, Francis Murphy, Hershel Parker, and William H. Pritchard, 2 vols. (New York: W.W. Norton, 1979). The second edition (1985) added Nina Baym to the editors; the third edition (1989) added Patricia B. Wallace.

8. Letter to Glen Johnson, January 26, 1989.

9. *The American Tradition in Literature*, ed. Sculley Bradley, Richmond Croom Beatty, E. Hudson Long, and George Perkins, 4th ed., 2 vols. (New York: Grosset and Dunlap/Distributed by W.W. Norton, 1974). The *American Tradition* continues in print; its sixth edition is published by Random House.

10. "The Shaping of a Canon: U.S. Fiction, 1960-1975," in *Canons*, p. 386.

11. 1979 Acknowledgements, I, vi. See Abrams, "The Deconstructive Angel," *Critical Inquiry* 3 (1977): 425-38.

12. They chose fourteen: See Jay B. Hubbell, *Who Are the Major American Writers?* (Durham: Duke University Press, 1972), p. 279.

13. Edmund Wison, *The Fruits of the MLA* (New York: New York Review, 1968). Wilson's pamphlet is an expansion of articles in *The New York Review of Books*, September 26 and October 10, 1968; Ronald Gottesman's letter in response was published in the issue of December 19, 1968.

14. Pearce, *The Continuity of American Poetry* (Princeton: Princeton University Press, 1961); Waggoner, *American Poets from the Puritans to the Present* (Boston: Houghton Mifflin, 1968).

15. Herrnstein Smith, p. 27; Sollors, pp. 255-56.

16. Russell J. Reising, *The Unusable Past: Theory and the Study of American Literature* (New York: Methuen, 1986), p. 25.

17. Floyd Stovall, ed., *Eight American Authors: A Review of Research and Criticism* (New York: Modern Language Association, 1956). The authors are Poe, Thoreau, Emerson, Hawthorne, Melville, Whitman, James, and Twain. A revised edition, edited by James Woodress, appeared in 1971.

18. See Eliot's comments on poetry anthologies in "What Is Minor Poetry?", *On Poetry and Poets* (New York: Farrar, Straus & Cudahy, 1957), pp. 35-40.

19. Figures are approximate. The anthologies not previously cited are the *Harper American Literature*, ed. Donald McQuade, Robert Atwan, Martha Banta, Justin Kaplan, David Minter, Cecelia Tichi, and Helen Vendler, 2 vols. (New York: Harper & Row, 1987); and *Anthology of American Literature*, ed. George McMichael with Frederick Crews, J.C. Levenson, Leo Marx, and David E. Smith, 4th ed., 2 vols. (New York: Macmillan, 1989). The Macmillan's first edition appeared in 1974.

20. Jackson Bryer, ed., *Sixteen Modern American Authors: A Survey of Research and Criticism* (Durham: Duke University Press, 1974). The authors are Anderson, Cather, Hart Crane, Dreiser, Eliot, Faulkner, Fitzgerald, Frost, Hemingway, O'Neill, Pound, Robinson, Steinbeck, Stevens, W.C. Williams, and Wolfe. The first edition, 1969, was called *Fifteen Modern American Authors* and omitted Williams. For an account of the poll, see Hubbell, *Who Are the Major American Writers?*, pp. 276-84.

21. Robert A. Rees and Earl N. Harbert, eds., *Fifteen American Authors Before 1900* (Madison: University of Wisconsin Press, 1971). The authors are Adams, Bryant, Cooper, Crane, Dickinson, Edwards, Franklin, Holmes, Howells, Irving, Longfellow, Lowell, Norris, Taylor, and Whittier.

22. The *Harper American Literature*, brochure (1987), pp. 3-4.

23. Frank Kermode, *The Classic* (New York: Viking, 1975).

24. Nina Baym, "Melodramas of Beset Manhood," *American Quarterly* 33 (1981): 123-39.

25. See Graff, *Professing Literature*, p. 72; and Bruce Kuklick, "Myth and Symbol in American Studies," *American Quarterly* 24 (1972): 435-50.

26. Nina Baym, *Woman's Fiction* (Ithaca: Cornell University Press, 1978); David S. Reynolds, *Beneath the American Renaissance: The Subversive Imagination in the Age of Emerson and Melville* (New York: Knopf, 1988).

27. Quotations are from the 1989 *Norton* headnotes to Jewett, Gilman, Chopin, and Freeman.

28. 1989 *Norton*, II, 965; this preface was new in the second edition, suggesting it was written by Nina Baym.

29. Altieri, "An Idea and Ideal of a Literary Canon," in *Canons*, pp. 41-64; Hirsch, *Cultural Literacy: What Every American Needs to Know* (Boston: Houghton Mifflin, 1987); Kermode, *The Classic* and later volumes; Booth, *A Rhetoric of Irony* (Chicago: University of Chicago Press, 1974) and *The Company We Keep: An Ethics of Fiction* (Berkeley: University of California Press, 1988); Rorty, *Contingency, Irony, and Solidarity* (Cambridge: Cambridge University Press, 1989).

30. See, for example, several articles in *Profession 88* (New York: Modern Language Association, 1988), as well as the materials regarding the *Heath Anthology* discussed below.

31. Golding, in *Canons*, p. 283; Herrnstein Smith, in *Canons*, p. 33.

32. Godfrey Hodgson, *America in Our Time* (New York: Doubleday, 1976).

33. Paul Lauter, "Reconstructing American Literature: A Brief History," *Newsletter* of *The Heath Anthology of American Literature*, Spring 1988, pp. 1-2. The last phrase is from a letter of Paul A. Smith to me, February 3, 1989.

34. Paul A. Smith, "A Hopefully 'Winning' Note from the Publisher," *Newletter* of *The Heath Anthology*, Spring 1989, p. 1.

35. See Gail Godwin's review, *New York Times Book Review*, April 28, 1985, p. 13.

36. *Heath Anthology* table of contents, "revised 1/10/89." I thank Paul Smith for providing me with this listing, which has been checked against the published volumes.

37. See Crews, "Whose American Renaissance?" pp. 75 and 78. The *Heath* prints eight chapters of *Uncle Tom's Cabin* plus forty pages of other works by Stowe.

38. Wayne C. Booth, *Critical Understanding: The Powers and Limits of Pluralism* (Chicago: University of Chicago Press, 1979), pp. 270-71; Booth refers his concept to the then-forthcoming Lawrence Lipking, *The Life of the Poet* (Chicago: University of Chicago Press, 1981).

Multiple Points of View:
A Study of French Comparative Literature Syllabi

Yves Chevrel

1989: The French *"Agrégation de Lettres Modernes"* celebrates its thirtieth birthday. This means that it has been possible, during these last thirty years, to try to develop a new way of training future humanities teachers. I do not know if we can speak of a "democratic pressure," but it was certainly not "scholarly play" that led some innovators to introduce a new discipline, comparative and general literature (CGL), into a rather conservative teaching system.

A few words are necessary to explain under what conditions humanities teachers are trained in France, in order to appreciate the "revolution" brought in by the new type of examination. There are several ways of becoming a humanities teacher (*professeur de lettres*) in secondary schools (*colleges* and *lycées*) in twentieth-century France. The *agrégation* is one of the most valued routes because of its high requirements, and also because it gives entitlement to a higher salary. This involves a competitive examination, both oral and written, taking place once a year, which recruits teachers for the whole French territory, among candidates who are completing their fifth academic year (most of them have actually more than five academic years behind them). The number of places is determined every year by the state: there is an average of one place for, say, from ten to thirty candidates, depending on the various disciplines (it is easier, at present, to become a teacher of mathematics than a teacher of philosophy, for example, because France needs more teachers of mathematics); we have such examinations in different disciplines, including history, physics, and English. As far as the humanities (*lettres*) are concerned, candidates have three options: the *agrégation des lettres,* the *agrégation de grammaire*, the *agrégation de lettres modernes.*

This division of subject speaks partly for itself. To teach humanities as a *professeur agrégé de lettres* up to 1960, you ought to have learned, and proved that you possess knowledge, of French, Latin, Greek (in each case, language and literature); the difference between *lettres* and *grammaire* was just a shifting of emphasis – more literature in the *agrégation des lettres*, more linguistics in the *agrégation de grammaire*. Soon after 1950, it appeared necessary, or at least useful, to offer a new way of becoming a *professeur agrégé*: in spite of strong opposition from many people attached to classical studies, it was decided to create an *agrégation de lettres modernes*, in which Latin (but not Greek) remained compulsory (candidates had to translate a short Latin text into French), and in which a CGL program was also compulsory, both in the written and the oral part of the examination. If we leave aside other considerations, such as the places of grammar and linguistics, the main patterns of the *agrégation des lettres* or *de grammaire*, on one hand, and of the *agrégation de lettres modernes*, on the other, are based on the following characteristics:

– Table 1 –

agrégation {des lettres {de grammaire	agrégation de lettres modernes
– 6 texts (or groups of texts) belonging to French literature (1 for the Middle Ages, 1 for the Renaissance, 1 for the 17th century, etc.) – 4 texts from Greek literature – 4 texts from Latin literature	same program – 2 syllabi of CGL (3-4 texts in each syllabus, studied in French version)

It is obvious that in the *agrégation de lettres modernes* CGL plays the role devoted to Greek and Latin in the older *agrégation des lettres*.

Since the *agrégation de lettres modernes* was created in 1959 (first examination 1960), sixty-five syllabi have been proposed (i.e., up to the examination of 1989), representing thirty examinations (during the first three years, 1960-62, there were four, then three programs of CGL). It may be of interest to list these programs, each of which has a precise title and involves a number of works (in table 2 only the authors' names are given to save space):

– Table 2 –

Year	Title of Syllabus	Authors
1960	1. Rousseau's influence on the literary sensibility of the end of the 18th century	Bernardin de Saint-Pierre, Goethe
	2. Positivist mind and antiromantic reaction among writers of the 2nd half of the 19th century	Renan, Taine, Leconte de Lisle, G. Eliot
	3. Rome in Trajan's century	Pliny the Younger, Juvenal
	4. Athens in the days of Socrates	Aristophanes, Plato
1961	5. Stoic thought in the Roman Empire	Seneca, Epictetus
	6. Three ancient legends:	
	- Electra	Aeschylus, Sophocles, Giraudoux
	- Medea	Euripides, Seneca, Corneille
	- Amphitryon	Plautus, Molière, Giraudoux
	7. The East in the philosophical literature of the 18th century	*The 1001 Nights*, Montesquieu, Voltaire, Beckford
	8. Anti-intellectual reaction and exaltation of the self at the end of the 19th century	Nietzsche, Barrès, Gide

Continued

1962	9. Italianism and Latin humanism in the days of Du Bellay	Ovid, Petrarch, Du Bellay, Ronsard
	10. Pastoral dream	Theocritus, Virgil, Garcilaso de la Vega, Chénier
	11. Fantastic imagination during Romaniticism	Hoffmann, Nodier, E.A. Poe, Pushkin
1963	12. Ancient and classical tragedy	Aristotle, Horace, Corneille, Racine, Fénelon, Euripides, Garnier, Goethe, Milton
	13. Italy in Stendhal's novels	Stendhal
1964	14. Caesar in literature, from the Renaissance to Enlightenment	Caesar, Suetonius, Plutarch, Shakespeare, Voltaire, Montesquieu
	15. The "nouvelle" in Europe, from Maupassant to K. Mansfield	Maupassant, T. Mann, Chekhov, Pirandello, Mansfield
1965	16. The novel of roguery	*Lazarillo de Tormes,* Fielding, Lesage
	17. Interpretations of history	Thucydides, Livy, Vico, Herder, Michelet
1966	18. The country of shadows and the world of punishment, from the ancient to modern epic	Homer, Virgil, Dante, Milton, V. Hugo
	19. Bourgeois drama	Lillo, Diderot, Lessing
1967	20. Men and agricultural labor in literature	Hesiod, Virgil, J. Thomson, G. Sand
	21. Don Juan	Tirso de Molina, Molière, Pushkin, Lenau
1968	22. Ideal cities	Plato, T. More, Campanella, Fénelon
	23. World War I in the novel	Barbusse, E.M. Remarque, G.A. Borgese, Hemingway

Continued

1969	24. The tragedy of honor and revenge	Seneca, Calderón, Corneille
	25. Childhood	R. Rolland, Kipling, Tolstoy
1970	26. Electra	Aeschylus, Sophocles, O'Neill, Giraudoux
	27. The historical novel	W. Scott, Balzac, Manzoni, Pushkin
1971	28. Metamorphosis	Apuleius, L. Carroll, Kafka, Asturias, Ionesco
	29. Moral anxiety and social uneasiness at the end of the 19th century	Becque, Ibsen, Chekhov, G.B. Shaw
1972	30. Critical insights on ideas and customs	Petronius, Erasmus, Fontenelle, Swift, Feijoo
	31. Man and city	Bjelij, Dos Passos, Döblin, Kawabata
1973	32. Baroque theatre	Shakespeare, Calderón, Corneille
	33. Novel and novelistic creation	Dostoevsky, Gide, A. Huxley
1974	34. Autobiographical aspects of the novel	Goethe, Foscolo, Chateaubriand
	35. Descent to Hades and raising of dead	Homer, Virgil, Dante, Claudel
1975	36. The literature of roguery	Quevedo, Lesage, Grimmelshausen
	37. Theatre and cruelty	Euripides, J. Ford, Kleist, A. Artaud
1976	38. Epidemic	Thucydides, Lucretius, Defoe, Giono
	39. Decay and the novel	Huysmans, Wilde, D'Annunzio

Continued

1977	40. Political farce	Aristophanes, Jarry, Brecht, Bulgakov
	41. Christ's figure in the novel	Dostoevsky, Pérez-Galdós, Kazantzakis
1978	42. State and power	Aristotle, Machiavelli, Hobbes, Rousseau
	43. Imaginary travel	Lucian, Cyrano De Bergerac, J. Verne
1979	44. Madness on stage	Shakespeare, Pirandello, A. Camus
	45. The fairy tale	Apuleius, Perrault, Grimm, Andersen
1980	46. Theory and practice of the Romantic drama	Manzoni, Pushkin, V. Hugo
	47. The martial epic	Homer, Lucian, *Chanson de Roland*, *Nibelungenlied*
1981	48. Prometheus	Aeschylus, Shelley, Goethe, Gide
	49. Jealousy in the novel	Dostoevsky, Svevo, Proust
1982	50. Master and servant in the comedy	Plautus, Molière, Goldoni, Brecht
	51. Fantastic narrative in the age of Romanticism	Lewis, Hoffmann, Gautier, Gogol
1983	52. Electra	Sophocles, Euripides, Hofmannsthal, Giraudoux
	53. Novel and history	M. Yourcenar, A. Carpentier, I.B. Singer
1984	54. Forms of comedy	Terence, Tirso de Molina, Musset, Pirandello
	55. The novel of adultery (2nd half of the19th century)	Flaubert, Tolstoy, Fontane

Continued

1985	56. Passionate love on stage	Shakespeare, Wagner, Claudel
	57. The trip to the moon	Lucian, Kepler, Cyrano De Bergerac, Godwin
1986	58. The poet as a critical consciousness of his time	Blake, Holderlin, A. Breton, O. Paz
	59. The picaresque narrative	*Lazarillo de Tormes*, Lesage, Defoe
1987	60. Heroic values on stage	Sophocles, Shakespeare, Corneille, Kleist
	61. The "Bildungsroman"	Goethe, Dickens, Flaubert
1988	62. Banishment and poetry	Ovid, Du Bellay, Ungaretti, Seferis
	63. Specular plays of the 20th century novel	Gide, Nabokov, Calvino
1989	64. The legend of Faust	Marlowe, Calderón, Goethe, Valéry
	65. Death and narrative	Tolstoy, C. Fuentes, S. Beckett

To appreciate the novelty or the originality of such curricula, it is necessary to know according to which rules the programs have to be guided. There are three main requirements, which are not at the same level: the first is actually compulsory, the other belong to "unwritten laws": 1) all texts must be read and studied in a French version. This means that foreign texts must have been translated and be available in inexpensive editions (in 1989 there were about 3500 candidates for the *agrégation de lettres modernes*). Therefore, one of the first questions to deal with when a commission sets out to produce CGL syllabi is to know whether reliable translations exist. It is, of course, imperative to take the quality of translations into account; in 1972, for example, *Berlin Alexanderplatz* was put on the program, but the only French translation of Döblin's novel was disastrous, not only because of the many mistakes, but because the translator simply cut out many passages without noting the fact. 2) In each program there must be a French work. But in 1972 and 1977 we find a program without such a text. 3) In one of the two yearly programs there must be a text translated from Greek or from Latin. There are three exceptions, the years 1973, 1986, and 1989.

Taking these things into consideration, a few remarks can be made about the evolution of the programs at a quantitative level. First, we observe that at the beginning there was a huge quantity of texts; the climax came in the 1961 programs. The candidates had to study eighteen different works, written by seventeen authors (Giraudoux was present twice: *Electra* and *Amphitryon 38*); this was a heavy burden. Since 1965 we have a reasonable average of three or four texts in each program. Secondly we note, still in the beginning years, that French and classical literatures play the leading role; 1960 (first year): ten authors, among them four French, two Greek, two Latin, and only one German and one English author; 1961: from the eighteen mentioned texts, nine are French (W. Beckford's *Vathek* included: the tale, as it is known, was written originally in French), three are Greek, four are Latin, and we find an Arabic work: Galland's

- Table 3a -

French	74	mentions
English	35	"
Greek	28	"
German	27	"
Latin	23	"
Italian	17	"
Russian	15	"
Spanish	15	"
Neo-Latin	3	"
Modern Greek	2	"
Arabic	1	mention
Danish	1	"
Japanese	1	"
Norwegian	1	"
Yiddish	1	"

translation of *The Thousand and One Nights* and a German work by Nietzsche. From that point on things change: it may be said that after 1968 there is an actual balance between various literatures (the 1978 programs are an exception: seven texts, of which three were written originally in French, two in Greek). When we look at the sixty-five programs that have been listed, we note that fifteen different languages are represented. They are shown in table 3a, in decreasing order (the given figures represent the authors, not the works, since an author can have more than one single work in a program).

If we consider that the first three years (1960 to 1962) represent an exceptional formula (more than two programs, deliberate emphasis on French and Classical literatures), and if we take only the years 1963 to 1989 into account (fifty-four programs), we may establish the following figures:

- Table 3b -

French	57	mentions
English	33	"
German	24	"
Greek	21	"
Latin	16	"
Italian	16	"
Spanish	14	"
Russian	14	"
(the rest without changes)		

These figures show clearly that eight languages represent more than 95 per cent of all texts proposed. It is not surprising that French literature leads numerically, and it is obvious that the programs are mainly focused on Western culture. We point out only 2 exceptions among 244 mentions (*The Thousand and One Nights*, and Kawabata's *Kyoto*); if Russian literature, which is the only representative of Slavic languages, is well represented, it may be surprising that several important literatures of the Western world have been "excluded" *de facto*: e.g., Dutch, Portuguese, and Swedish literatures, not to speak of Chinese or of Indian.

May we consider the above as features of what we could feel inclined to call the French view of world literature? It is fair to keep in mind the constraints listed above (see p. 143), and the general difficulty of shaping a CGL program. It is possible though to give a more precise overview of the main authors as they show up in these programs:

- Table 4 -

Goethe	6	programs
Shakespeare	5	"
Corneille	5	"
Pushkin	4	"
Sophocles	4	"
Euripides	4	"
Virgil	4	"
Molière	4	"
Gide	4	"
Giraudoux	4	"
Tolstoy	3	"
Dostoevsky	3	"
Pirandello	3	"
Calderón	3	"
Lesage	3	"
Voltaire	3	"
Aeschylus	3	"
Homer	3	"
Seneca	3	"

The result is that ten authors represent, with forty-four works, 18 per cent (almost one-fifth) of all texts, and nineteen authors, with ninety-nine works, 40 per cent of all texts. Among these nineteen authors we find six French, four Greek, three Russian, two Latin, and only one German, one English, one Italian, one Spanish. All these nineteen authors are "great" writers, and it is small wonder that we find Goethe, Shakespeare, Corneille, Pushkin, at the top. A question may arise: Are not French authors like Gide or Giraudoux somewhat overestimated? Or, if such a question seems inappropriate, are they not what we could call "CGL program authors"; Gide because of his reflections on the novel (two of the four mentioned works are *Les Faux-Monnayeurs* and *Paludes*), Giraudoux because he often chose to deal with ancient myths (*Electra* appears in three programs, *Amphitryon 38* in one), which was also the case of Gide with his *Prométhée mal enchaîné*.

If we try to establish by which authors French, English, German, and Spanish literatures are represented (in these four instances the literature comes from more than one country), we note that in almost all cases French literature means, in fact, literature produced in France (in the so-called "hexagone"). Exceptions: Rousseau (but the works of the Swiss writer were written during his residence in France), W. Beckford, S. Beckett; there is nobody from Quebec, nor from Africa. The same emphasis on the literature of the metropolis occurs in the English texts, only five American writers: E.A. Poe, O'Neill, Dos Passos, Hemingway, Nabokov, and in the German texts, three Austrian writers – Lenau, Hofmannsthal, Kafka; one writer from East Germany – Brecht; and nobody from the German part of Switzerland. But it may be of interest to underline that contemporary Hispanic literature is represented only by Latin American authors: Asturias, Carpentier, Fuentes, and Paz.

Leaving the problem of the authors represented, we may ask another question: What are the main features of a CGL program? Looking back at the list of sixty-five syllabi, we find that three types clearly predominate: 1) the study of a theme, a motive, or a myth: Don Juan, Electra, Faust, jealousy, or metamorphosis, etc. This kind of study seems to be a favorite among French comparatists: about one-third of all programs; 2) the study of some aspects of a literary genre, most often seen in a diachronic perspective: picaresque, theater of the Baroque, and martial epic; 3) the synchronic study of a moment of the literary or of the intellectual evolution: moral anxiety and social uneasiness at the end of the nineteenth century, fantastic narrative at the age of Romanticism.

As may be seen from the last instance, there are "cross-programs," i.e., programs that belong to two or even three of the major types; therefore it is not easy to give an exact account of the number of items for each type. A few other tendencies can be noted: philosophical problems, influence of a writer, and problems of literary creation. It also seems that there is a trend to consider diachronic more often than synchronic problems. This is, of course, related with the emphasis put on the study of themes, which also offers many possiblities to introduce Greek or Latin texts.

The chronological range of the texts runs from Homer's *Iliad* to I. Calvino's *Se una notte d'inverno un viaggiatore*. Take note that all periods are not equally represented (see table 5).

Three blocks emerge: classical antiquity, and the nineteenth and twentieth centuries. The authors of these last two periods represent together more than 45 per cent of all texts. There is a lack of interest in the time between the end of the classical period and the Renaissance, and we note a growing interest from the sixteenth to the nineteenth centuries.

- Table 5 -

Classical Antiquity	51	mentions
Middle Ages	6	"
14th Century	6	"
15th Century	6	"
16th Century	16	"
17th Century	28	"
18th Century	31	"
19th Century	62	"
20th Century	50	"

A final classification may be attempted about which genres are most represented. The column titles are: 1. Narrative Prose; 2. Theater; 3. Poetry; 4. Political and Philosophical; 5. Criticism; 6. History; 7. Diary, Letters.

- Table 6 -

Language	1.	2.	3.	4.	5.	6.	7.	total
French	29	25	33	22	4 (+2)	-	-	74
English	17	12	3	2	-	-	1	35
Greek	2	13	5	4	1	3	-	28
German	12	11	2	2	-	-	-	27
Latin	3	5	9	-	1	3	2	23
Italian	7	4	4	2	- (+1)	-	-	17
Russian	11	4	-	-	-	-	-	15
Spanish	7	5	2	1	-	-	-	15
N. Latin	1	-	-	2	-	-	-	3
M. Greek	1	-	1	-	-	-	-	2
Arabic	1	-	-	-	-	-	-	1
Danish	1	-	-	-	-	-	-	1
Japanese	1	-	-	-	-	-	-	1
Norwegian	-	1	-	-	-	-	-	1
Yiddish	1	-	-	-	-	-	-	1
	94	80	33	22	6 (+3)	6	3	244

In column 5 (criticism) the bracketed figures refer to critical texts that were also present in a program consisting mostly of creative works.

It is easy to draw conclusions: narrative and theatre together make up more than 71 per cent of all texts, and poetry represents only a little over 13 per cent. If we add the relatively important place of philosophical and political essays (like Machiavelli's *Prince*, or Hobbes's *Leviathan*), which represent 9 per cent of the texts, we can conclude that problems strictly related to language – study of poetical texts – play a minor role in these programs. This has to do, of course, with the fact that the texts are to be read in a French translation.

The analysis of the previous figures, especially of tables 5 and 6, leads to the following comments: the CGL programs of the *agrégation de lettres modernes* are oriented towards narrative and the drama, but maintain a balance between modern and contemporary works, on one hand, and older texts, on the other. French comparatists seem aware of these facts: in the last decade we have nine syllabi with narrative texts, eight syllabi with dramatic works, but we also see an attempt to reintroduce poetry: three syllabi, in which we find not only "great" books, like the *Iliad*, the *Aeneid, Chanson de Roland, Nibelungen*, but also modern poets, like Paz, Seferis, Ungaretti, and "difficult" poets like Blake and Hölderlin. On the other hand, French comparatists do not forget writers like Manzoni, Sophocles, Aeschylus, Terence, Shakespeare, even Kepler, and we find these names together with those of M. Yourcenar, I.B. Singer, I. Calvino, Nabokov, C. Fuentes, and S. Beckett, among others.

In a country like France, where the classical tradition is so strong, CGL programs give a wide opening to world literature and, in this respect, it may be asserted that their role is irreplaceable. For many future teachers of literature, it is an almost unique occasion to acquire information on literature other than French, in addition to the French. This can be shown if we compare the French literature programs that have to be studied by all candidates (see table 1) with the French works belonging to the CGL programs of the *agrégation de lettres modernes*. An exact comparison cannot be done owing to the fact that the regulations are not the same in both cases. As each program of French literature must contain 6 authors (each represented by one or several works) belonging respectively to the Middle Ages, the sixteenth century, the seventeenth century, etc., we have, in the last three decades (1960-89) 180 authors mentioned, against only 74 authors in the CGL programs.

Even if a point by point comparision cannot be made, it is possible to observe that the "canons" of French literature are not exactly the same in both types of programs. If we leave aside the Middle Ages, we can establish the following table:

- Table 7 -

	French lit. programs	CGL programs	Both programs
16th c.	Montaigne (5) Rabelais (4) Marot, Marguerite de Navarre, M. Régnier (2), D'Aubigné, Monluc, Turnèbe, Sponde, Sosève(1)		Ronsard (5/1) Du Bellay (3/1) Garnier (1/1)
17th c.	La Fontaine(4) Pascal (3) Bossuet, La Bruyère (2) Boileau, Scarron, La Fayette, Sevigne, La Rochefoucauld, Retz (1)	Fénelon, Cyrano De Bergerac (2) Fontenelle, Perrault (1)	Corneille (5/5) Molière (4/4) Racine (4/1)
18th c.	Marivaux (5) Beaumarchais (3) Prévost, Saint-Simon, Laclos, Senancour (1)	Lesage (3) Beckford, Bernardin de Saint-Pierre (1)	Voltaire (6/3) Montesquieu (2/2) Rousseau (4/1) Chénier (1/1) Diderot (4/1)
19th c.	Verlaine, Vigny, Baudelaire, Nerval (2) Sainte-Beuve, Lamartine, Mallarmé, Rimbaud, Zola, Barbey d'Aurevilly (1)	Barrès, Becque, Gautier, Jarry, Huysmans, Leconte de Lisle, Maupasant, Nodier, Renan, G. Sand, Taine, J. Verne (1)	Chateaubriand (2/1) Flaubert (3/2) Hugo (4/2) Balzac (2/1) Musset (2/1) Michelet (1/1) Stendhal (2/1)
20th c.	Péguy, Alain-Fournier, Apollinaire, Colette, Bernanos, Eluard, Montherlant, Saint-John Perse, Malraux, Supervielle, Gracq, Sartre, Desnos, Mauriac, Senghor, Aragon (1)	A. Artaud, Barbusse, Beckett, Ionesco, R. Rolland, M. Yourcenar (1)	A. Breton (1/1) Camus (1/1) Claudel (3/2) Gide (1/4) Giono (1/1) Giraudoux (2/4) Proust (3/1) Valéry (2/1)
	52 writers	25 writers	26 writers

(The bracketed figures behind the names of writers indicate the number of programs in which they were mentioned. For example, "Montaigne (5)" means that Montaigne was proposed in five different programs of French literature; in the last column, the first figure refers to the programs of French literature, the second to the CGL programs. For example, "Ronsard (5/1)" means that Ronsard was proposed in five different programs of French literature and in one CGL program.)

The most important consideration is perhaps not the last column, which could give an overview of the main references to French literature, but the first two columns of table 7. There are "exclusions" that are not surprising: Montaigne, Pascal, Bossuet, Sainte-Beuve, for example, may be considered as representative of genuine French literature and thought, and it would be difficult, perhaps, to introduce them into a CGL program. On the other hand, Perrault, W. Beckford, J. Verne, and H. Barbusse are not representative of the literature of their century. It may be noted, however, that CGL programs have introduced authors like Cyrano De Bergerac, A. Jarry, A. Artaud, or S. Beckett, who still are considered as somewhat "marginal," and received rather bad treatment from the critics or the historians of literature. So CGL programs can also lead to a discovery, or a new reading, of French literature.

This becomes more evident if we go into some detail and consider the works mentioned in the two types of programs respectively. Let us take only works of the seventeenth century. Corneille and Racine, eminently representative of the "classics," have been studied in CGL programs not only for their plays, but also for their critical works: Racine's forewords to his tragedies, Corneille's *Trois discours sur la poésie dramatique*. On the contrary, Voltaire and Diderot, who are represented by their narratives in the French literature programs, have also been studied as dramatists in CGL programs: *La Mort de César*, and *Le Fils naturel*. CGL programs tend to propose "other" views, less traditional, of some great writers: in a CGL program a work is never studied for itself nor in relation with the whole work of its author, but always within a group of texts that can change the meaning of a single work. It is not the same thing to study *L'Illusion comique* as a play anticipating the classical masterpieces of Corneille's maturity, or as a play belonging, like *A Midsummer Night's Dream* or *La Vida es sueño*, to a Baroque *Weltanschauung*. Molière's *Don Juan* is, of course, a play of the legend of Don Juan (CGL program of 1967), but can also be seen as an instance of the comical feature "master/servant" (CGL program of 1982). Inserting a given text into a CGL program leads to other views of this text. I tried to demonstrate this on the occasion of Cyrano De Bergerac's novel *Etats et Empires de la Lune*, when I answered an article by my friend Jacques Prévot, who proposed a reading of the text that, in my opinion, excluded every comparative perspective (see *L'Information littéraire*, 37/1, 1985, 6-11: J. Prévot's article *"Cyrano de Bergerac au concours"*; and 37/3, 1985, 102-8: my article *"L'Autre Monde à l'épreuve de l'étranger"*).

The purpose of the present article was to provide a survey of some trends of comparative and general literature in France, and I selected a very limited, but representative sample: sixty-five CGL programs, which give a kind of institutional image of the discipline, because they appear in official journals and publications of the French *Ministère de l'Education Nationale*; these programs give an idea of what CGL can be, especially to non-specialists of the discipline.

I tried to be objective, and therefore often chose a "quantitative" point of view. In my commentaries I tried to underline, in a few words, what the discipline can supply: discovery of other literatures, a different knowledge of French literature, the desire to go further in the reading of other literary works. The limits of the programs studied are self-evident, and already mentioned – they are the expression of a part of Western literatures and cultures and include poetry rather seldomly; in addition to this we must be reminded that the students read the texts in translation.

Notwithstanding these limits, such programs always raise questions – true questions. They suggest that literary canons are not established once and for all, that the problem of literary value is a real one, that changes of paradigms are possible. To teach *one* literature only through masterpieces of this literature too often leads to limit oneself to one single point of view, to satisfy oneself with a closed and narrow *corpus* of texts. We know that an *opera aperta*, an open work, is perhaps one of the findings of the twentieth century: would it not be worthwhile to think of an *open literary canon*?

Laocoön IV:
An Essay Upon the Pragmatics of Art and
the Limits of Criticism

Raymond Adolph Prier

The mere act of reflection necessitates a confusion of the aesthetic object with its critical reduction. Nowhere is this more evident than in the recent misprision of "canonicity" and, by extension, "the canon." On the other hand, seldom has the relationship between the aesthetic object, its choice, and its criticism been better perceived and more fruitfully employed than in the work of Goethe, whose cultivation of the interstices between the past and the present yielded an answer that must ring true in contemporary "canonic debates," which are, of course, ultimately debates about *human values*.

The intention in the following pages is to examine three critical approaches to a specific aesthetic object: the Laocoön. I wish to evaluate the critical limits of what is, in effect, Winckelmann's, Wölfflin's, and, hence, the modern academic's examination of the sculpted object, of Lessing's eighteenth-century semiotics in his *Laocoön or Upon the Boundaries of Painting and Poetry*, and of Goethe's and Meyer's aesthetics in and about their *Propyläen*. I shall ultimately center special emphasis in Goethe's "Upon the Laocoön."[1]

This is a semiotic essay written against most modern semiotics; a rhetorical deconstruction against deconstructionist rhetoric; a purveyor of a Goethian, pre-Husserlian sense of "object" against Heidegger's overbearing "Truth," upon which Derrida predicated his antilogocentrics. This is a pragmatist's essay of which the primary concern is not so much what a phenomenon *is* as what it *does* and of which the purpose is to examine the value of a human work of art, in contradistinction to the limits of its criticism, in order to comment upon what that examination implies. In short, why is metaphorics good for critics but bad for human beings?

"And if one says, one has indeed seen as
one wanted to see, that is a foregone
conclusion" (Wölfflin, *Grundbegriffe* x)

1. The Re-appearance

Although the Laocoön group came into being at least some 1450 years
before, we moderns first saw it – or, to be more nearly exact, most of it – in
1506 when it was discovered in a part of Nero's golden house that Titus
had a bit later appropriated for his own. Around that time Pliny had commented upon such a Laocoön sculpture and had even listed its artists:
Hagesander, Polydorus, and Athenodorus of Rhodes (*Naturalis Historia*
36.37).[2] Despite, moreover, the group's somewhat shattered condition –
one of its arms was not "found" and added until the present century (Pollack 277-82; Magi 21-22) – the recognizable figures of two adolescent
boys, two snakes, and a large central mature male, all pressed to or drawn
toward slabs that could be an altar, immediately suggested the Laocoön
narrative in Virgil (*Aeneid* 2.199-227). Hence, the moderns, from their very
first point of dis-covery identified the group on the grounds of a *poetic referent*. Thus did we first see the Laocoön, and already the metaphors of literature lurked in the wings.

Because the Laocoön group was unquestionably ancient, the imagination of Renaissance antiquarians was touched, and even Michelangelo
himself became highly agitated:[3] the statue was a wondrous dis-covery; it
had to be re-stored. Yet, even the suggestion of such an act meant that the
work ran the risk of being sub-ordinated to a modern *stylistic* re-vision, in
this case to a "planigraphic" neoclassical "ideal" (Howard, "Reconstruction" 369). But "revision," under one guise or another, had long been the
name of the Renaissance game. After all, Lorenzo Valla's philological
deconstruction of the *Donation of Constantine* had appeared a good sixty-
five years before. The Renaissance moderns had *arguments* in favor of
what was "ancient" over what was not. It was not until later, however, that
the same analytic semiotics were applied to the Laocoön's re-construction,
whether suggested or executed by Michelangelo, Bernini, or Cornachini.
The point here is this: the semiotics of criticism remained the same. Upon
what are Valla's or Howard's stylistic arguments based except the rhetorical supposition that "what 'is' is not," whether or not one accepts the Der-

ridian claim that Being and its Heideggerian ontology be "logocentric" and hence open to "relevant" multiplicity at the margins?

The Renaissance taste for the ancient was predicated, until the time of the early-middle Goethe, upon an "idea," the methodological interpretation (read "hermeneutics") of which, as a recent critic has noted, rested upon the "cultivation of memory" (Greene 31). Such an activity, as Petrarch sensed well (*Ad Familiares* 23.19), is profoundly *metaphorical* and allows a critical evaluation of "ancient" over "modern" works of art. From such a complication arose Winckelmann's idea of "the beautiful ancient" and its radiant realization in the Laocoön.

Winckelmann was, however, more than a lover of the ancient Greek; he created the modern study of the history of art and brought to it two contradictory views of the world: the discursive metaphorics of the post-Petrarchan historian and the descriptive metonymics of the archeologist. As a late Renaissance scholar, he predicated his work upon a detailed knowledge of the anecdotal and semi-critical metaphorics of Pausanias, Pliny, and Vitruvius, in addition to a general knowledge of Greek and Latin texts ranging from Homer through the Silver Latins. (He showed a decided proclivity toward Plato's.) As a practical observer, however, he evinced a strong interest in the mechanical techniques involved in manufacturing and production (*Geschichte* 249-61; Leppmann 282-83). The vocations of the historian and the archeologist are, therefore, in constant tension in his work and were to lead to such apparently puzzling reflections as the last sentence of his otherwise Pindaric description of the Belvedere Torso, where he signifies a strong desire to "balance" the metaphorics of his previous text, his "idealistic description" (*Idealischen Beschreibung*), with one argued "according to technique" (*nach der Kunst*) (*Bibliothek* 41).

Winckelmann's major metaphorical complication, however, did rest in his use of "the ideal." As a somewhat recent critic has noted, his overwhelming tendency was to arrange his evidence by an "assigned priority to the statements of ancient writers, and, after them, to his own visionary concept of classical Greek" (Leppmann 290). What is more interesting is the havoc Winckelmann's "vision" wreaked upon his historical narrative. First it throws him into a purely metaphorical relationship between his argument and any ancient text. Second it necessitates an adherence to the metahistorical stylistics of dating.

As early as 1756 he argued, for instance, that Greek statues were "a true mark (*Kennzeichen*) [read "signified"] of Greek writings (*Schriften*) ... from the Socratic School" (*Gedanken* 24). By 1764 and the publication of his major work, *The History of the Art of Antiquity*, he will be inextricably trapped within the problematic metaphorics that the comparison of ancient texts and ancient artefacts inevitably produces. It was Lessing, after all, who complained that, in the case of the Laocoön, Winckelmann had "allowed Pliny to say more than he really wanted to say," that he had made "extensions" (*die angefuhrten Beispiele*) to the ancient's assertions in the *Naturalis Historia* (Lessing XVII.2.949). Winckelmann evidently is metamorphorizing beyond the language of the text. But to what end?

The clue rests in Lessing's end: his disagreement with Winckelmann's dating of the Laocoön group to the fifth century B.C. school of Polyclitus (*Geschichte* 347 fn. 2), *Dating is the problem here, and dating must imply a sense of history*. Winckelmann's Platonic and neo-Platonic insertion of the "beautiful ancient Greek" into the annalistic flow of a simple narrative of history introduced a "moment" that necessitated a much more complex, anachronistic narrative. Past moments had to lead to the ideal itself; future moments had to descend from it. Gibbon, who cultivated Winckelmann's acquaintance in Rome, relies on exactly the same metaphorical imagination. It is this metahistorical premise to which Winckelmann subordinated the Laocoön group as well as any ancient text.

A metahistorical premise is metaphorical because it is highly imaginative. Both Winckelmann and the father of twentieth-century art criticism, Heinrich Wölfflin, however, drew upon such fragile metaphorics. Both further obscured not only aesthetic objects from the viewer, but also the inherent tension between history and archeology. Wölfflin simply opted for another theoretical schema and, in conjunction, an historical narrative that interposes itself even more radically between the aesthetic object and the viewer than Winckelmann's "beautiful ancient." The later critique also dictated the ground rules for most modern academic art historical and archeological comment that has been applied to the Laocoön in the twentieth century.

Wölfflin, in his *Principles of Art History* (1915), was driven by a deconstructive, sometimes hidden agenda. Theoretically he was opposed to the eighteenth century "idea of the ancient" and its critical metaphorics, but to my reading, he never addressed that particular metaphor *per se* in either Winckelmann or Goethe. He transferred the Renaissance concern with "the ancient" to one with "the classical," which he considered "an historical problem" (*Gedánken*, "Die Schönheit des Klassischen" 47), in order to address a more manageable opposition between "classical" and "modern." His new opposition – and the stuff of his theory consisted of the rhetoric of opposition – then afforded him an opportunity to shift his focus to the opposition between "northern" and "southern." Although such a shift did necessitate the uncomfortable identity of "classical art" with "Italian art" (*Gedanken*, "Die Schönheit" 28), with it he is free to voice a full glorification of "northern art." It is in this that his published address on Goethe's *Italian Journey* becomes important.

What strikes the reader most forcibly about "Goethe's Italian Journey" (*Gedanken* 49-57) is its unwillingness to comment on any of Goethe's aesthetic views during or after 1793/4, that is during or after the time Goethe, with Voss's help, directly confronted the text of Homer and when he must have begun to form plans for the *Propyläen*. Instead, claiming that "the Roman Goethe is for us the classical Goethe" (*Gedanken*, "Reise" 50), Wölfflin interprets the Goethian aesthetics, in effect, only in terms of an eighteenth-century ideal Goethe shared before 1793 with Winckelmann and, to some extent, with Lessing. It soon becomes clear that the purpose of this blinkered consideration is to turn his audience's attention to the "notion of form" (*Begriff der Form*) and Goethe's early organic theory of "structural form" (*Bildungsform*) as it came to a specific head in his Sicilian musings upon the "original plant" (*Urpflanze*). At this point, Wölfflin identifies both Winckelmann and Goethe in a common interest: 1) as proponents of an opposition between "north" and "south" and 2) as given over to the exposition of the "history of style" (*Stilgeschichte*) (*Gedanken*, "Reise" 53).

Wölfflin will accept the "metaphorics of style," but repudiate the efficacy of his transformed metaphor "north-south." Again the agenda is hidden. He claims that the Goethian *idea* of the "sunny south" had become so strong *for all the Germans, but only Germans*, that it overshadowed, as it were, all German art – especially the "romantic" variety (*Gedanken*, "Reise" 55-56). Our critic will claim that he perceives such a shadow over *Iphigenie, Tasso, Gotz*, and *Werther* (!). Away with such fancy for the moderns: "We travel today differently than Goethe and are proud *of it*" (*Gedanken*, "Reise" 56, stress mine). "To be sure, Italy cannot be our home. ... The kingdom of Heaven is in you." It "comes home" much better in German: "Heimat freilich kann uns Italien nicht sein. ... Das Himmelreich ist in euch" (*Gedanken*, "Reise" 57).

The time is 1926. Wölfflin's underlying deconstructionist agenda is German, and, for this reason, his better known and otherwise possible claim that "Each people, nevertheless, has its own feeling for form (*Formgefühl*)" becomes suspect (*Gedanken*, "Nationale Charaktere" 109; *Grundbegriffe* 252-53).

Yet, Wölfflin's declaration that "one sees always in forms [*Formen*]" (*Gedanken*, "Grundbegriffe" 7) would have led nowhere, however, had it not been for his insistence that the history of art deals primarily with "Forms of the Imaginative idea" (*Vorstellungsformen*) (read "metaphorics") rather than "sightforms" (*Sehformen*) (*Grundbegriffe* ix) and that any talk of "intuitive form" (*Anschauungs*form), "sightform" (*Sehform*), and the "development of seeing" (*Entwicklung des Sehens*) was entirely analogistic (read "metaphorical") (*Gedanken*, "Kunstgeschichtliche Grundbegriffe: Eine Revision [1933]" 19-20). Ironically Wölfflin evinced an awareness of the metaphorics of sight while, at the same time, blindly advancing the even more abstract metaphorics of his own formal theory.

The constitutive force in Wölfflin's metaphorics always lay in the deconstructive instability of rhetorical opposites, generally between the characteristics of an "outer" appearance and an "inner" perception and interpretation (*Gedanken*, "Grundbegriffe" 7), but more "formally," in *The Principles of Art History*, within the major tectonic oppositions of linearly-painterly, flatness-depth, closed form-open form, multiplicity-oneness, clarity-unclarity. These, once again, he linked to the diachronics of history, from which he could speculate on "periods," "cessation," "recommencement," and "development" (*Grundbegriffe* 249-52):

> The history of forms (*Formengeschichte*) never stands still. ... Nothing maintains its affect (*Wirkung*). What today appears lively tomorrow will no longer be completely so. (*Grundbegriffe* 246)

> The imaginative idea (*Vorstellung*) of the real changes itself just as does the imaginative idea of the beautiful. (*Grundbegriffe* 244)

What is at issue here? One needs little critical finesse to be aware of Wölfflin's imposition of a major, complex theoretical metaphor between any viewer and any aesthetic object. *The point, however, is that he does so perforce of a total deconstruction of that viewer.*

The agenda is, therefore, relativistic. Wölfflin denies the validity of any form predicated upon sight (*Sehform*) in the name of a formal, imaginative metaphoricity (*Vorstellungsform*) – a critical position, as we shall see, one may trace to Lessing. Once lodged in the general area of metaphor, moreover, Wölfflin, again like Lessing, may resort to narrative – in this case the narrative of a "history" devoid of the primacy of human viewer. So in the self-perpetuating relativity of his own stylistics, our critic makes the vicious claim, "if one says, one has indeed seen as one wanted (*wollte*) to see, that is a foregone conclusion" (*Grundbegriffe* x; *Gedanken*, "Revision," 24).

Human sight is willed. It is *not* a necessary and reliable given. Taste is relative. Judgment is relative. The human being is depraved and at the mercy of metaphoricity run amuck.

Winckelmann and Wölfflin, however, have broadcast their legacy to present-day art historians and archeologists who, like the former, have continued to introduce the hermeneutic play of classical texts and classical philology into their musings upon the Laocoön. In short the aesthetic artefact is "viewed" on the same Barthian plane as the written text. Poetic and prose referents still stand as the metaphorical base for aesthetic interpretation and always are argued at the expense of the aesthetic object and the viewer.[4]

Take for instance Pliny's text of the *Naturalis Historia*. Lessing might well have criticized Winckelmann for his idiosyncratic "extensions," but not until recently, with the discoveries at Sperlonga of several sculpted pieces and an inscription bearing the name of Pliny's artists, has Pliny's text again been used as something approaching a reliable source (Pollitt 122; Winkes 294; von Blankenhagen, "Laocoön" 273-75). Formerly, deconstructionist academics second-guessed any direct, uncomplicated reading of his text with arguments ranging from his inherent disregard for contemporary sculpture,[5] to an absence within his list of artists' names of a patronymic genitive, or to whatever else might have come to mind (Richter 67-70).

What does Richter's philological deconstruction of Pliny's text accomplish? For the art historian-cum-archeologist, it once again allows access to Winckelmann's deceptive, wholly metaphorical diachronics of dating. There is involved, however, little archeological metonymics (read "direct juxtaposition of the aesthetic object and the viewer"), so the date of the Laocoön's composition wandered to 50 B.C. by the end of the first third of the present century (Bieber 12), to 150 B.C. by 1951 (Richter 69), and to

180 B.C. *or before* by 1964 (Howard, "Prototype" 134-35). The playful metaphorics of opinion becomes a loose can(n)on on deck, and one is inclined to suggest, considering the progressively deconstructive dependence of one critical argument upon its predecessor, whether in "opposition" or "apparent agreement," that *après* Howard *le déluge*. (One is left taking heart in the retrograde: Conticello avers an original from 100 B.C. [48-49]; Andreae hypothesizes that the group is a copy of a bronze *original* [104].)

What is the substantive issue here? The primary experience of human sight and its ability to establish the Laocoön's cultural *value*. This issue is not, moreover, limited to the matter of hypothetical copies or reconstructions of the statue itself. (After all, such considerations are at best "theoretical" and, even in Plato, at least one step removed from sight.) The worrisome point is the blatant claim of one human being in the name of style that another human being cannot *see* the group's physical presence or its physical detail (e.g., Havelock's denial of Howard's Renaissance planigraphics [149] or von Blanckenhagen's defense of his "view" on the grounds of what he *sees* and what Andreae, Corticello, Saeflund, and Magi *do not* [Review 103]). This kind of claim portends much more than mere critical disagreement.

Clearly the metaphorical nature of stylistic diachronics *based on likenesses* has so far removed itself from a pragmatic viewing of the aesthetic object that sight itself is somehow "lost." Metaphorically, of course, ever since Teiresias, Oedipus, and the rhetoric of the New Testament, we have been told that we "see" but do not "see," in short told that human sight is relative and, hence, deconstructible. For critics and cardinals this has been a good game indeed. Pragmatically and aesthetically it is nonsense. *To relativize an aesthetic object is to ignore it.*

Yet, stylistic diachronics is only one semiotic problem the Laocoön poses. Much worse are those references to Greek and Latin poetic texts that have been brought to bear from its very creation. To be sure Winckelmann, Lessing, and the contemporary critics (e.g., Havelock 148; von Blanckenhagen, Review 103; Pollitt 121-22) did not instigate such play, but in their inability to realize the deconstructive relativity of such comparisons, they do point ultimately to one of their own: Lessing and his naive acceptance of Horace's *ut pictura poesis*.

2. A Selective History of a Very Bad Metaphor

> Since a poet is an imitator (*mimētēs*), just
> as a painter [imitating life] ... he must imi-
> tate [portray] (*mimeisthai*) a sum of
> three things. ... These are proclaimed by
> diction (*lexei*) in which [lie] both glosses
> (*glōttai*) and metaphors (*metaphorai*) ...
> (Aristotle, *Poetics* 1460b8-12)

Horace's *Ars Poetica* is, with the exception of its hexameters, much more
an essay than a poem. It deals with the components, history, means, ends,
and song of poetic *words*. It neither challenges nor denies the theoretical
metaphoricity of sight and appearance and employs any possible metaphorical relationship between poets and painters only *twice*. Each instance, however, will introduce for Lessing and for us a major aesthetic
problem.

First Horace opens his poem with the flourish of painters and poets (1-
37), and in the context of this traditional appeal to a simple and consistent
creative idea (simplex ... et unum – 23), he will allow to both the *choice of
their own subjects*: "Painters and poets have always had an equal share in
daring whatever they willed" (9-10). Second, far into his essay, he introduces the following:

> As a picture, a poem: one is more appealing the nearer you *stand* to it;
> another so when you *stand* further *apart*. This loves obscurity, this
> wants to be *viewed under light* and is not intimidated by the sharp criti-
> cism of a *judge* [*iudicis argutum* – "semiotic cunning"?]. This pleased
> one time; this will please even if repeated ten. (361-65, stress mine)

It has been suggested lately that Horace's forced and peculiar set of
rhetorical oppositions imply "the spectator's impression" of a work of art
(Leach 5), and this is secondarily true. Yet, such an essentially Wölfflinian
sophistic, by necessity of its empirical notion that one "simply sees" a
painting or sculpture and that some art requires the oppositional rhetoric
of "closeness," "distance," "darkness," or "light," leaves metonymic language totally out in the cold or, if pushed, under an unbearable pressure to
conform *spatially* or *physically* to the rules of the physical representation as
did the technopaegnia of Hellenistic times. It also imposes upon language
the metaphoricity of sight.

Yet, one must never forget that Horace's essay is in poetry and over-whelmingly *about* poetry, not pictures. So even given the relative weakness of most metaphors or analogies before Petrarch, that is even given the theoretical possibility that Horace founded his own questionable meta-phor or analogy upon a viewer's non-reflected and relative relationship to the "physics" of light and space, three clear problems still arise *from his use of words*: it signifies the *differences* between poetry and art, not their *likenesses*; it raises the question of a *proper viewing*, not simply "an impres-sion"; and it emphasizes the semiotic play of judgment (*iudicis argutum*). Horace and Lessing clearly had a great deal to say about one and three, but not about the proper power of sight – perforce, one should venture, of the self-limiting semiotics lodged in their opening premise: *ut pictura poesis*.

No reader interested in the eighteenth century can deny the parallels between the semiotic positions of Wolff, Baumgarten, G.F. Meier, Men-delssohn, and Lessing (Wellbery 1-98), but eighteenth-century semiotics, no more than the deconstructionist-Saussurian variety of the twentieth-century, can explain away the several glaring difficulties that gleam close beneath the surface of Lessing's text, not the least of which is exacerbated by his failure to have ever looked upon either the "original" or a model of the Laocoön group (McCormick xxviii). Clearly Lessing did not appreciate the vagaries of the metaphor upon which his own essay is based – not, to be sure, that *ut pictura poesis* was not a popular topos in eighteenth-cen-tury England and France. Then too what strikes the contemporary reader of Lessing's essay as unproductive is his ignorance of Homeric Greek and the synaesthetics of its aural-oral semiotics,[6] from which, if he had been better informed, he could have drawn some exceedingly striking relation-ships between art and language indeed. Specifically, moreover, it soon dawns on the reader that the metaphoric semiotics of Lessing's text pro-vides him with no better insights into the choice of poetic or artistic *sub-jects* (*Gegenstände*) than did Horace's. The same must be said for Lessing's re-emphasis of Shaftesbury's and Mendelssohn's *aesthetic moment* (*Augen-blick*) (Keller 67-68; Wellbery 90).

Lessing's *Laocoön* arose from a compelling love of "things Greek." It also flounders on it. The reader senses this long before he stumbles on the definitive proof: Lessing's blatant emphasis upon Winckelmann's then re-cently published *History of the Art of Antiquity* (1764) that throws the con-clusion of Lessing's essay, as we have it (XXVI-XXIX), into not only little more than an academic review of that extraordinary work, but also a critical aporia that, one suspects, must have been somehow instrumental in barring the author from completing his original conception of his project. (After all Winckelmann *had* seen the Laocoön group and a great deal more!)

A more learned reader, however, will already have been alerted to a fault in Lessing's relationship to the Homeric Greek when, in attacking the superficial metaphorics of Caylus' "painting in words," he attempts to draw Homer's *description* (*Beschreibungen* – XVI.2.881) solely into the area of *the flow of verbal narration* (*Flusse der Rede* – XVI.2.881), where he can equate it with the progressively diachronic "telling of a history or story" (*Geschichte* – e.g., XVI.2.876 or 880), in itself and, in some respects, more legitimately open to the inherent metaphoricity of words. The distinction Lessing attempts to make here is as important for most modern semiotics as it is aesthetically unsatisfactory in itself.

Lessing confuses a poetic description *of* a work of art with an Homeric description of and as a work of art. On the one hand, he notes perceptively that in the description of the sceptre in *Iliad* 2.101-8, Homer does not provide a "description for a book of heraldry" (*Wappenkönigbeschreibung*), but a diachronic "history of the sceptre" (*Geschichte des Szepters*) (XVI.2. 879). Yet, on the other, in the greatest Homeric description *as* a work of art, the Shield of Achilles (*Iliad* 18.478-608), does Homer again depend upon such annalistic diachronics? It is here that Lessing falls short.

Lessing was primarily concerned with comprehending an aesthetic object as an *ideal* whole (*Begriff von dem Ganzen* – XVII.2.883; Wellbery 207-9), but at the same time he was misled by the *metaphorics of language inherent in any prose style*, especially his own, and adhered to the idea that when one deals with words one may describe the whole only through an at best hypotactic and always serial, linear narrative. In fine, when it comes to the semiotics of *poetic description*, he argues, all is caught in a verbal narration of successive *imitations* ("in ihren fortschreitenden Nachahmungen" – XVI.2.875-76). Also, as for artistic "representations" of the poetic go, one must never forget that Lessing adduces the Senecan and Petrarchan trope that makes an imitation only faintly resemble an "original": "And so their [the painters'] works become copies (*Abdrücke*) of the *Homeric*, not in the [mimetic] relationship of a portrait to the original, but in the [imitative] relationship of a son to his father: alike, but different" (XXII.2.919). Again we have the proof for literature and art that *ut pictura poesis* presupposes essential, imitative differences, not solely mimetic identities, in its very positing.

Lessing's adherence to poetic narration, therefore, will cause the careful reader of his essay to doubt his pragmatic grasp of Homer's Greek. While some could be convinced that Virgil in his description of the Shield of Aeneas might have predicated the metaphorics of ornamentation upon it long after its "historical completion" (XVIII.2.896), no one who knows Greek can avoid the fatal contradiction Lessing's weak analysis poses to his diachronic theory of poetic narration, when he is forced to rely upon an imagined "consecutive making" that involves ten different "pictures" upon *Achilles'* Shield (XIX.2.899).

To begin with, although Lessing cites the catalogue-markers that order the Homeric Shield (*en men eteuxe* [aorist], *en de poiēse* [aorist], *en d' etithei* [imperfect], *en de poikille* [imperfect], etc. – XIX.2.899), he is ignorant of the fact that the aorist does *not* imply consecutive action. Secondarily he does not know that such an "atemporal tense" draws action centripetally towards likeness, not difference. Homer's language is in its very essence *paratactic, not hypotactic; poetic, not prosaic; metonymic, not metaphoric.* The Shield of Achilles is not a "poetic painting" simply because it does not give a painter a description of an heraldic armament to paint, but because it is an *ecphrasis,* the externally *a*ffective value of which Horatian metaphorics could not fathom.

The semiotic metaphoricity of prose tends to obscure the metonymic value inherent in Homeric poetry. Lessing was certainly not the man to bring the differences of his semiotic play in line with the identities that a view of a whole work of art necessitates, be it the Laocoön or, for that matter, any aesthetic object. Hence both he and his twentieth-century commentator (Wellbery 199-200) fail to appreciate a subtle distinction that remains in the master's critique when he endeavors to push aesthetic similarities in poetry and art to their furthest limit: Poetry "in its progressive imitations" (*in ihren fortschreitenden Nachahmungen*) can use only a single attribute of human bodies [one may also read "of a subject at a time"] and must make its "choices" (*wählen*) accordingly. Painting "in its coexisting compositions" may only create a "single moment" (*einen einzigen Augenblick*) and, hence, "must make use of (*nutzen*) the most pregnant one (*den prägnantesten*)" (XVI.2.875-76).

So immediately before the reader spring the two key issues that Lessing's metaphorics uncover: "subjects" and "the pregnant moment." Yet, the disturbing difficulties they impose should not obscure from the reader the fact that Lessing, seemingly in spite of himself, has *not*, in the end, identified the aesthetic natures of poetry and art, for it is not quite the same to choose (*wählen*) a model and make use of it (*nutzen*), nor is it the same to conjecture a poetic description as a series of "progressive imitations," which Lessing will later describe as "elements ordered after one another in succession" (*Elemente, nacheinander geordnet* – XX.2.902) and painterly creation as a "coexisting composition," latter of "elements in juxtaposition" (*sie [Elemente] nebeneinander geordnet* – XX.2.902). "Nacheinander" stresses the metaphoric; "*nebeneinander*," the metonymic. For the early-to-mid-eighteenth-century semiotician and for the deconstructionist-Saussurian such a distinction obviously "signifies" little.

This privileging of metaphor, moreover, undercuts the *Laocoön*'s two major aesthetic propositions: aesthetic subjects or *choices* and the pregnant moment. Again it obscures the aesthetic object from the viewer. Again it does so in spite of what Lessing ostensibly desires to say.

He speaks at one point of a viewer's "first glance" (*mit dem ersten Blicke* – XI.2.859). We are soon to find, however, that this seemingly direct aesthetic experience is not a simple one, but mediated *by the painter's intended choice* (*Vorwurf*), which in its turn should be "familiar" (*bekannt* – read "traditional"). Goethe and Heinrich Meyer will fret this proposition for everything it is worth, but what is important for the argument at this point is that Lessing is not interested so much in the immediate viewing of an aesthetic object as in *its thematic* selection by the artist, an action that, in fact, for all his reference to a viewer's "glance," steps back from that "glance" by interposing the conscious decision of critical choice and a further problem, namely why an artist, whether a poet, or a painter, made that choice.

The same critical play surrounds Lessing's discussion of the "pregnant moment," and again the proposition becomes problematic because the reader is never quite sure of the value of the "pregnant moment" Lessing wishes to address. Of a critic who at one point argues that the most exteriorized moment is the worst (*Lessings Laokoon*, Nachlass A.4.2.391) and then turns to the necessary freedom of imagination it will allow the viewer (III.2.798-99), perhaps little more may be said than that his view of the physical is very low (Wellbery 116). It is not, however, Lessing's avoidance of the hyletic that should hold our attention here so much as the inherent metaphoricity of argument inherent in *ut pictura poesis*. Once more, as was the case with the academic critic, the rhetorical metaphorization of sight reduces the artist's dependence upon the generated plastics of space to a second order: ("... in his [the artist's] art we can see only what has been generated [*entstanden*]" – XVI.2.882). How could a greater metaphorical gulf be posited between art and poetry, between the viewer and the aesthetic object, than this?

It is not an easy task to pinpoint exactly what Lessing wants to say about the similarities between art and poetry in his *Laocoön*. In some ways it is even more difficult to pinpoint what he wants to say about their differences. On the one hand, as is the case with Horace, it is clear that his first love is poetry (for Lessing also read "prose"); on the other, why? From the point of view of aesthetic choice alone, one should entertain the proposition that a kind of aesthetic freedom dictates his preference, but on closer examination we see that while Lessing argues on the part of the artist for a freedom *from* second-rate choices; e.g., from those of a religious nature (IX), he interposes the metaphorically eidetic, image-making ability of the imagin-ation (*Einbildungs-kraft*) in free play (*freies Spiel*) between the viewer and the aesthetic object:

> The more we see (*sehen*), the more must we be able to think in addition (*hinzudenken*). The more we think thereto (*darzudenken*) the more we believe (*zu sehen, glauben*) to see. ... To indicate to the eye the most exteriorized (*Äusserste*) [moment] is called binding the wings of phantasy. (III.2.798-99)

One sees what one thinks, and one thinks with a diachronically metaphorical succession of words. Can stylistic metaphors be far behind? Yet, surely Lessing calls upon the metaphors of sight in a rationalist's attempt to "perceive" the whole, and to transfer such an argument into a full-blown deconstructionist "freedom of imagination" on the part of the viewer (Wellbery 168-70) is at best premature, although certainly not impossible somewhere down the metaphorically semiotic road on which Lessing seems to be leading us. The more pressing problem is this: Given such a devaluation of an artist's use of space to a single moment of unchanging duration ("*unveränderliche Dauer*" – III.2.799), itself subordinated to an inherent metaphoricity of language and thought, *how can the artist's "moment" not be enchained by the totalitarian claim of the viewer's "free play" to a set of arbitrarily selected and passively accepted aesthetic choices*? Goethe and Meyer were to take somewhat opposite sides in their answers.

What Goethe and Meyer evolved in their respective efforts, however, was a critique that dissipated the metaphorics of sight in language through an appeal to sight's immediate metonymics, in short one that steers us *to* the aesthetic object rather than *away from* it. It was to take the form of one of the most bizarre joint projects in the history of aesthetics: the *Propyläen*.

3. Fretted and Unfretted Statements on the Pragmatics of Art

From the Klopstock incident in *Werther* through the epiphany of the *Mater Gloriosa* in the last scene of *Faust*, Goethe privileged the immediate value of human sight as an aesthetic and, ultimately, internal and external visionary experience. Like Winckelmann, he attributed a great deal of value to the literary and artistic artefacts of antiquity. Hence, in his analysis of the Laocoön group, he returned in his way to the earlier critic's "beautiful ancient" and his emphasis upon the "human soul" (*Seele*) and "human acts" (*menschliche Handlungen*) (Winckelmann, *Gedanken* 22-24). In so far as Goethe undercuts the metaphoricity of Horace's and Lessing's aesthetic argument through a relative elevation of human perception and human values, he opts generally for the earlier, passionate and less formally semiotic critique. Clearly Lessing's playful aesthetics were not entirely to Goethe's taste; yet, on the other hand, neither were Winckelmann's *until they would undergo a very pragmatic wash*.

In short, Goethe distrusted critical metaphorics. His aesthetic experiences were lodged in the processes with which he addressed his own work. Therefore, in an attempt to bridge and, hence, dissolve the aesthetic gulf created by the critic between the viewer and the aesthetic object, he devised the *Propyläen*-scheme, in which, from its very inception, he perceived himself as versed in "the reflection (*Nachdenken*) and discourse (*Gespräch*) of theory and method" and Meyer as versed in "observation" (*Anschauung*) and its "consideration" (*Betrachtung*) (Goethe to Meyer, July 14, 1797, WA 4.12.188-89). That the contributions to the journal suggest that Meyer's interest is more critical and Goethe's more authentically visual might confuse only someone who forgets the nature of the project.

Goethe opens the journal with a striking metaphor of man and place. The *Propyläen* becomes the cultural antechamber of the temple of Athena herself, into which he draws the reader and the contributors towards a common "place" (*Platz*), up the steps, through the door and entrance. This antechamber is "the space (*Raum*) between the inner and outer, the holy and profane" where they all will "absent themselves as little as possible from classical ground." He dubs his title "symbolic" (*symbolisch*) (*Propyläen* 7-8) and calls upon the artist to regard all about him and make a "practical use of such experiences so that, after a continual practice and in a state of ever sharper observation)," he will, as much as possible, "make use of it for himself" and, "later share it happily with others" (*Propyläen* 9). Goethe also promises "pure observations," which he admits difficult to produce "without soon employing [the process of] reflection (*Betrachtungen anstellen*)" (read "metaphorical discourse") (*Propyläen* 9).

It soon becomes clear that a profound humanism lies behind the journal's aesthetic purpose: "the human being (*der Mensch*) is the highest, indeed the intrinsic subject of the plastic and graphic art" (*Propyläen* 16). Thus when Goethe adduces the old, ultimately non-Wölfflinian saw, "What one knows, one really sees" (*Was man weiss, sieht man erst*) (*Propyläen* 18), he is in effect calling for an intense and special visual, almost biblical, knowledge that in itself will penetrate to the very constitution of the human body *and* being to reveal the "manner" (*Art*) by which a work is carried out (*Propyläen* 19). This pragmatic evaluation, however, puts him at odds with the hermeneutics of his time, for as if to denounce the metaphorics traced above, he argues *against* the moderns' grasp of the ancients, whom, he declares, they call their teachers while at the same time attributing "to their works such inaccessible perfection" that they, in the end, "distance themselves, in theory and practice (*in Theorie und Praxis*), nevertheless, from the principles which they steadfastly executed" (*Propyläen* 28). (Exit Winckelmann and Renaissance metaphorics.)

Goethe's aversion to cultural and critical metaphorics becomes even sharper as he argues that one is able to speak of works of art with profit "only when present" (*nur in Gegenwart*) (*Propyläen* 34). (Exit Lessing.) Only from this "highest and most certain notion of art (*Begriff von Kunst*) can a history of art (*Kunstgeschichte*) rest" (*Propyläen* 35). "Every art requires the whole man" (*den ganzen Menschen*); the highest possible level of art, all humanity (*die ganze Menschheit*) (*Propyläen* 39). (Reenter a Winckelmann denuded of "the beautiful ancient" with deadly implications for Wölfflin's "relative viewer.")

Yet also, "Happy the artist who does not go astray in the undertaking of work, who understands to choose (*wählen*) [what is] aesthetically satisfying (*Kunstgemässe*), or better to execute it" (*Propyläen* 23). For the journal, Goethe interestingly ceded a fuller discussion of this problem to Meyer.

Goethe did, however, have his say in Meyer's task, and it is important to note just how far he was willing to develop it. The letter of June 14, 1797, mentioned above, was accompanied by a very short essay or précis entitled, "Upon the Subjects for Plastic and Graphic Art." This is the same title of the long essay by Meyer that trails over from the first into the second issue of their journal (*Propyläen* 72-117, 231-67).

From his essay's first sentence, it strikes the reader that Goethe will elevate the importance of the metonymic *viewer and creator* in the complex consideration at hand: "From the plastic and graphic arts one desires meaningful (*deutlich*), clear (*klar*), determined (*bestimmte*) [read "objective"] re-presentations (*Darstellungen*)." He then imposes upon the artist, first, the intuitively correct choice and then, second, the highest execution (*Ausführung*) of subjects (*Gegenstände*). The essay's one-sentence second paragraph allows a most extraordinary condition: Goethe declares that "the most advantageous subjects" (one must argue both for artist and viewer) have *a life of their own*, that is a "sensuous being" (*sinnliches Dasein*) ("Über die Gegenstände der bildenden Kunst" [subsequently "Gegenstände"] WA 1.47.91).

Paragraph three begins with the first, "type," "topos," or "species" (*Gattung*), and it appears that both Goethe did, and we should, hold all his topoi in a strict Aristotelian sense as secondarily categorial, perhaps even to the point of entertaining the strong possibility of their *limited* ontological status (Aristotle, *Categories* 2a11-27). Goethe's categories are 1) the "natural," which because of its physiological and sometimes ordinarily expressive (*gemein pathetisch*) nature is part of, but not identical to, 2) the "ideal." The "ideal" partakes of the soul-spirit's (*Geist*) most human, *inner* ties with "Nature." It is at this point that Goethe adduces the accomplishments of the Dutch and the Greeks and specifically remarks upon the *subject* of the Laocoön ("Gegenstände" WA 1.47.91-92).

Suddenly the essay takes an unhappy turn into what is, in effect, a mixed category or set of subcategories: cycles of subjects that have a certain "mystical" bent. (In categorial terms, the vagaries of this "detour" will be to Goethe's misfortune.) He offers, as particular examples, the Muses with Apollo and Niobe with her daughters in which, he claims, the natural and ideal have coincided in their "consummate perfection." The second categorially vague topos is much more interesting. Here, Goethe argues, are subjects that become neither understandable nor interesting unless tied and explained in succession (*durch eine Folge*). He points to the art of bas-relief, a painting of troops accompanying the Emperor Sigesmund, and representations of antique myth.

Is Goethe sinking, as did Lessing, into the metaphors of narrative? Has *ut pictura poesis* crept in the back door? It has, and Goethe is unhappy with it. Backpedaling to the experience of the inherent excellence of the single representation, he notes that any *one* particular labor of Hercules is, after all, a perfectly good subject because the narrative cycle is well enough known in itself ("Gegenstände" WA 1.47.92-3). In other words *we the viewers can supply the narrative; the art work is removed of the burden.* In terms of Goethe's categorial argument, however, it is important to note that his equivocation in this matter pertains not to the aesthetic moment but to his categories, or, more precisely, to *the metaphorics or semiotics of categorization with which he is clearly unhappy.*

In semiotic terms what bothers him is, in effect, Lessing's metaphoric identification of the aesthetic moment within the imagination, for he turns forthwith to the center of a *metonymic aesthetics.*

He returns to the implicit referent of his essay's opening sentence, that is the viewer and creator and notes that his three previous categories have dealt solely with the object (*Objekt*). He wishes now to move the discussion towards not only the *treatment* of the subject but also towards "the spirit [essence?] of the handling itself" (*der Geist des Behandelnden*) ("Gegenstände" WA 1.47.93). This distinction is more exact in German than in English, but it introduces here what one critic has called the "polar notion" of "meaning in the spiritual-mental" (*Bedeutung im Geistigen*) and an "[infinite] appearance in the evident" (*Erscheinen im Sichtbaren*) (Keller 97). *Goethe is dealing here with the semiotics of the meaningful and the problem of direct referentiality.* This is not Lessing's semiotics of *ut pictura poesis*, and especially not Wölfflin's and von Blanckenhagen's semiotics of the relative referent. Goethe's binary intuition turns the metaphorics inherent in his own criticism away from its tendency toward extended metaphoricity and back upon the paratactic metonymics of a return of the signifier in the signified, in short *back to the aesthetic object itself*. He appropriately dubs this new category "the symbolic" ("Gegenstände" WA 1.47. 94).

His argument thereto is this: If certain subjects be "pure and natural," "best and highest," and are in this way represented or "placed-there-before" (*dargestellten*), "they appear (*scheinen*) to stand purely [uncovered] for themselves (*bloss für sich zu stehen*) and are, in addition, meaningful in the deepest [sense] (*im Tiefsten bedeutend*)" ("Gegenstände" WA 1.47. 94). Certainly we are moving here toward a full statement of phenomenological intension, and we come even nearer as Goethe continues by subordinating allegorical subjects to symbolic ones in the name of the former's "indirect" characteristics and the latter's "direct" ones.

The essay ends with an unconcealed attack upon the metaphorics of *ut pictura poesis*. Goethe insists that the plastic or graphic artist should "compose" (*dichten*), that is perform creative acts, and not "make poetry" (*poetisieren*). The painter is not like a poet, "who in his works must, strictly speaking, set in motion his imagination (*Einbildungskraft* [!])" and "by a sensual representation also work for [!] the imagination" ("Gegenstände" WA 1.47.95). (Exit Lessing and his linguistic metaphorics). Yet, it is not until the essay's last sentence that Goethe at last gathers the fortitude to throw over the whole concept of categories and its hierarchy of subjects entirely. He adds to his first three categories a fifth (the inane attempt to create aesthetic objects from the "highest abstractions," that is to metonymize the highest degree of the metaphoric and, in effect, to turn Aristotle's categorial ontology on its head). All these four of his five categories he dubs "blameworthy" (*tadelnswerth*) ("Gegenstände" WA 1.47.95). *True positive value lies in the symbolic*.

Given Goethe's obvious frustration over his own critical attempts at categorization, it is little surprise that he handed over the final essay on the matter to Meyer, who faithfully assumes Goethe's categories to the letter (*Propyläen* 74-75), whether they be blameworthy or not, and dutifully fills them up with examples, including more of those that indicate the consecutive representations of narration (*Propyläen* 84-87). Would these have put Goethe entirely at ease? Meyer also introduces additional vague subcategories and, thus, reveals a tendency to semiotic multiplicity that Goethe so abruptly dismisses in his own essay on their common rhetorical subject.

As for Meyer, the tendency builds upon itself with a startling virulence in the journal's next issue, where he professes to examine categories (plural) that are "below the purely human" (*tiefer* [not "deeper"] *als die rein menschlichen*) (*Propyläen* 231). His last category will consist of the painfully non-aesthetic trash heap of "contradictory subjects" that are so unclear in choice and execution that (sin upon sin) "the meaning must be produced by the viewer" to complete the unhappy work itself (*Propyläen* 244-67).

What is at point here? Neither Meyer's nor our own "contemporary art," although his words must certainly have brought to Goethe's mind thoughts of Füssli ("Gegenstände" WA 1.47.95). Clearly what Meyer, as Goethe, refers to is *the relative inefficacy of the imagination in the human confrontation with the aesthetic object:*

> A picture, regarded as a work of art stirs us only through that which is really placed-right-there (*wirklich dargestellt*). What we at the same time imagine [or "reflect"] (*Was wir uns dabei denken*) belongs not to it (*gehört nicht ihm*), but to us in addition (*gehört uns an*). (Meyer, *Propyläen* 245, stress mine)

It was, after all, Meyer's resistance to visual metaphorics and his ability as an observer that could verify Goethe's own visual observations and, hence, his aesthetic judgments.

Both Meyer and Goethe, *in purely critical terms*, therefore, tend to elevate the aesthetic object onto a par with critical judgment, which, by necessity, must attribute to that aesthetic object qualities it had not possessed theretofore in the history of aesthetic criticism.[7] What confronts us here arises from Goethe's struggle with aesthetic objects and his own reflection thereto. It is this Janus-faced tension that will cause him to privilege an immediate, paratactic, and metonymic confrontation with any aesthetic object and its *affect*. Later he will codify this self-reiterating experience in the notion – artefact of the *Urbild* (Benjamin 1.1.110-11). It always remains, however, a locative instinct between the viewer and the viewed, which Goethe explains in his journal's first essay, "Upon the Laocoön."

Unlike Lessing, Goethe had viewed a model of the Laocoön group in Mannheim in 1771 (*Dichtung und Wahrheit* WA 1.28.84-7). Moreover, before composing his essay, he had sent the willing Meyer off in order to verify, not what he *thought about* the group, *but what he had seen*. The good Meyer's reply in March of 1796 found its way into the journal's second issue in 1799, and it is doubly important, both in that Goethe saw the necessity of its publication and in that it represents a "direct sighting" of the statue that records much of its 1506 appearance and the history of its "restoration." (The piece is even helpful today.) Thus armed, Goethe attempted a foray against the statue itself.

Expectedly the essay's opening pages review Goethe's positions upon the relationship between art and human nature (*die menschliche Natur*); upon the aesthetic necessity of what we should probably call "bracketing" ("It is a great advantage for a work of art if it is free-standing [*selbstständig*] and if it is closed in itself"; and upon the related representation of the aesthetic moment (*Darstellung des Moments*) (*Propyläen* 54-55, 57-58, 59-60). What is unexpected, however, arises at that point where he turns to a clear phenomenological aesthetics, right down to the primacy of human sight, to the *intention* of the aesthetic object, and to the necessary human knowledge derived therefrom:

> In order to grasp correctly the *intention* (*die Intention*) of the Laocoön, one places oneself at a suitable distance before it with eyes shut (*mit geschlossnen Augen*); one opens one's eyes and shuts them again immediately; thus will one see (*sehen*) all the marble in *movement*. ... As it [the group] now stands there, it is a fixed bolt of lightning, a wave enstoned in the *moment* (*versteinert im Augenblicke*). ... the same affect is produced if one sees the group at night by torchlight. (*Propyläen* 60, stress mine)

The importance of this short paragraph upon the eighteenth-century's then recently established "History of Art" is revolutionary. That it would have to be stated in the first place reveals a great deal about the nature of criticism and aesthetic experience before Goethe; that it privileges human sight and a phenomenological affectivity of the aesthetic object itself indicates strongly that Goethe knew something about aesthetic experience Lessing did not. His following *description* of the Laocoön group assumes an immediacy in prose that Homer created in poetry in his/our Shield of Achilles. Goethe knew very well the difference between an *ecphrasis* and a *pictura*.

It is an essentially human perception that lies behind Goethe's lightning bolt or, we might say, "shutter's click" of the aesthetic experience. It recalls not the dead, reflecting apparatus of a camera, but the live, metonymic, visually intent power of the viewer. His "kairetic" locus of experience supersedes the metaphorical reflectivity of an "inner chamber's room," a *camera obscura*, as it were, the ironic possibilities of which Goethe knew well (*Wahlverwandtschaften* WA 1.20.316-17).

The reader might wish to follow Goethe's directions, for the experience involved can be a startling one. It maximizes the focus and intent of sight, minimizes reflective thought, and vests the aesthetic object with an immediate "life of its own," a phenomenological intention. Such an affectivity applies whether in full light or in the flickering light of a candle. So man *must* see denuded of the metaphorical opposition of light and dark that Wölfflin only wills to a critical norm.

Goethe will, therefore, in the remainder of his essay depend upon what is, in effect, pragmatic human experience. Our direct observation of the Laocoön, he claims, must yield the artist's representation of sensuous causes and effects (*Propyläen* 62), and therein he has handed us the "highest expressive manifestations" (*der höchste pathetische Ausdruk*), in which smolders a remarkably non-rhetorical "energy of life," an "electric shock" (*electrischer Schlag*) (*Propyläen* 63) we are forced to perceive, not by our critical metaphorics or even, interestingly enough, by antique perfection, but by what is humanly physical or moral. Goethe sees in this reflexive instinct the form of opposition (*es ist ein Gegensatz*) "of which one has no idea without [human] experience" (*Propyläen* 63). Only in the name of this common human experience, then, will he allow the human metaphorics of reflection, and his extended musing about "the peak of the represented moment" (*Propyläen* 66) transforms the Laocoön group into a powerful narrative of our "suffering ... fear, terror, and compassion" (*Propyläen* 68). Metaphors have found a common level with the aesthetic object.

Ultimately, of course, one has the rhetorical option to deny the humanist reading Goethe proposes, just as one might deny that of a Marxist, feminist, or deconstructionist. After all a reading is only a reading. What is exceptional about Goethe's, however, is its direct predication upon the metonymics of sight, rather than upon its metaphorics, by which it is aided, not hindered, by the metaphorics of the written word or argument.

He underlines this fact when he avoids closing his essay with a further observation upon the statue itself, but turns, in effect, to "the relationship of [aesthetic] subjects for poetry (*Verhältniss des Gegenstandes zur Poesie*)" (*Propyläen* 70). In short, how does Virgil fare in this eighteenth-century semiotic battle?

Goethe, like Lessing, strikes here a deep wedge between art and poetry in general, but, in this particular instance of the Laocoön group, he, unlike Lessing, will attribute to Virgil's poetics a *damning metaphoricity: As a referent* by which to judge or evaluate the sculptured object itself, Virgil's "history of Laocoön" (*die Geschichte Laokoons*) becomes extremely problematic. It is, after all, for Virgil *only a "rhetorical argument"* (*ein rhetorisches Argument*, stress mine) that gives vent to "hyperbole" (*Übertreibung*). Goethe concedes that as a means to an end one might accept the language, but he declares, in a last sentence as tantalizing as the last of his "Gegenstände," that he is none too sure that the Laocoön event (*Begebenheit* – read "moment") is a proper subject for poetry at all (*Propyläen* 70-71).

Non ut pictura poesis. The reader cannot help asking what might be "proper poetic subjects," but who can be confident that we should immerse ourselves once again in the semiotics of categories and choices? Goethe, as a reader and author, selected his own "proper" literary subjects, and although he appears willing enough to broach the phenomenology of the literary work of art in "Upon the Laocoön," it is significant that he is unwilling to develop it. To avoid a rat's nest of metaphoricity is always the better part of valor.

> One, two, three, but where, good Timaeus, is the fourth. ...

This essay is purely critical and has few claims to be a work of art or an aesthetic object – hence the title "Laocoön IV." In its Goethian emphasis upon metonymy, moreover, it has done little more than reargue his case for the par value of the aesthetic object and its critical reduction. One could, I suppose, have given the piece some kind of "polar designation," such as "IV/V" or "Moments Metaphoric *and* Metonymic," but such semiotic images are seldom compelling. The present title should signify little more than a clarification of Goethe's own reflections, not a desire to advertise abstractions more nearly pure than the attempt itself.

This essay is not "metacritical" but "encritical" or "implodic" in the sense of the implosion of a criticism turned upon itself. If it might appear to have the distinction of using semiotics differently than the deconstructionist-Saussurians, it can make no claim other than that it turns Jakobsonian metaphorics and metonymics on their axial heads. If the essay exposes anything new, it is probably the hardly unexpected insistence that all criticism, written in prose or poetry, may be regarded as equally metaphoric, whether the specific work be that of Wölfflin, his academics, Horace, Pliny, Winckelmann, Lessing, or Goethe. As far as the humanistic reduction itself is concerned, I can only claim its value as one human being among many, as I find myself in the process of making pragmatic judgments, for that matter, of any aesthetic moment in the world's "canon." The choice of objects and moments within that canon rests on human intention and, hence, *experience*.

Why is this choice any better than yours? It's not. Why is this choice any better than that of the playfully metamorphorizing critic? It is, and to this point, which was after all its primary critical focus, this essay has much to say and should be allowed to stand entirely on its own.

It opened with the statement: the mere act of reflection necessitates a confusion of the aesthetic object with its critical reduction. By its close it has shown that the state of affairs is even more unsettling than that. Critical reductions on the order of Winckelmann's, Lessing's, or Wölfflin's, ignore and deny the aesthetic object in a smokescreen of inappropriate rhetoric that interposes itself between any particular aesthetic object and its viewer. In addition it interposes itself between the aesthetic object and the general category of "aesthetic objects" that might be reduced in the framework of any Aristotelian categorial ontology. (Not, to be sure, that I should ever speak well of the Philosopher's ontology were it not for the rhetorical perversities the theory of being has suffered under the onus of Heidegger and Derrida.) In the case of Goethe's own critical reflections, one may only argue that they are as fairly and pragmatically oriented toward the aesthetic object and its function as any can be.

Whose canonic taste, then, should we follow? Goethe's, Wölfflin's, Derrida's, or, to be absolutely democratic and fair in our play, a computer's? Goethe's is the best choice. He knew much more about the aesthetic experience and how to confront the viewer with an aesthetic object. As for the others?

I ask the reader the following question: How can a critic whose primary rhetorical premise destroys or propagandistically re-interprets the affect and immediate perception of an aesthetic object, in turn, select a "canon" composed of aesthetic, humanly affective, and perceived objects?

RHETORIC FAILS. THE TRUTH IS THAT S(HE) OR IT CAN'T.

Notes

1. I make no attempt here at a full either archeological or philosophical-art historical listing of the Laocoön problem. If the reader misses references to players in the game, please turn to the sources I have indicated in the bibliography.

2. References to the *Naturalis Historia* are to the Teubner edition of Pliny's works; all other classical citations may be found in the latest edition of the respective author's Oxford Classical Text.

3. A letter by Cesare Trivulzio of June 1506 reveals a caveat that has had to be admitted or explained away even today (Pollitt 310 fn. 16): both Michelangelo and Giovanni Cristofano Romano saw that the piece was in more than one piece and not the *one* Pliny claims (Bieber 1-2).

4. In the following examination of the limits of the academic critique I have made no attempt to include every participant in the debate. Characteristics are more interesting than numbers.

5. The passage in which Pliny mentions the Laocoön group is somewhat an afterthought or digression (Nec deinde multo plurium fama est. ... "After this [assumed to be enumerative in tone, not temporal] few accrue much renown ... " [*NH* 36.37. 1]). Where lies the overt textual evidence to argue that Pliny is *not* speaking of contemporary sculptors?

6. I have recently attempted a discussion of this unusual linguistic problem and its ramifications for modern literary theory: *Thauma Idesthai: The Phenomenology of Sight and Appearance in Archaic Greek* (Tallahassee: Florida State University Press, 1989).

7. It will become an invaluable antimetaphoric aid for Goethe in Die *Wahlverwandtschaften* (1809), in which "the artist" as creator and organizer, both inside and outside the narrative, will play outrageously with the *ironic significance* of *the tableaux vivants*. Nowhere in literature is the complex relationship between the aesthetic object and its human reception better represented than in Goethe's narrative that surrounds Ottilie's Nativity Scene (*Die Wahlverwandtschaften* WA 1.87.270-73).

Works Cited

Benjamin, Walter. *Gesammelte Schriften*. Eds. R. Tiedemann and H. Schweppenhäuser. 6 vls. Frankfurt am Main: Suhrkamp, 1974-85.

Bieber, Margarete. *Laocoon: The Influence of the Group since its Rediscovery*. New York: Columbia UP, 1942.

von Blanckenhagen, Peter H. "Laokoon, Sperlonga und Vergil." *Jahrbuch des deutschen Archäologischen Instituts* 84 (1969): 256-75.

von Blanckenhagen, Peter H. Review of Conticello, Baldassare, and Andreae, Bernard, *Die Skulpturen von Sperlonga* (Berlin: Mann, 1974). *American Journal of Archeology* 80 (1976): 99-104.

Conticello, Baldassare and Andreae, Bernard. *Die Skulpturen von Sperlonga*. Berlin: Mann, 1974.

von Goethe, Johann Wolfgang. *Werke*. Ed. by commission of Grandduchess Sophie von Sachsen. 133 vols. Weimar: Bohlau, 1887-1919. (Cited as WA).

von Goethe, Johann Wolfgang. Ed. *Propyläen: Eine periodische Schrift*, Intro. and Appen. by Wolfgang Frhr. von Löhneysen. Darmstadt: Wissenschaftliche Buchgesellschaft, 1965 (or. ed. Tübingen: J.G. Cotta, 1798-1800).

Greene, Thomas. *The Light in Troy: Imitation and Discovery in Renaissance Poetry*. New Haven/London: Yale UP, 1982.

Havelock, Christine Mitchell. *The Art of the Classical World from the Death of Alexander the Great to the Battle of Actium*. London: Phaidon, 1971.

Howard, Seymour. "On the Reconstruction of the Vatican Laocoon Group." *American Journal of Archeology* 63 (1959): 365-69.

Howard, Seymour. "Another Prototype for the Gigantomachy of Pergamon," *American Journal of Archeology* 68 (1964): 129-36.

Keller, Heinrich. *Goethe und das Laokoon-Problem*. Frauenfeld/Leipzig: Huber, 1935.

Leach, Eleanor Winsor. *The Rhetoric of Space: Literary and Artistic Representations of Landscape in Republican and Augustan Rome*. Princeton: Princeton UP, 1988.

Leppmann, Wolfgang. *Winckelmann*. New York: Alfred A. Knopf, 1970.

Lessing, Gotthold Ephraim. *Gesammelte Werke*. Ed. Wolfgang Stammler. 2 vols. Munich: Carl Hanser, 1959.

Lessing, Gotthold Ephraim. *Laocoön: An Essay on the Limits of Painting and Poetry*. Trans. Edward Allen McCormick. Indianapolis/New York: Bobbs-Merrill, 1962.

Lessing, Gotthold Ephraim. *Lessings Laokoon*. Ed. Hugo Blümer. 2nd ed. Berlin: Weidmann, 1880.

Magi, Filippo. *Il Ripristino del Laocoonte*. Vatican: Poliglotta, 1960.

Pollack, L. "Der Rechte Arm des Laokoon." *Archäologischen Instituts, Römische Abt. Mitteilungen des Deutschen* 19 (1905): 277-82.

Pollitt, Jerome Jordan. *Art in the Hellenistic Age*. Cambridge: Cambridge UP, 1986.

Richter, Giesela. *Three Critical Periods in Greek Sculpture*. Oxford Clarendon, 1951.

Wellbery, David E. *Lessing's Laocoön: Semiotics and Aesthetics in the Age of Reason*. Cambridge: Cambridge UP, 1984.

Winckelmann, Johann Joachim. *Abhandlung von der Fähigkeit der Empfindung des Schönen in der Kunst, und dem Unterrichte in derselben*. Dresden: Walther, 1763 (facsimile. *Studien zur deutschen Kunstgeschichte* 349 [1971]).

Winckelmann, Johann Joachim. *Anmerkungen über die Geschichte der Kunst des Alterthums*. Dresden: Walther 1767 (facsimile. *Studien zur deutschen Kunstgeschichte* 344 [1966]).

Winckelmann, Johann Joachim. From *Bibliothek der schönen Wissenschaften und der freien Künste* 5 (1759): 1-41 (facsimile. *Studien zur deutschen Kunstgeschichte* 349 [1971]).

Winckelmann, Johann Joachim. *Gedanken über die Nachahmung der griechischen Werke in der Malerei und Bildhauerkunst*. Dresden: Walther, 1756 (facsimile. *Studien zur deutschen Kunstgeschichte* 330 [1962]).

Winckelmann, Johann Joachim. *Geschichte der Kunst des Alterthums*. Dresden: Walther, 1764 (facsimile. *Studien zur deutschen Kunstgeschichte* 343-44 [1966]).

Winkes, Rolf. Review of Bieber, Margarete. *Laocoon: The Influence of the Group since its Rediscovery* (Detroit, Wayne State UP, 1967). *American Journal of Archeology* 72 (1968): 293-94.

Wölfflin, Heinrich. *Gedanken zur Kunstgeschichte. Gedruktes und Ungedrucktes*. 3rd ed. Basel: Benno Schwabe, 1941.

Wölfflin, Heinrich. *Kunstgeschichtliche Grundbegriffe: Das Problem der Stilentwicklung in der neueren Kunst*. 6th ed. Munich: Hugo Bruckmann, 1923.

Arnold's Legacy: Religious Rhetoric of Critics on the Literary Canon*

Pierre A. Walker

In his famous response to T.H. Huxley, "Literature and Science," Matthew Arnold argued that despite the scientific revolution in the nineteenth century, letters should still form a significant part of a person's education. In the Middle Ages, said Arnold, religion had satisfied certain innate parts of the human psyche. Subsequently, when scientific discoveries made it no longer possible to believe in religion, these instincts would have to be satisfied by something else, namely "humane letters." Physical science, wrote Arnold paraphrasing Huxley, proved fatal "to the notions held by our forefathers." Only "humane letters" could "establish a relation between the new conceptions [of science], and our instinct for beauty, our instinct for conduct" which religion had previously allied itself to so profoundly (66).

Arnold's point that "letters" would replace religion seems to have been proven true by the pervasiveness of religious rhetoric in criticism today. As Edward Said writes,

> When you see influential critics publishing major books with titles like *The Genesis of Secrecy, The Great Code, Kabbalah and Criticism, Violence and the Sacred, Deconstruction and Theology*, you know you are in the presence of a significant trend. (291)

The trend is especially significant in the debate that has been raging among literary theorists about the canon because to talk about a "literary" canon is to use terminology taken from theological discourse. The "canon," according to the *Oxford English Dictionary*, is "the collection or list of books of the Bible accepted by the Christian Church as genuine and

* This article was first published in *Stanford Literature Review* 5 (1988), *1-2*, pp. 161-77. It is reprinted here by kind permission.

inspired" and, by extension, "any set of sacred books." The word is borrowed by scholars and students of literature and refers to those texts that are valued more than others. It is significant that "canon" is preferred and not the "tradition" that T.S. Eliot, F.R. Leavis, and Raymond Williams used, because it signals that the discourse about which literary texts are authoritative is virtually the same as the discussion about the religious canon. What is more, critics who write about the literary canon do more than just borrow the word "canon" from religious discourse; they adopt an attitude of reverence towards their subject that is proper to the religious devotee. My argument is that the prevalence of this attitude proves all the more that Arnold was right; literature has indeed attached itself to people in the way Arnold said religion used to.

In order to give a proper account of some of the forms this reverence takes, I propose to consider the theoretical writing on the literary canon of a variety of critics: Frank Kermode, Harold Bloom, Terry Eagleton, and Jane Tompkins. In respect to the literary canon, these theorists can be divided into two camps. Bloom and Kermode are really explicators, historians, and theorists of canonization; their projects are to produce a model of what brings about a canon. Because they do not castigate the elements of the traditional literary canon as part of their project, I label them "right-wing" canon theorists. I label Tompkins and Eagleton "left-wing" because they are representative of feminist and Marxist attacks on a traditional canon that they would like to replace with something radically different.

The religious attitude of the right-wing canon theorists takes two forms; on the one hand, religious texts and the institutions that use and control them become a point of reference for what happens to literary texts, and on the other hand, literary texts and their authors become the outright objects of reverence.

Frank Kermode is exemplary of the point of reference approach to the canon. In his "influential" article (Altieri 38) "Institutional Control of Interpretation," he offers the canonizing and exegetical labors of the Church as "a model we would do well to consider as we attempt to understand our own practice" (172). While the Church made its "nomination" (172) of texts centuries ago, and has permitted virtually no variation since, canonization of Christian texts has had two results that have clear parallels in literary studies: the text, and its author, becomes sacred, and it is subjected to "repeated exegesis" (172).

The first result is clearly what has happened with James Joyce and *Ulysses*, the early readers of which Kermode calls "an enthusiastic cult" (*Gen esis* 49). In 1921, *The Observer* spoke of Joyce's "restricted" but "intense ... cult" (quoted. in Magalaner and Kain 165), and John Galsworthy reflected "bitterly in 1925 on the changing tides of taste, in which Dostoevski replaces Turgenev, Proust is seen to usurp the place of France, 'and a Joyce replace the Deity'" (Magalaner and Kain 169).

The phrase "enthusiastic cult" is equally applicable to the prolific activity that *Ulysses* inspires today. The abundance of guide books, which give "literary *pilgrims* ... guidance through the cities associated with Joyce" (Staley 238; italics added), note-books, concordances, and study-aids to *Ulysses* is unequalled in any twentieth century literary work and has a clear parallel in the many concordances, guides, and geographies to the Bible. The checklists of the *James Joyce Quarterly* announce titles such as: *Joyce and the Bible*, "James Joyce, Heretic," "Torn by Conflicting Doubts: Joyce and Renan," "The Voice of Esau: Stephen in the Library," "James Joyce: the Advent of Bloom," "The Way of the Cross in *Ulysses*," *My Brother's Keeper*, and "Ulysses the Divine Nobody." Frances Restuccia, in an article on "secular typology in *Ulysses*," calls Joyce an "artist-god" (441) which suggests that Joyce is no less revered today than in 1920, when Sylvia Beach "worshipped James Joyce" (Beach 35), and "Joyce was, of course ... god" for Robert McAlmon, William Bird, Ernest Hemingway, Archibald MacLeish, and Scott Fitzgerald (Beach 40).[1] For many years, two Jesuits were on the editorial board of the *James Joyce Quarterly* – William T. Noon and Robert Boyle – and the religious ties of Harry Blamires, Chester Anderson, and Kevin Sullivan are well known.

Even Joyceans of more secular backgrounds take part in Joyce studies as in a religion. Certainly no modern author – and perhaps none in English literature – is the object of as much ritualistic behavior. June 16 is the single most important day of the year, and the name "Bloomsday," with its apocalyptic ring (contrasting with the evocation of spring), is very appropriate. One cannot doubt that the annual meetings of the James Joyce Society or the biennial International James Joyce Symposiums that always occur on and around Bloomsday are ritualistic. The description of the First International Symposium in the *James Joyce Quarterly* sets that event on "Bloomsday, Dublin, 1967" and not on June 16, clearly showing that the symposium did not take place in anything as vulgar as calendar time.

The second result of the canonization of scripture, according to Kermode, is "repeated exegesis." Once the words in a text are held sacred, they become open to commentary and interpretation at the same time that their authenticity can be questioned less and less. The situation is the same in literary studies; it is unfashionable now to argue that an inconsistency in a text is caused by an inaccuracy (the clocks in *Julius Caesar*, for example), but it is quite acceptable to make it the basis of an intricate interpretation.

Kermode's writing on canonization and academic literary criticism abounds with religious terminology. He calls interpretative power, "the power of divination," those who do not belong to the academy are "the laity" ("Institutional Control" 169), and Louis Kampf is one of the "boy bishops." F.R. Leavis – or is it Yvor Winters – "is the Marcion of the canon" (179), his impact Kermode describes as "evangelical success," and "New Criticism and *Scrutiny* were (and still are) pretty successful heresies" (180). In *The Genesis of Secrecy* (the title itself has religious implications), Kermode describes the difference between readers of the "spiritual sense" and readers of the "carnal sense" (1-21). The latter read only the text's surface, while the former, who are also described as having "circumcised ears" (*Genesis* 5), are interested in a text's concealed meanings.

Harold Bloom's use of religious language is perhaps the most extensive of all, despite his having been one of the last holdouts for the word "tradition" over "canon" (although he often borrowed the word "Kabbalah" from Jewish theology). Bloom begins his 1984 article on canon-formation, "Criticism, Canon-Formation, and Prophecy: the Sorrows of Facticity,"like the Gospel of John, with a word: "I begin with my search for a word" (1). Bloom finds his word, but contemporary criticism, he feels, is not so successful in its quest:

> The quest of contemporary criticism is for method, and the quest is vain. *There is no method other than yourself.* All those who seek for a method that is not themselves will find not a method, but someone else whom they will ape and involuntarily mock. Poetry and fiction share with criticism the mystery that poststructuralist speculation seeks to deny: the spark we call personality or the idiosyncratic, which in metaphysics and theology once was called presence. ("Criticism" 9)

This passage would only seem slightly mystical, rather than explicitly religious, if the author had not pointed out a few pages earlier that God's "name is presence" (6). Thus, the personal, idiosyncratic, and mysterious spark that criticism shares with poetry and fiction was once called God. Contemporary criticism seeks and does not find method because it is seeking for the wrong thing, but Bloom is saying that if critics seek the deity (or, at least, what was once called such) within themselves, their quest will be successful.

When writing about specific critics and critical schools, Bloom's language is full of religious and reverential vocabulary. On feminism and its effect on canon-formation, he writes:

> I prophesy that the first true break with literary continuity will be brought about in generations to come, if the burgeoning religion of Liberated Woman spreads from its clusters of enthusiasts to dominate the West. (*Map* 33)

Bloom makes this statement as a prophecy, depicting feminist criticism as if it were an eastern god like Jesus or Dionysus whose enthusiastic followers were bringing it to, and conquering, the West.

Speaking of Emerson, Bloom writes: "I revere him" (*Map* 28). M.H. Abrams and Northrop Frye are "two of my heroic precursors" ("Criticism" 11). The Hebrew Bible is "consumed in Frye's great Blakean Code of Art, a fiery furnace worthy of the authors of *The Four Zoas* and *Fearful Symmetry*. Even the uncanny originality of [the] J[ahvist] is melted down in the visionary flames of Toronto" ("Criticism" 12). It is no surprise that Bloom says about Frye: "I worship that great critic's stance and style" ("Criticism" 15). Bloom's most reverent rhetoric is reserved for Freud: "We pay tribute to Freud involuntarily, as we do to all the powerful mythologies and idealism. ... Our Elijah or Supreme Critic was Freud, who preferred to see himself as Moses" ("Criticism" 2, 17).

When Bloom writes about the canon and its formation, religious discourse is as abundant as in his remarks on critics and criticism in general. The literary canon consists, he says,

> of individual parts, those strong enough to force their way against facticity [i.e., taking metaphors, such as Freud's model of mental processes, literally and actually believing our heads are made up of objects called ego, superego, and id] into a canon that is complete without them, and must be compelled somehow to need them. ("Criticism" 13)

To illustrate the formation of the literary canon, Bloom, like Kermode, looks to scripture: "I turn to the one inevitable work in Western literary culture, the Bible" ("Criticism" 4):

> But to describe just *how* any revisionist struggles against facticity from within, I need to resort to the authentic precursors of so dialectical an agon. These precursors were the line of Hebrew prophets, from Elijah to the Jesus of the Gospels, which returns me to J, the Jahvist, as the textual founder both of this facticity and the prophets who emerged from it. ("Criticism" 10)

Bloom turns to the Bible for the same reason as Kermode; the similarity between the literary and the sacred canon is so compelling. Bloom sees Stevens and Shelley, for example, struggling against, and from within, the influence of their tradition just as he pictures the Hebrew prophets struggling with the influence of Genesis. Like Kermode, Bloom posits the same model for scriptural and literary canon-formation. Kermode concludes that canonization of a literary text licenses the interpreter to engage in the same kind of commentary as the exegete of scripture, but Bloom shows us, by the religiousness of his own language, that texts belonging to the literary canon are candidates for reverence.

Bloom only somewhat acknowledges the canonizer's role:

> Gossip grows old and becomes myth; myth grows older and becomes dogma. Wyndham Lewis, Eliot and Pound gossiped with one another; the New Criticism aged them into a myth of Modernism; now antiquarian Hugh Kenner has *dogmatized* this myth into the Pound Era, a canon of accepted titans. (*Map* 28; italics added)

For the most part, though, Bloom (and T.S. Eliot even more so before him, in "Tradition and the Individual Talent") understands the better or stronger poets as prevailing automatically, independently of any political activity of those – today the academic community – who shape the canon. He downplays the role that the institution plays in forming its canon, a role that Kermode does recognize. This is an important point, for the politics of the canon-forming institution are fundamental to the arguments of Marxist and feminist critics when they propose radical changes in the literary canon; for them, too much attention is paid to Lewis, Eliot, and Pound, and not enough to Kenner's role in making them as important as they seem.

Pointing out the religiousness and reverence in Joyce criticism or in Kermode's and Bloom's writing on the canon may not seem a great discovery, because several – predominantly Marxist – critics have already railed against the reverential tendencies of traditional literary scholarship in general. In fact, these critics would argue that not only is literary study a displaced religion but that is precisely what is wrong with it. However, these critics only rail against the broad tendency; they do not examine specific critics or groups of critics. Such attacks have been evolving over the last fifteen years, at least, but in the last five years have turned into assaults against the canon and the limitations caused by a narrowing of focus onto a body of texts distinct from all other culture. Unfortunately, these attacks on the reverence of traditional literary criticism, whether allied to an attack on the literary canon or not, typically offer no alternative to the reverence itself, simply an alternative reverence.

Frederic Jameson writes that dialectical literary criticism is "an intensification of the normal thought processes such that a renewal of light washes over the object of their exasperation" (307). Marxist criticism means redemption and rebirth, in other words; it will make us all "see the light." Richard Ohmann, in *English in America*, urges his colleagues to "teach politically with revolution as our end" and "oppose the tyrannies of this culture and lay the groundwork for the next." This argument "is, among other things, a specimen of the literature of conversion" (*English* 335). The significant word is conversion. Ohmann begins his book with the story of his own conversion to the radical of the subtitle. The MLA's resistance to discussing politics and the Vietnam War revealed to Ohmann that an apolitical stance was really a conservationist and conservative one. At the book's end Ohmann proclaims with appropriate missionary zeal his new proselytizing project, his intention to convert the whole institution. In other words, he simply wants to replace one displaced religion with another.

Terry Eagleton comes closest to acknowledging Arnold's legacy. In *Literary Theory*, he attributes the rise of English studies to "the failure of religion" in the later nineteenth century (22). English was "to provide the social 'cement'" that "religion progressively ceases to provide" (23). In England F.R. Leavis (Eagleton would probably call him the Eusebius rather than the "Marcion of the canon," as Kermode does) and *Scrutiny*'s "moral and cultural crusade" made literary works into "sacrosanct objects" (23), while in America "the ideology of New Criticism" turned the poetic response into "an affective affair which linked us to the 'world's body' in an essentially religious bond" (46). "Leavis sought to redeem criticism by converting it into something approximating a religion" (44).

In his first chapter, Eagleton argues that it is impossible to say what literature definitely is. He then maintains that what is considered literature is considered as such not because of any inherent superiority but as a result of the politics of the institution that designates what is worthy of its study.

> The fact that this canon is usually regarded as fairly fixed, even at times as eternal and immutable, is in a sense ironic, because since literary critical discourse has no definite signified it can, if it wants to, turn its attention to more or less any kind of writing. (201)

The reason for the exclusion of films, parties, and advertisements "from what is studied is not because they are not 'amenable' to the discourse: it is a question of the arbitrary authority of the literary institution." As a result, "Shakespeare was not great literature lying conveniently to hand, which the literary institution then happily discovered: he is great literature because the institution constitutes him as such" (202).

Rather than "the dogmatism which would insist that Proust is always more worthy of study than television advertisements," Eagleton prefers "any method or theory which will contribute to the strategic goal of human emancipation, the production of 'better people' through the socialist transformation of society" (211). Rather than literary studies, Eagleton proposes cultural studies,

> but it should not be taken as an *a priori* assumption that what is currently termed "literature" will always and everywhere be the most important focus of attention. Such dogmatism has no place in the field of cultural study. (213)

The study of Proust and Shakespeare will not be replaced, but will be revitalized by "the broader and deeper discursive formation" of cultural studies (213).

It is important to understand that Eagleton, while condemning the "dogmatism" – and, by extension, the reverence and religiousness – of traditional literary criticism and its current canon "piously swaddled with eternal verities" (217), proposes to replace them with nothing other than a dogmatism and a religiousness of a different sort. Rather than participating in the ritual worship of Joyce and other authors in the literary canon, we will become missionaries proselytizing for 'human emancipation' and "the production of 'better people'."

Ironically, as Eagleton himself points out, this mission is in some respects as conservative, politically speaking, as the apolitical stance of the liberal humanists that he criticizes: "Like all the best radical positions, then, mine is a thoroughly traditionalist one" (206). His belief that the socialist transformation of society will "produce 'better people'" gives away his reactionism, for liberal humanism, with its "suburban moral ideology" (207), claimed that "dealing with literature is worth while [because] it makes you a better person" (207). Thus Eagleton is not asking that literary studies change in any way but one. He is not against the morally edifying value of this study, nor is he against the methods or manners in which this study is conducted, nor does he wish to end the reverence toward that which is studied; all he wants is the name of that study to be "cultural study" and not "literary study" and for "television," "the popular press," and "Robert Tressell" to receive as much reverence as Shakespeare and Proust (216). The results will be "human emancipation" and "the death of literature," which will, in fact, be its "liberation" and "redemption" (217). Thus Eagleton is trying to do exactly what he said Leavis did: "Redeem criticism by converting it into something approximating a religion" (44). From the apolitical (i.e., covertly political) redemptive power of literature that Ohmann criticized, Eagleton has taken us full circle to overt – and left wing – politics that are going to redeem literature.

Jane Tompkins, in the two penultimate chapters of her book, *Sensational Designs*, uses arguments similar in many ways to Eagleton's to propose a feminist canon. The villains in this attack are the authors of the "American Renaissance," and the heroines are Harriet Beecher Stowe, Susan Warner, Sarah J. Hale, Augusta Evans, Elizabeth Stuart Phelps, her daughter Mary, and Frances Hodgson Burnett. The first group authored "*succès d'estime*" (122) that had limited commercial success, while the second group, "whose names were household words in the nineteenth century" (123) wrote sentimental novels that were "tremendous hit[s]" (148) and "sold in the hundreds of thousands" (146). The works of the first group today constitute the canon of American literature of the 1850s, while those of the second group are considered "trash" (123). Most importantly, the first group is made up entirely of men, while women make up the second. This explains, for Tompkins, why Hawthorne, Melville, *et al.* are the canonical writers of today, while Stowe, Warner, and the others are ignored.

By choosing to deal exclusively with American literature in the 1850s, Tompkins loads the deck in her favor. The opposition between male-authored, commercially unsuccessful, yet now canonical texts and texts that were written by women, highly popular, and almost entirely forgotten today falls readily to hand in this period and permits Tompkins to argue easily that male-dominated academic literary criticism is responsible for the ascendance of the men and the near disappearance of the women authors. One wants to ask: where does Emily Dickinson – the most admired American poet for many, yet entirely neglected in her own life-time – fit into this picture? Will Tompkins extend her attack to a British canon that today favors *Frankenstein* over the works of Mary Shelley's more influential and famous contemporaries, Matthew Lewis and Charles Maturin? Would she favor John Galsworthy and H.G. Wells to Virginia Woolf?[2] I believe not, for, as we shall see, only in American literature of the 1850s can Tompkins have texts with all the necessary attributes: successful, non-canonical, written by women, and – most importantly – religious.

The two texts that Tompkins especially commends are Stowe's *Uncle Tom's Cabin* and Warner's *The Wide, Wide World.* The reason that these novels are considered "trash" today has nothing to do with their inherent worthlessness or the intrinsic esthetic value of the texts of the American Renaissance authors, according to Tompkins. It is because the traditional judgments of "the male-dominated scholarly tradition" (123) are "amplified versions of what Hawthorne and Melville said about their sentimental rivals"(148). A "long tradition of academic parochialism" (125) began with Hawthorne and Melville "who – successfully as it turned out – strove to suppress" (148) the work of these popular women writers.

The argument, here, is very similar to Eagleton's, above. "Shakespeare was not great literature lying conveniently to hand" and neither were the writers of the American Renaissance. Just as Shakespeare "is great literature because the institution constitutes him as such" (Eagleton 202), so, too, Melville, Hawthorne, and Whitman are great literature because "the male-dominated scholarly tradition" has successfully suppressed any contenders.

According to Tompkins, "the enormous popularity of ... the popular domestic novel[s] ... is a reason for paying close attention to them" (124). After all, *Uncle Tom's Cabin*, she says, "helped convince a nation to go to war and free its slaves" (141). Aside from this simplistic idea of the historical causes of the Civil War, there are two problems with Tompkins's argument that the initial popularity of a text is a justification for considering a text important. In his article, "The Shaping of a Canon: U.S. Fiction 1960-1975," Richard Ohmann shows that the commercial success of novels today is the result of as powerful, albeit very different, political forces as those that affect the canonical status of a text in the academy. Therefore, popularity is no more due to anything intrinsic to the text than is canonicity. If Tompkins is to argue that the nineteenth century sentimental novels require our attention simply because of their popularity, then she is implying that popularity is in itself a value. But if popularity is as much the result of the popularizers' successful activity as canonic status is due to successful canonizing strategies, it cannot be held up as a value any more than any other. Tompkins would have to convincingly establish that no political forces, of the type Ohmann describes in his article, were at the root of the commercial success of the novels of Stowe and Warner before she could begin to claim that these novels' popularity is sufficient reason in itself for them to be considered important today.

The second problem with Tompkins's attack on the canon of 1850s American literature comes from the success of her critique of the standards of literary evaluation that shape the canon. If one argues that we cherish certain literary texts over others because we have been indoctrinated to value particular kinds of literariness by "the male-dominated scholarly tradition" that trained us, and if one claims, therefore, that what we value is not inherently better in the context of the institution that determines literary value, then one has to consider what would happen if the institution should change sufficiently and reject the values it holds to now for those that Tompkins proposes. Would not the new system of values be just as liable to the same critique as the old one? If everybody were to subscribe to a new system of values, would it not be as a result of the same sort of institutional conditioning that has lead us to subscribe to the old values? In other words, if I have been conditioned to prefer *Moby Dick* to *Uncle Tom's Cabin*, then would I not have to have been conditioned just as much in a different way if I were ever to prefer *Uncle Tom's Cabin* to *Moby Dick*? If esthetic superiority cannot be inherent to any text but only the result of the conditioning forces of the reader's cultural and historical environment, then it becomes impossible to argue that any text – and any cultural artifact, by extension – is better, more important, more worthy of attention, study, inclusion in a curriculum, or publication than any other.

Barbara Herrnstein Smith has shown in "Contingencies of Value" and "Fixed Marks and Variable Constancies: A Parable of Literary Value" – that last title shows that even Smith has to express questions of canon formation in religious terms – that it is the accrual of many decisions to include one particular text as opposed to another in a syllabus or literary anthology, to re-publish a text while letting another go out of print, to study and write about one text rather than another that contributes to the formation of a literary canon. If, then, literary (or cultural) study rejects a canon on Tompkins's and Eagleton's grounds (that canons are created by interested parties and not discovered "lying conveniently to hand"), it must study with a uniform degree of attention and make equally accessible to readers absolutely every cultural artifact. Otherwise the series of unavoidable choices that Smith describes will come into play and a canon will form inevitably (though not disinterestedly). Of course it is impossible to devote equal attention to all cultural artifacts, and, therefore, a situation in which an acanonical cultural study existed is inconceivable.

Popularity is not defensible as a criterion for canonical status of a text, and it is not, in fact, what Tompkins proposes as the real justification for seriously considering *Uncle Tom's Cabin* and *The Wide, Wide World*. The real reason these works are important is the religious beliefs they convey.

> The one great fact of American life during the period under consideration was ... the revival. Sentimental fiction was perhaps the most influential expression of the beliefs that animated the revival movement and had shaped the character of American life in the years before the Civil War. Antebellum critics and readers did not distinguish sharply between fiction and what we would now call religious propaganda. (*Sensational Designs* 149)

There are two points about this passage. First, the notion that sentimental fiction was an "influential expression" and that certain beliefs "shaped the character of American life" must be explained. Just as with the argument that *Uncle Tom's Cabin* convinced the nation to go to war, the sense of history is highly simplistic. How much religious belief shaped (and shapes) American character, what is American character, what is an influential expression, and how and what did this particular expression of beliefs influence are very important questions that arise but unfortunately are not satisfactorily answered. The second point about this passage is its last line: "what we would now call religious propaganda." This phrase is ironic, which suggests that the author would rather not have religious tracts and sentimental fiction disparagingly labeled "propaganda." The significance of this ironic tone is that Tompkins appears to be adding to her active critique of the "male-dominated scholarly tradition" an implied critique of the absence of overt religious values on the part of the group referred to as "we."

Tompkins's display of the formal complexity of *Uncle Tom's Cabin* and *The Wide, Wide World* is very convincing and clearly shows the relationship between these texts and their authors' religious and millennial strategies. "Stowe's rhetorical undertaking is nothing less than the institution of the kingdom of heaven on earth" (141). However, the basic conclusion is that these novels are great because they are like the Bible and canonical religious literature: "Warner, for instance, never referred to her books as 'novels,' but called them stories, because, in her eyes, they functioned in the same way as Biblical parables" (149). It is not Warner, but Tompkins, who calls her novels "Biblical parables." Referring specifically to criticism that *The Wide, Wide World* is a fairy-story, Tompkins says: "The education of the sentimental heroine is no more a fairy-story than the story of Job or *Pilgrim's Progress*" (184). The conclusion to her analysis of *Uncle Tom's Cabin* is that "its distinguishing features, generically speaking, are not those of the realistic novel but of typological narrative" (135) and that "this novel does not simply quote the Bible, it rewrites the Bible as the story of a Negro slave" (134).

After turning *Uncle Tom's Cabin* into the Bible, Tompkins is able to turn motherhood into godliness. One difference between *Uncle Tom's Cabin* and the Bible is that "the principle of sacrifice is revealed not in crucifixion but in motherhood" (141). The god(dess) is Rachel Halliday, who Tompkins elsewhere calls "the presiding deity" ("Sentimental Power" 95) of the Quaker settlement and who "is God in human form" (*Sensational Designs* 142). Women "dominate the scene" (145), and men are reduced to "the anti-patriarchal activity of shaving" (quoted in *Sensational Designs* 146). Thus, "the removal of the male from the center to the periphery of the human sphere ... the most radical component of this millennarian scheme, which is rooted so solidly in the most traditional values – religion, motherhood, home, and family" (145), is accomplished. Religious – "the sentimental writers had millennial aims in mind" (185) – and feminist – "the removal of the male from the center" – goals are achieved together in the sentimental novels, and Tompkins's own goals are exactly those of the writers she champions: the removal of the male-authored secular texts from the canon of nineteenth century American literature and their replacement with evangelical fiction written by women.

In Kermode, Bloom, and Joyce criticism, I have tried to demonstrate that Arnold's legacy is still with us; traditional literary criticism is a displaced religion. The example of Eagleton, however, shows that even when attacking it, Arnold's legacy cannot be shaken off; reverence can only be replaced with a different reverence. Ironically, Tompkins is most successful at escaping Arnold's legacy because she neither criticizes the reverential attitude of traditional literary criticism nor promises that her radically different approach to reading will have a redemptive value. But while she does not fall into the trap of Arnold's legacy as Eagleton does, her goal of replacing the canon of the American Renaissance with the evangelical fiction of the period is an open embrace of religious values.

Tompkins is not the only feminist critic whose discourse or project is in some way religious. Quite similarly to Kermode and Bloom, Christine Froula (a Joycean, incidentally) begins her "undoing of the canonical economy" by establishing a parallel between the second-century struggle over the scriptural canon of the early Church fathers and the gnostics and the struggle today over the literary canon fought by traditional male-dominated literary criticism and feminist criticism: "The *revisionary* female theology promoted in *literary* writing by women implicitly counters the patriarchal theology which is *already* inscribed in literature" (324). Elaine Showalter writes that (in 1981) "feminist literary critics are wandering in the wilderness, [and] as Geoffrey Hartman tells us, all criticism is in the wilderness" (179-80) and she describes the "two poles of feminist literary criticism" that Carolyn Heilbrun and Catherine Stimpson identified as "Old Testament" and "New Testament" (179).

I have proposed these samples of religious rhetoric in order to suggest how pervasive it is among a variety of critical strategies. Since I have only looked at a few critics, it may not seem that all discussion of canon formation indulges in the kinds of religiousness I have cited here. There may, indeed, be many instances where religiousness is entirely avoided, but, I would counter, the few critics I have concentrated on here are by no means the only ones whose critical discourse is of a religious type. To paraphrase the passage by Edward Said quoted above, when Barbara Herrnstein Smith calls her examination of literary value "a parable," when a Joycean like Gerald Bruns publishes an article about Hebrew scripture and canons, when Geoffrey Hartman writes about criticism in the wilderness, you know you are "in the presence of" (and we recall how Bloom said that God's "name is presence") a significant trend.

Jacques Derrida writes:

> The history of metaphysics, just as the history of the West ... must be thought of as a series of substitutions of center for center. ... The center receives, successively and in a regulated manner, different forms or names ... *eidos, arché, telos, energia, ousia* (essence, existence, substance, subject) *aletheia*, transcendentality, conscience, God, man, etc. (410-11; my translation)

After Arnold, T.S. Eliot, F.R. Leavis, and the American New Critics consolidated and propagated the substitution of culture for religious scripture, and the situation today is that,

> without willing the change, our theoretical critics have become negative theologians, our practical critics are close to being Agaddic commentators, and all of our teachers, of whatever generation, teach how to live, what to do, in order to avoid the damnation of death-in-life. (Bloom *Map* 29)

The critics who attack the canon and the religiousness of literary study must realize that their own position is often equally, if not more, religious and dogmatic. "Once an intellectual, the modern critic has become a cleric in the worst sense of the word," says Said (292), but the Marxist's attempts and inability to alter this situation make it seem inescapable; the legacy of Arnold is still with us. Ironically, it is critiques like Eagleton's that contribute most to making the literary canon appear eternal and sacred. Perhaps all is not lost; after all, the literary canon is not "eternal" and "immutable," as Eagleton would have it (201); it is in a state of constant fluctuation and controlled by far less "dogma" than the canon of the Christian churches.

Notes

1.   Beach is no doubt guilty of projecting her own adoration of Joyce a little too
     strongly onto the contemporaries she mentions here; this worship is not at all ap-
     parent in Hemingway's own memoir of the expatriate days, *A Moveable Feast*, but
     he, of course, had his own cult to think about at the time he was writing that book.

2.   I am perhaps guilty of mis-representing the overall argument of Tompkins's book
     by limiting my attention to the two penultimate chapters and not considering the
     rest. However, I do not think this is unfair. The two chapters were published in
     slightly different form as separate articles first ("Sentimental Power: *Uncle Tom's
     Cabin* and the Politics of Literary History" and "The Other American Renais-
     sance"), and this means that they are meant to stand on their own at the same time
     that they contribute to a greater overall project. The replacing of a male-oriented
     canon with a female one is only part of the book's overall project, which is to pro-
     pose nothing less than a whole new way to read and evaluate literature, and Tomp-
     kins is to be commended for proposing specific books and for actually presenting a
     way of reading them. This is in contrast with Eagleton's scheme, which only men-
     tions alternatives in the vaguest and most general way and gives no clue as to how
     cultural study is to be done.

Works Cited

Altieri, Charles. "An Idea and Ideal of a Literary Canon." *Critical Inquiry* 10
     (1983): 37-60.

Arnold, Matthew. "Literature and Science." *Philistinism in England and America.*
     Ann Arbor: U Michigan P, 1974. Vol. 10 of *Complete Prose Works of Matthew
     Arnold.* Ed. R.H. Super. 11 vols. 1960-77.

Beach, Sylvia. *Shakespeare and Company.* 1956; Lincoln: U Nebraska P, 1980.

Bloom, Harold. *A Map of Misreading.* New York: Oxford UP, 1975.

Bloom, Harold. "Criticism, Canon-Formation, and Prophecy: the Sorrows of Fac-
     ticity." *Raritan* 3:3 (1984): 1-20.

Bruns, Gerald L. "Canon and Power in the Hebrew Scriptures." *Critical Inquiry*
     10 (1984): 462-80.

Derrida, Jacques. *L'Ecriture et la différence.* 1967; Paris: Points-Seuil, 1979.

Eagleton, Terry. *Literary Theory: An Introduction.* Minneapolis: U Minnesota P,
     1983.

Eliot, T.S. "Tradition and the Individual Talent." *The Sacred Wood.* 1928; New
     York: Barnes & Noble, 1950, 47-59.

Froula, Christine. "When Eve Reads Milton: Undoing the Canonical Economy."
     Critical Inquiry 10 (1983): 321-347.

Hartman, Geoffrey. *Criticism in the Wilderness.* New Haven CT: Yale UP, 1980.

Jameson, Frederic. *Marxism and Form: Twentieth Century Dialectical Theories of Literature.* Princeton NJ: Princeton UP, 1971.

Kermode, Frank. "Institutional Control of Interpretation." *The Art of Telling: Essays in Fiction.* Cambridge, MA: Harvard UP. 168-84. Rpt. from *Salmagundi* 43 (1979): 72-86.

Kermode, Frank. *The Genesis of Secrecy: On the Interpretation of Narrative.* Cambridge MA: Harvard UP, 1979.

Magalaner, Marvin, and Richard M. Kain. *Joyce: The Man, the Work, the Reputation.* New York: New York UP, 1956.

Ohmann, Richard. *English in America: A Radical View of the Profession.* New York: Oxford UP, 1976.

Ohmann, Richard. "The Shaping of a Canon: U.S. Fiction 1960-1975." *Critical Inquiry* 10 (1983): 199-223.

Restuccia, Frances. "Not Foreknowledge, Simply Knowledge: Secular Typology in *Ulysses.*" *James Joyce Quarterly* 20 (1983): 429-42.

Said, Edward W. *The World, the Text, and the Critic.* Cambridge MA: Harvard UP, 1983.

Showalter, Elaine. "Feminist Criticism in the Wilderness." *Critical Inquiry* 8 (1981): 179-205.

Smith, Barbara Herrnstein. "Contingencies of Value." *Critical Inquiry* 10 (1983): 1-36.

Smith, Barbara Herrnstein. "Fixed Marks and Variable Constancies: A Parable of Literary Value." *Poetics Today* 1 (1979): 7-22.

Staley, Thomas F. "Notes and Comments." *James Joyce Quarterly* 19 (1982): 235-38.

Tompkins, Jane P. *Sensational Designs: The Cultural Work of American Fiction, 1790-1860.* New York: Oxford UP, 1985.

Tompkins, Jane P. "Sentimental Power: *Uncle Tom's Cabin* and the Politics of Literary History." *Glyph: Johns Hopkins Textual Studies* 7 (1981): 97-102.

Tompkins, Jane P. "The Other American Renaissance." *The American Renaissance Reconsidered: Papers from the English Institute,1982-1983.* Eds. Walter Benn Michaels and Donald Pease. Baltimore MD: Johns Hopkins UP, 1985, 34-57.

"Canon," Theme, and Code*

Christopher Clausen

For the past three or four years, the loudest sound in most university
English departments has been the clamor of battle between bands of adversaries – sometimes organized into regiments, often mere raiders from
the hills – over what has recently come to be known as the canon. The
canon, as that formerly religious term is now used, means the body of literary works that are commonly taught and written about. The more vocal
side in this conflict asserts that the canon is overwhelmingly conservative,
white, male, European, and obsolete; that the purpose of those who teach
it is, whether consciously or not, to instill in their students the values of an
imperialistic Western society; and that standards of literary merit are mere
rationalizations for perpetuating the rule of bourgeois white males over
everyone else. The more timid party to the debate asserts on the contrary
that not to have grappled with certain authors – Homer and Shakespeare
are the two most often mentioned, but there are others – is to be less than
educated; that the quotas of affirmative action are an inappropriate basis
for organizing a literary syllabus; and that the goal of the "canon revisers"
is less literary than political, less to educate than to indoctrinate. From the
pages of the *Chronicle of Higher Education* to those of the *Wall Street Journal*, from the *New York Times* to *Newsweek*, the battle has been raging,
with each party trying to spike the guns of its adversaries and figure out
where the high ground is, there to set up – what else? – its own canon. A
tiny third group, ignored by nearly everyone, points out that there is not
now and has never in recent times been anything rigid enough in American departments of English to be called a canon; that the selection and
character of books taught or written about change constantly, even chaot-
ically; and that the same debate, minus a lot of theoretical jargon, has
been going on for longer than English departments have existed.

---

* "'Canon,' Theme, and Code" first appeared in *Southwest Review*. Copyright 1990 by
Christopher Clausen.

This controversy, although important, will not in itself be my subject. Instead I want to look at certain questions raised by the debate, questions that have always been with us but have been made more acute by the rhetoric of the canon revisers. At their more moderate, they ask us to define what we mean when we call a book great, and they wish us to teach students not so much literature itself as how to "situate ourselves" in relation to what they invariably call the text.[1] At their more extreme, they come close to asserting that literary works have value and meaning only for the period, culture, class, sex, or ethnic group that produced them. ("Once you have subtracted from the accidents of class, race, gender, and political circumstance," Stanley Fish asks rhetorically, "what is it that you have left?"[2]) It is an oddity of the humanities today that those scholars who are most egalitarian in their sympathies – who denounce any apparent slight to members of racial minorities, women, or the abstract "other" – have become so hostile to the notion of universal works of art, ideas, or ethical principles. A belief in transcultural values would seem far more consistent with their social radicalism than the assertion that nothing has any validity beyond its culture of origin, since only universal moral principles can support their egalitarianism in a convincing way. If all beliefs and practices are culture-bound, then we lack any reasoned basis for criticizing local traditions (past or present) that sanction rape, slavery, or the murder of rebellious students. Extreme cultural relativism has in fact been one of the intellectual props of conservatism at least since Edmund Burke and has recently been invoked by the Chinese government in the face of human-rights criticisms. The moral and intellectual universalism that underlay the revolutions of the eighteenth century (not to mention the Universal Declaration of Human Rights in the twentieth) provides a much stronger underpinning for adversary politics or a multi-cultural society. On what other basis besides the possibility of universal meaning can we understand or care about the works of an alien culture? More to our immediate point, the possibility that literary works can have universal features provides an intellectually coherent framework for serious discussion of "canon" questions and for much else in literary criticism. Here I shall be exploring, in a tentative and partial way, a single aspect of that possibility.

I

One service rendered by the canon revisers has been to make us more thoughtful about the question "What constitutes literary greatness?" if only by demonstrating that no firm consensus exists. A more analytically satisfactory formulation of the same question might be, "What intrinsic qualities – aesthetic, intellectual, moral, or otherwise – help a literary work outlast the historical and cultural circumstances in which it was created?" A commonplace of Marxist criticism is that "texts" are the products of a particular cultural/historical context, and that to understand them one needs to "recontextualize" them – that is, recover as best one can the most relevant features of that context. But why do some works and not others continue to interest readers in a vastly *different* context? Political and social ideology, another favorite concept of Marxist critics, may be discounted immediately. If one looks at the large and extremely diverse body of works that are or have been taught by English departments, one finds no ideological consistency. Jane Austen would in modern political terms be called a conservative. George Eliot would be considered today, as she considered herself, a liberal. George Bernard Shaw was clearly a radical. No amount of critical finesse can obscure these differences. Yet all three writers have been taught and studied for many years, often in the same courses.

The emphasis on ideology carries with it the assumption that to explain a work's appeal, we should once again contextualize it – that is, consider not so much what the individual author thought he was doing or saying, but rather the social circumstances and institutions that influenced a book's composition and then led to its being widely read, taught, and admired. Those institutional factors naturally vary according to time and place, but the implication is that a highly valued work is always one that pleases a powerful group by defending that group's values or status in a compelling way. Thus, the argument goes, Homer's epics became the center of classical Greek literary education because they embodied the ideals and interests of the "ruling class"; Shakespeare was popular among eighteenth-century literary critics because he expressed their nostalgia for an idealized hierarchical and agrarian society; and so forth. Today the most powerful cultural institution is the university, and the institutional reasons for the "canonization" of certain books by English departments have been much discussed of late; Gerald Graff's book *Professing Literature* discusses the canon debate, among other things, in terms of the history of English departments themselves.

Emphasizing institutional reasons for the survival of some literary works and the demise of others seems at first glance to promise an escape from subjectivity: instead of examining "intrinsic" factors in particular works, whose significance may be largely in the eye of the beholder, we can answer the question objectively through historical research. Furthermore, it is clearly true that at some periods, works produced by members of certain social groups, or works that did not fit a narrow set of aesthetic criteria, have been neglected or undervalued by the cultural institutions of the time. But for my purposes here, the institutional explanation has two important defects. First, instead of replacing the question of intrinsic qualities, it merely evades it. If Homer survived in ancient Greece for institutional reasons – because he pleased the most powerful people – then we have to explore in some detail why his epics pleased them more than other epics, which is the intrinsic question all over again. We seem to be back to ideology again, with the additional burden of explaining why these two poems served a particular set of ideological purposes better than any potential competitors. The institutional explanation, while not altogether false, does not get us very far by itself.

The second defect in the institutional explanation is that, at best, it explains only the short-term survival of a work. The ruling class in ancient Greece may indeed have made a classic out of Homer for its own institutional and ideological reasons, but that ruling class has now been dead for upwards of 2,000 years. Similarly, the culture that "produced" Homer, and in which we try (with mixed success) to recontextualize him, has been dead for an even longer time, yet people still read him, and not only in universities. The question we are exploring is not why a given book is initially successful in its own time and culture, but why some books continue to be read and admired in a time or culture that is drastically different. There can be any number of good reasons for reading, valuing, or teaching a contemporary work, quite apart from any prediction about its likelihood of enduring. When one reads or teaches a pre-modern book, however, one is almost by definition affirming its continued relevance to the present, however one wishes to describe that relevance. An exception can be made for the pure historian, whose interest in a work may focus entirely on its pastness, its reflection of the times in which it was created. Most academic and non-academic readers of literature, however, read with a different set of motives – to be amused, informed, and inspired in a complicated variety of ways and mixtures.

The greater the diversity of cultures or institutions that value an author like Homer over long periods of time, the less satisfactory institutional explanations for his continued prestige become. Almost nobody today believes in the kind of society or government that we find in Homer; merely understanding how anybody could have believed in it requires a good deal of imagination. The *Bhagavad-Gita* has been widely read and admired in the West since it was first translated in the eighteenth century; most of its Western readers think it a major work of the world's literature. Few of those readers are Hindus, and hardly any believe in the caste system that is a major feature of the poem and its culture. Furthermore, the *Gita* has made its way in the West without the support of any powerful institution, let alone a ruling class. The ideological explanation and its twin brother, the institutional explanation, are simply inadequate to answer the question of why some literary works from distant times and places are still considered great. It would be naive to deny that governments, social groups, and educational institutions have often made use of particular literary works for their own purposes; it is equally naive to explain the continuing attraction of such works purely in terms of their usefulness to institutions.

What intrinsic qualities should we look for, then, to explain the power that Homer, the author of the *Gita*, Virgil, Lady Murasaki, Dante, Chaucer, Shakespeare, Goethe, Jane Austen, Wordsworth, and a few score other pre-modern authors continue to exert over us? The problem here may be that literature is too varied, too richly diverse an assortment of things to yield a single answer. Even if we define *literature* narrowly to mean poems, plays, and works of prose fiction, the range of such works over the last three thousand years is so enormous that to identify any particular quality or set of qualities as the indicators of permanent importance is apt to mean forcing the evidence. Given the amount of cultural and individual variation among the world's great authors, as well as the large role of accident in all human affairs, this situation is exactly what we should expect to find. Even within the same time and place, we find bewildering variations in style, form, ideology, and, of course, level of talent. The history of culture is a worthwhile enterprise, but by itself it will neither explain the poem nor tell us what the poem is worth. The writers we call great do not all say the same things, still less create interchangeable works. Any theoretical master key to such profusion could open only a very small door, like the garden door that Alice was too large to crawl through.

The probability that there is no master key, however, does not mean there is no way into the garden. A good burglar can pick almost any kind of lock and give himself the run of many mansions, as long as he keeps an eye out for the alarm switch and the dog. I recommend the burglar critic over the critic with a key every time, for the man with a lock pick never suffers from the illusion that he owns the estate. Furthermore, the man with the key is apt to throw a tantrum and break down the door when he finds a lock his key will not open, while the burglar quietly lets himself in through the kitchen window.

II

The lock pick I propose to use here is the notion of theme. "Theme" as I use the term means simply – unoriginally – the central idea that gives cohesion to a work, its guiding concept. Often there are secondary themes as well, in which case the themes of a work exist in some relation to each other, whether of subordination, congruence, or opposition. Although the theme of a work is intrinsic, it also unites that work to the outside world, the context. "Theme" is a much better word here than "ideology" because it need not imply a total view of the world, still less a dogmatic one, and because it carries no automatic political connotations, although nobody would deny that some themes are political. The author may even be an original thinker, although then again he or she may not; it depends on the work.

The poet Louis Simpson has described theme as the most important element in a poem, the "urgent thing" for the poet to say and the reader to apprehend:

> In great poetry – writing that moves us to feel and think deeply – there is a theme or pattern of thought expressing a general truth that appears to have been arrived at through experience. ... Discovering the theme is the nearest we can come to the central mystery of the poem – all the other parts depend on this. It would seem best, therefore, in reading to go straight for the theme, to see the most important thing about the poem before we become engrossed in the details.[3]

Although "thematic criticism" retains in some circles the unfavorable sense of looking superficially at the most easily paraphrasable elements of a work, the intellectual content of literary works is today a much more acceptable object of criticism than it was in the heyday of the New Criticism. Too often it gets studied in rigidly ideological ways, but at least it gets studied. Emphasizing intellectual content does not mean denying that poems, plays, and novels have aesthetic, nondiscursive features that are also intrinsic and also worthy of study – precisely those features that the New Critics valued almost to the exclusion of everything else. Moreover, aesthetic features can be interpreted as having intellectual significance, while ideas and the rhetoric of argument can be evaluated aesthetically; it all depends on which lock pick you happen to be using.

Stein Haugom Olsen, a philosopher, maintains like Simpson that theme is an essential, defining characteristic of literary works. He goes on to divide themes into two categories. "Topical thematic concepts" are of local and temporary significance. They characterize literature that deals with manners or problems peculiar to a society, an era, a particular group. Dickens's novel *Hard Times* or Upton Sinclair's *The Jungle* could be described as works organized around "topical thematic concepts." Such works typically do not outlast the topics that inspired them, although there are exceptions, such as *Hard Times* itself. Contrasted with "topical thematic concepts" are "perennial thematic concepts," or "mortal questions." The latter, in Olsen's words, "are typically philosophical or theological concepts if one understands both the term 'philosophical' and the term 'theological' in a broad sense." Such concepts do not date, at least not to the extent that topical concepts do. They constitute, Olsen says, "the fingerprints of the culture"; when they change, the whole culture changes.[4] These mortal questions form the thematic basis for literary works that last, although merely writing about such questions does not in itself insure immortality. (There is always the work's richness and quality of execution to be considered – what in its highest reaches we refer to as genius.) Sophocles' *Antigone* is a good example of a work animated by "perennial thematic concepts." Olsen does not claim that such "mortal questions" outlast whole cultures, but it would be perfectly consistent with his argument to say that at least some of them do.

Like most useful critical distinctions, the discrimination between topical and perennial thematic concepts makes explicit something we were already aware of, at least dimly, and helps us think more clearly about why some literary works endure. But matters become more complicated when we try to formulate the themes of actual works in such a way as to identify the category to which they belong. We then discover that we are dealing with a continuum rather than a polarity, with plenty of ambiguities huddled near the middle of the spectrum. The examples given above – mine rather than Olsen's – work fine until one tries to formulate the theme of a didactic novel such as *Hard Times*. Is it something like "The sufferings of the industrial proletariat in early-Victorian Britain are intolerable"? That would certainly be topical. Is it more accurately "Education that consists of all fact and no imagination leads to disaster"? That sounds a little less topical. Or, if we take Louisa as the protagonist, is the real theme "Life without love deforms people"? That begins to sound nearer the perennial end of the spectrum.

Of course all of these themes are present in *Hard Times*, and my way of stating them is overly simple in each case. The fact that *Hard Times* has lasted, at least for a while, and most industrial fiction of the nineteenth century has not might be taken as evidence that perennial themes are more prominent in it than topical ones. On the other hand, it might only mean that as late-twentieth-century readers we wrongly believe our own topical concerns and concepts to be perennial. Where we think we see permanent dilemmas, we may merely be seeing our own.

Before we try to decide what kinds of themes might be (in human terms) timeless, we had better look more carefully at what we mean by a theme. Earlier I defined it as "the central idea that gives cohesion to a work, its guiding concept." Clearly this means more than a subject; saying that "war" was the theme of the *Iliad* would not get us far. It is usual to state a theme in propositional form, as I did earlier with *Hard Times*. Some critics, especially those of a formalist bent, prefer to say instead that the theme is a statement of an issue, a question, a dilemma or situation that a work explores. Homer announces in the first lines of the *Iliad* that his subject will be "the anger of Peleus' son Achilleus / and its devastation" (Lattimore translation). Some readers will be content with this formula as the theme. It is sometimes feared that to put the theme of a literary work in the form of a proposition oversimplifies that work, reduces plot and character to the status of rhetorical devices, and overemphasizes philosophical or didactic qualities.

Using the propositional form, however, allows us a much more complete and precise statement of the theme. What Homer's own formulation leaves out, as any mere announcement of subject must, is the most important and distinctive part of the theme – what the work does with its subject, what conclusions it arrives at, how it interprets the raw material, which in this case is Achilles' anger and its consequences. Suppose we say instead that the theme of the *Iliad* is the following proposition: "The anger of a powerful but immature hero causes disaster to his best friend and to many others, while bringing closer his own death and the fall of a great city." There we have not just a topic but an idea that is entirely present in the poem, that invites consideration as a general truth but does not insist, does not reduce the poem's artistic dimensions, and clearly guides its progress from beginning to end. In short, we have a theme. *The major theme of a long-enduring work may be framed differently by different readers at different times: in that sense any formulation of it is relative. But provided it meets these tests, it is not wholly subjective: it rests on the evidence of the text and avoids treating the work as a cross-cultural Rorschach test.* A theme baldly stated omits a great deal – all the subtlety, specificity, and gravity of its own working out – but what it includes is essential and distinctive.

The *applicability* of that theme is immensely wide – as wide, in the case of the *Iliad*, as the world's experience of immature warriors, violence, and the fall of cities – but the poem to which it gives coherence is neither an allegory nor a philosophical treatise. Yet the poem is nonetheless, in Olsen's terms, philosophical: it interprets mortal questions. While critics often point out that a poem or play cannot be paraphrased as a treatise, it is less often noticed that a treatise (on military ethics, for example) is equally resistant to paraphrase as a play or poem. All texts of any complexity, not just literary ones, change their meanings to a greater or lesser degree in paraphrase. Yet the themes of both the treatise and the poem may be accurately stated as propositions. Where the theme of the poem is what Olsen calls "perennial," then the poem is philosophical; but it is philosophical in the manner appropriate to a poem, not in the manner appropriate to a treatise. Its "argument" proceeds by plot and action, metaphor and symbol, not by logical demonstration.[5]

A timeless theme, then, is an interpretation of a deeply significant problem, situation, dilemma of human life – a mortal question – that can apply in any time or culture. As the philosopher William Casement says:

> While the details differ according to locale, there are certain basic issues that have always confronted human beings. They are common to all human beings in all times. These issues are portrayed in literature, and portrayed best in great literature. The decision Antigone faced was that of choosing between conflicting demands of state versus conscience, the latter being influenced by religion. This decision is not unique to ancient Greece or to the ancient world in general. It could be found applicable for people of any nation or any religion at any time.[6]

All human cultures beyond the hunter-gatherer stage have government; all have religions and funeral rites; all have systems of ethics. To say that, humanly speaking, conflicts recognizably like Antigone's can occur and represent mortal questions in any time and any place is no exaggeration. Of course history and culture will affect the forms such themes take; that goes without saying. To assert that a theme is "timeless" is not to divorce it from history; it is rather to say that such a theme has significance, even topical significance, within virtually any historical context.

Notice once again that in discussing the theme of *Antigone* we are not just talking about the conflict itself, the *subject* of the play. The theme of *Antigone* is that, given the positions of the characters involved, the conflict must lead to a tragic outcome – to the death of Antigone herself and the weakening of the state. From Antigone's dilemma there is no honorable escape. So that I will not be suspected of finding such themes and conflicts only in Western literature, let me point out that the dilemma in the *Bhaga-vad-Gita* is equally mortal and timeless. There the hero Arjuna wishes, for what seem perfectly good reasons, to avoid killing his own kinsmen in battle. But there is no acceptable alternative, and the god Krishna persuades him to do his duty – a duty that may seem the opposite of Antigone's but actually has much in common with it. This essay could have been written (though not by me) using entirely non-Western examples.

Must such conflicts always have tragic outcomes? History suggests that the likelihood is great; but when a theme is put in abstract form, its universal validity becomes a fruitful subject for argument. A timeless theme is not a divine revelation, whatever Arjuna may have thought, but rather a *permanently plausible interpretation of mortal questions* and an invitation to examine the fundamental circumstances of human existence. We are always free to critique both the theme and the work. Powerful works with timeless themes survive in part because they repay the most searching criticism from the greatest variety of theoretical and existential standpoints. We test the theme and the work itself against not only other works of literature but our own experience of life and history. Because a major work of literature has many secondary themes – some topical, some perennial – this testing is immensely complicated, but it is nonetheless one of the activities by which we evaluate the books we read.

A timeless theme is one that reminds us forcefully of the basic conditions of human life – its aspirations and its limits. Those conditions are larger and deeper than any culture or historical period. The broadest context that all men and women share is an ambiguous world into which we are born helpless; in which we love, hate, struggle, and suffer; in which we grow older and die. All cultures interpret these irreducible facts, often in strikingly different ways, but no culture can change them. For human beings, they are universal in the strictest sense. Because the most powerful aspirations inevitably come up against the most intractable limits, the literary bearer of such themes is often a hero: a man, occasionally a woman, who is stronger, braver, more determined than the average person. The hero can accomplish deeds that seem marvellous to his audience. He extends the limits of human possibility, but unless he is explicitly supernatural he cannot abolish them.

Gilgamesh will conquer monsters but fail to capture the secret of eternal life. Hector will lose his final battle. Troy will fall. Achilles will die young. Beowulf will overcome Grendel, but when he grows old the dragon will defeat him and doom his people to extinction. Whatever we value most – strength, family, our city, life itself – will ultimately be lost; only glory, at most, will survive. A certain kind of literature flows naturally from this realization: first epic, then tragedy. Thematically they have much in common. The epic or tragic protagonist is deeply at odds with some overpowering realities, suffers disaster, and is immortalized by the poet. Oedipus will not escape his fate, nor Antigone her conflict of duties. King Lear cannot overcome the helplessness of old age, nor Macbeth the logic of his ambitions. By using as their protagonists immoderate figures who are larger than everyday life, the authors of epics and tragedies dramatize in the most powerful way the limits of what any human being can accomplish.

By emphasizing an ancient complex of themes embodied in two ancient literary forms, I may seem to be implying that timelessness is a thing of the remote past, impossible for modern writers to achieve, and furthermore, that timeless themes point us in a conservative direction. Both implications seem to me wrong. My list of works includes some well known epics and plays whose survival is now well established; it is far from exhaustive, either as to period or as to forms. I have, after all, said nothing here about lyric poetry, that least topical of genres. Nor do I mean to imply that all epics and all tragedies embody timeless themes as I have been defining them. *Paradise Lost* is a great poem, but its theme is not timeless. Christian cosmology of any variety is far from universal, and the dilemmas of free will that arise from it long ago lost their status as mortal questions for most people even in Christian countries. Furthermore, as Samuel Johnson put it more than two centuries ago, "The man and woman who act and suffer are in a state which no other man and woman can ever know." A mortal question must be one that we can at least imagine ourselves beset by. (Any man in time of war can imagine himself in Hector's situation, or Priam's; any woman can imagine herself in Andromache's or Hecuba's, Penelope's or Nausicaä's.) A work organized around beliefs or circumstances that are peculiar to one or a few cultures cannot be universal no matter how well executed it may be.

Tragedies are still being written today, if not epics; and we have our own epic form, the novel. The theme that J.R.R. Tolkien found in *Beowulf* – *Lif is laene* (life is transitory) – is as much a presence in contemporary literature as it was a thousand or three thousand years ago. Because they arise out of universal dilemmas, timeless themes are almost infinitely adaptable to the circumstances of different societies; that is what makes them timeless.

Furthermore, we have that other epic, the *Odyssey*, with all its comic offspring – just as universal, just as profound as all the gloomier epics. The protagonist of the *Odyssey* is nearly unique among epic heroes in coming to a happy ending because he does not seek immortality, empire, or even the glory of being first among the Greeks. He fights against the gods only briefly and by mistake. He strives with monsters only when forced to. Among all epic heroes, he has the most limited ambitions: he merely wants to go home. He is also the smartest of epic heroes, and his intelligence is most strikingly manifested in his appreciation of the limits to his own power over circumstances. Odysseus is the one major epic hero who shares many of the qualities of the sage, also an archetypal figure but an altogether more prudent one who takes care *not* to find himself at odds with the way the world is organized. As a hero, he is nearly the opposite of Gilgamesh and Achilles, and equally timeless, as Dante, Tennyson, and James Joyce (among others) have demonstrated.[7]

To the protagonists of comedy, romance, and fairy tale, more is often possible than to the heroes of epic and tragedy because they so often learn to demand less. All these forms, at their most profound, deal in mortal questions. Love is as serious a matter as war – the cause of Homer's war – and, in its myriad of culturally varying expressions, a far more common experience. In the comedies of Shakespeare and Jane Austen, Sterne and Joyce, Mark Twain and Saul Bellow, the limits of human life are exactly what they were in epic and tragedy, but the protagonists rarely push as hard against them, and the result is usually a modest triumph at the end. This possibility was always present in epic. Both the Greeks and the Trojans are repeatedly reminded of the domestic life they have forsaken in their pursuit of glory. In an even more ancient culture, when Gilgamesh, the first epic hero, sets out on his vain search for immortality, the goddess gives him some unheroic advice: "Let your clothes be fresh, bathe yourself in water, cherish the little child that holds your hand, and make your wife happy in your embrace; for this too is the lot of man."[8] And, we might add, this too is a timeless theme, one that allows equally for an emphasis on human finitude and on the possibilities of social transformation. The dream of Utopia, a society as happy and just as human beings can make it, here shows a glimpse of its own timeless possibilities.

III

Much contemporary literary criticism speaks of themes and forms as culturally devised "codes" awaiting decipherment by the omniscient critic. This view of literature and criticism is inherently self-dramatizing and self-flattering; which of us would not prefer to think of ourselves as engaged in counter-espionage rather than merely in understanding old poems? Still, poets have long been suspected of being spies on the human condition, and there may be some advantages to thinking of the critic as a counterspy as well as a burglar. For one thing, the concept of literature as a system of codes carries with it the implication that literary works can be decoded – that their meanings can be rendered intelligibly in another code, the idiom of another time, another culture. Without this minimal degree of universality, the discipline of comparative literature across cultural boundaries would be impossible. The "text" is not inherently "undecidable" or "indeterminate" – at least not always; it can be translated satisfactorily, if not perfectly, unless the code has been lost. Just as a mathematical or chemical formula is a highly conventional code for saying something in the clearest and most economical way, so is a haiku or an epic. In each case, the form evolved to express the content; in each case, the form itself has aesthetic value to those who understand it. And in each case, the properly trained reader can recover much, if not all, of the encoded meaning.

In this terminology, a timeless theme would be one that could be translated into the greatest possible number of other codes – the languages and literary forms of other times, other cultures – without losing either its intelligibility or its standing as a "mortal question" for a significant audience. I have already quoted a philosopher's reasons for thinking that the theme of *Antigone* falls into this category. For purposes of contrast, let us briefly consider a work of our own time with what appears to be a similar theme. George Orwell's novel *1984* certainly deals with resistance to tyranny on the part of a comparatively isolated individual. The subject, unhappily, does not date. But does that make the theme timeless in the same sense as *Antigone*'s? If we formulate the theme of *1984* as a proposition, we seem to come out with something like: "Given the technological resources available to a fully developed totalitarian dictatorship, individual resistance is doomed to failure, unless at some vague date in the future the relatively uncorrupted lowest class should rise up against it." Although the dilemmas embodied in this theme are without doubt "mortal questions" for the contemporary world, they are not timeless, for the technological resources of surveillance and control that make totalitarianism and the plot of *1984* possible did not exist before the twentieth century. Winston Smith's plight and its outcome could not have occurred in earlier times. In that sense, *1984* embodies a topical rather than a timeless theme.

We should always remember that a timeless theme is at most a necessary but not sufficient condition for literary survival. There is no reason to think that the level of literary talent or frequency of genius is any less in the modern world than it was in Sophocles' time or Shakespeare's, and the access of potential genius to enabling forms of education is much greater today. Yet *1984*, whether or not it could fairly be described as a work of genius, raises a suitable question on which to close. It is this: does the pervasiveness of recently invented forms of technology in the contemporary world limit the ability of contemporary authors to create universal works about timeless themes? Many modern works, *1984* among them, could not be intelligibly translated into the codes of the past. That in itself may not matter much; the possibility of Sophocles reading Orwell cannot arise. The larger question is whether a culture so dominated by rapidly changing technology has special difficulties in creating literature that will be intelligible to the future, and whether its themes will still seem to be "mortal questions." The technology of *1984* is already so badly dated as to affect one's appreciation of the theme. It is not simply that the technological "furniture" of the novel now seems old-fashioned; that happens with the literature of every era. It is rather that the theme and plot themselves derive from technology of a particular kind. Is this situation inevitably common in works, however well executed, that reflect a civilization such as ours? Is it possible that the most lasting of our fiction will be that which deals with the past or with people who lead comparatively primitive lives, little touched by modern technology? Such works are certainly prominent in our literature; consider the best novels of William Faulkner or Toni Morrison.

These questions are worth asking, if only to make us humble. Trying to answer them would be the opposite of humility. Even well trained counter-spies cannot possibly decipher codes that have yet to be devised.

Notes

1. See, for example, the quotation from James Kincaid with which Gerald Graff concludes *Professing Literature* (Chicago: University of Chicago Press, 1987), p. 262.

2. Stanley Fish, quoted in the *Chronicle of Higher Education*, 28 September 1988, p. A16. See also Cary Nelson, "Against English: Theory and the Limits of the Discipline," *Profession 87* (MLA), pp. 50-51. For a counterattack on extreme cultural determinism, see Paul Hernadi, "Doing, Making, Meaning: Toward a Theory of Verbal Practice," *PMLA*, CIII (October 1988), pp. 749-58.

3. Louis Simpson, "The Poet's Theme," *Hudson Review*, XLI (Spring 1988), pp. 100-101. For a more technical recent discussion of the variant uses of this much-used term, see Horst S. and Ingrid Daemmrich, *Themes and Motifs in Western Literature: A Handbook* (Tübingen: Francke Verlag, 1987), pp. 239-41.

4. Stein Haugom Olsen, "Thematic Concepts: Where Philosophy Meets Literature," in A. Phillips Griffiths, ed., *Philosophy and Literature* (Cambridge: Cambridge University Press, 1984), pp. 87 and 85.

5. Olsen, at the end of his article cited above, goes on to assert that in reading literature, we do not apply its thematic concepts to the world outside the work. He therefore stops short, in New Critical fashion, of allowing literary works the philosophical status that his emphasis on theme had seemed to claim for them. On the question of whether lyric poems, as distinct from narrative works, have propositional themes, see Gerald Graff, *Poetic Statement and Critical Dogma* (Chicago: University of Chicago Press, 1970).

6. William Casement, "Literature and Didacticism: Examining Some Popularly Held Ideas," *Journal of Aesthetic Education*, XXI (Spring 1987), p. 110.

7. For epic heroes in general, see C.M. Bowra, *Heroic Poetry* (London: Macmillan, 1966), especially chapter 3; for Odysseus in particular, W.B. Stanford, *The Ulysses Theme* (Ann Arbor: University of Michigan Press, 1968).

8. N.K. Sandars, trans. and ed., *The Epic of Gilgamesh* (Harmondsworth: Penguin Books, 1964), p. 99.

Literary Canons and Social Value Options

Virgil Nemoianu

Is the discussion on canons and canonicity in literary matters as exciting and beneficial a phenomenon as many believe? Whatever the answer, it must be tinged with at least some doubts, or even some gloomy apprehensions. Certainly an opening towards areas of the secondary, of marginality and heteronomy, and a more generous valuation spread over broader areas of textuality are events that will be saluted by the scholarly and the playful alike. Not so a certain grim rancor and a demolishing urge that are soon recognized inside the process and that seem directed more at literature and literariness than at any specific work in itself. The deconstructive affect turns into sedulous dismantling and brutal levelling. It would almost seem as if some pressure of increased cultural entropy imposed relentless war against those creative and antientropic areas (such as literature) that always refuse to align themselves totally and to obey some given socioideological imperatives. Trying to abolish literature is undoubtedly wrong in itself, as must be any attempt to diminish human potentials and complexity, but it may well turn out to be wrong also in an unexpected and contrary way. Literature may well be called an institution, but surely not in the same sense in which we call the House of Commons an institution. Yet explicit and crystallized structures are called into life precisely through the opposition against an assumed institutional status. Hegemonic structures once established, can truly begin to play an oppressive part, manipulated by social configurations that, innocent no longer, will no longer acquiesce in the previously benign neglect of the literary domain.

Can we in any way turn the canonicity debate back into the ludic negotiation between scholarly axiology and democratic receptiveness that it ought to remain if its vitalities and disorders are to function as enhancements of societal and personal abundance? I believe that some distinctions and some explications can lay the ground work for fairer and more joyful kinds of play and exercise. Many such distinctions will be simple reminders (of etymologies, of historical dates), others will be comparisons, and others contrastive suggestions; together they may well constitute a frame – brittle and incomplete – for continued civilized conversation between literature and its society. This is what I will try to do and what I think most of this volume's contributors have also been doing from very different methodological and geohistorical perspectives.

I

Etymology is seldom adduced in discussions about literary canons: perhaps because a close look at word history very convincingly suggests that a literary use of canons was – until ten or fifteen years ago – almost always metaphorical or connotative, and semantic overlappings were partial and occasional. An even cursory look at the *OED* and other sources shows that, significantly, on both occasions when the word entered the vernacular (from Latin into Anglo-Saxon under Alfred the Great and, with a slightly different spelling from Norman French into Middle English), "canon" was used (as it was in the Latin and Greek sources) with reference to ecclesiastical and civil law, and to sacred writings. This limited and precise usage is confirmed by occasional subsequent extensions: the temporary (and abandoned) use with reference to trigonometrical tables, or the sense of rigidity, austerity, and order conveyed in the musical compositions called "canons." It is only fairly late, in the eighteenth century, that linguistic "secularization" on a larger scale can be observed and canons (as "prototypes" or "models") are mentioned in architecture, medicine, manufacturing, and other fields.

It cannot be mere coincidence that "canon" and "canonical" were used much *less* in literature and literary criticism than in virtually any other cultural area. This is not to deny that, after Arnold in England, or Schopenhauer in Germany, literature as a whole was sometimes elevated to the status of sacralized activity, one that was supposed to act as a substitute for religion. But we should also keep in mind some qualifying circumstances. One is that activities, sensations, and experiences were suggested as worthy of an exalted status most often, authors slightly less often, and works *per se* (i.e., the typical units of canonical propositions) least often. Another is that theological positions towards the substitutive enterprise were conspicuously lacking in enthusiasm, as they had always been ambiguous towards literature in general, as a debatable infringement of the

Second Commandment (against graven images). Kierkegaard's pointed distinction between genius and apostle[1] can stand as a model for a more widely spread unease. As against this, it was argued by some in the nineteenth century (from Chateaubriand to Solovyov, not to mention the more specialized Alois Gugler or H. Scheeben) that the transfer and humanization of religious values or states has an incarnational and mediating utility.

The fact remains that it is virtually impossible to find even one example of *full* substitution, that is, of actual sacralization or sanctification, or of a fully prescriptive canon. Even the efforts of T.S. Eliot or Harold Bloom in the twentieth century appear – when looked at closely – tentative and vague. Literary canons remained always *as if.* They were either frankly metaphorical, or relativized by implied linguistic markers of distance, approximation, and diminishment.

One good way of bringing home the difference between literary "canons" and real canonical decisions is to remember what the stakes of a truly canonical dispute can involve. In the second century the brilliant young radical Marcion of Sinope proposed to the Christian community in Rome that it reject as uncanonical the Hebrew Bible in its entirety and confine its teaching to the authority derived from the Gospel of Luke and selections from Pauline letters and the three other Gospels. His was not a whimsical and arbitrary fabrication of ideas. Rather, it was based upon a thoughtful and highly sophisticated argument (with textual, as well as ideological bolstering) that proclaimed the Jewish God of the Old Testament as radically flawed and tyrannical, one who must be superseded and replaced in the here and now by the mercy and perfection of the recent Good News. Sternly anti-Judaic, Marcion emphasized the liberating and revolutionary components of Jesus' message and argued eloquently against any possible continuity and compromise with the millenia-old monotheistic Scriptural tradition. Marcion's system (in which the modern reader tends to discover retrospectively anti-Semitic positions, as well as radicalisms of all stripes) led to a short but intense conflict in Rome. Within four years Marcion was excommunicated and formed his own semi-Gnostic movement that flourished for a few decades in the second half of the second century A.D. and then lingered on for a few other centuries. The incensed Christian community was obliged to formulate a true complete Biblical canon, embodying and crystallizing its more conservative practice of and faith in Jewish-Christian continuities, a model that underwent only marginal changes over the ensuing eighteen centuries.

It is easy to imagine what incalculable historical differences would have ensued from a victorious Christianity with a Marcionite coloring[2] and with radically curtailed Marcionite canons. Certainly the fate of the Jewish people would have been deeply affected, but it is equally likely that an accelerated, "unencumbered" Marcionite Christianity would have shaped historical mentalities and attitudes in ways that would have made subsequent evolution almost incommensurable with events as we know them.

Other similar textual-canonical splits can be adduced. Mohammed's and Buddha's careers with their world-historical consequences can be described in a few respects as Marcionite gestures that *were* crowned with success. Hermeneutical canons, rather than textual ones, separated Luther and Calvin from S. Carlo Borromeo and the Tridentine Council, but these were equally momentous in channeling future historical evolutions.

By contrast all the "canonical" disputes in literature, such as the Romantic rehabilitation of Shakespeare, Dante, Cervantes, Gothic architecture, and chivalric romance seem to have added mere coloring and nuance to a history that was advancing in any case. Even more interesting (and a little droll) is the previous turning point in European literature, when the question was debated whether vernacular authors deserve equal ranking with those of classical – Greek/Latin – antiquity. The "*Querelle des Anciens et Modernes*" (approximately 1659 to 1700 pitting chiefly Boileau against Perrault and Fontenelle) or Swift's *Battle of the Books* (written c. 1697, published 1704) marked these conflicts that generally ended with the victory of the old "canons," a victory that availed nothing at all, since the classics lost ground (slowly), while the "moderns" gained ground and standing (at a fast rate).

This later example is of somewhat greater sociocultural moment in molding future configurations, and yet the difference from previous cases taken from the history of religion and law remains considerable. It can be said to be a qualitative difference, and in any case it is an indication of the huge difference between "canons" and canons, by the objective measurement of the size of outcomes.

Given these rather obvious circumstances, what is the purpose of canon disputes in literature and, more fundamentally, what is the nature and the function of these "canons?"

II

We can best circumscribe the field of literary canonicity by distinguishing three levels of discussion and, corresponding to them, levels of meaning. One has already been alluded to: it refers to the symbolic battles and manipulation in which transferred values are pitted against each other, and the literary is merely a vehicle for conflicts of an entirely different nature. In certain ways this is a gross and ignorant way of discussing literature, but in others it may well be symptomatic of deeper and more obscure movements of history. I would prefer to leave a discussion of it for somewhat later in this essay and deal first with the crucial distinction between the other two levels: *curriculum* and *canon*.

Curricular works are those that are chosen to be taught in class, to be included in anthologies, those that are read by and fed to large numbers of individuals in a linguistic and social community at any given time. Living curricular authors are those showered with praise and prize, honor and success. Sully-Prudhomme wins the first Nobel Prize in literature in 1901, Cronin and Warwick Deeping, Lloyd Douglas, Louis Bromfield and Charles Morgan are among those who dominate Anglo-American publishing between the two World Wars. Kotzebue dwarfed Goethe and Schiller in popularity and power of attraction in the first decade of the nineteenth century. In California, the poet George Sterling was believed by the powers that be to be the equal of Dante and Cervantes, and the maximum of public pressure was summoned in order to impose upon everybody this conviction.[3] In France François Coppée and Alphonse Daudet were the darlings of school textbook readings during their lifetimes and ten or fifteen years later. In the Romanian literature of the 1870s and 1880s, Samson Bodnarescu was considered a close second to Eminescu, and both inferior to Vasile Alecsandri.

Curricular authors of the past are chosen for utilitarian reasons, to satisfy some needs – political, ethical, practical – and to create bridges of compatibility between an essentially recalcitrant phenomenon and the needs or preferences of structured societies with their ideological expressions. Purely random causes – availability of manuscripts or editions, idiosyncrasies of influential readers, offensive or attractive peculiarities of writers' biographies – also play a role in the ups and downs of curricular structures. Finally a most important cause of curricular formation is the *forma mentis* of a given age: the prevailing prejudices and sensiblities,

writing styles and aesthetic tastes (primarily defined by creative production, not by either critical elites or reading masses) attract some writers of
the past into curricula, boost their reputation and reshape radically their
interpretation, while others are diminished, barred from general recognition, and misunderstood. Curricula are, in a sense, negotiated accords
between the definitional and hegemonic features of a given historical time
and place and the broader and inchoate canonical domain proper.

The curricular lists of the early Middle Ages seem nowadays little short
of bizarre. One rather typical example of the earlier twelfth century
includes along with Virgil, Horace, Juvenal, Ovid, Sallust, and Lucan, predictable Christian authors such as Boethius and Prudentius, but on equal
footing with these the grammarian Donatus, "Homerus" (i.e., a Latin con-
densation of the *Iliad* in approximately 1100 lines), religious didactic poets
of the first millenium such as Sedulius, Juvencus, Theodulus, Prosper of
Aquitaine, and Arator. Cicero is also present, but only with *De Amicitia*
and *De Senectute,* Ovid's *Metamorphoses* are deleted, Roman satirists are
presented as admonitory authors who at some secret level must have preferred Christianity to Paganism, and *all* authors are subjected to the heavily allegorical interpretation developed for use on Scriptural texts.[4]

Similarly, in the second half of the English nineteenth century, to recall
yet again the very well-known example against which the high-modernists
so effectively protested, general critical esteem as well as curricular options were directed towards shorter Romantic lyrics, in particular those of
Shelley, Keats, and Coleridge. Shelley, Milton, and Spenser loomed large
as favorite figures, while Pope and the Metaphysicals continued the steady
decline they had begun soon after 1750. Social and aesthetic needs imposed sentiment and vague suggestion against rationalist indeterminacy
and orderly agilities. Inside the seventeenth century Herrick dominated
Donne and Marvell (or even Dr. Johnson).[5]

Canons on the other hand are both smaller and larger, and certainly
less tangible. They incorporate values, questionings, intentionalities, plots,
and constants of human nature. Truly canonical works are selected on the
basis of a chaotic and natural process that remains ultimately unpredictable even though it is shaped by a number of parameters. Of these I will
enumerate quickly a few. The first is majority preference: canonical works
are those chosen by most readers in a historical cross-section (not necessarily at any given point in time, but in an ongoing polling). The second is
the multiplicity of attached meanings: *Hamlet* has to carry the burden of

hundreds or indeed thousands of meanings (directorial, critical, and others) and does not break down under them, a feat that is difficult to imagine in the case of a Mickey Spillane production for instance. A third is a lively interaction and compatibility with different value fields and kinds of discourses, but not full alignment with them. History, religion, ethics, the sciences, political and economic textualities, various artistic idioms – all find their counterparts, their rhymes, or their contrasts in Sophocles' *Antigone* or in George Eliot's *Middlemarch* in ways that escape Maurice Dekobra or Louise de la Ramée. Another one – probably the most irritating to some critics – is an ability to establish aesthetic durability and transcendence. What is meant by this is not only the special fusion between any aesthetic creation and the search for transcendence that is inherent in any human culture known to us,[6] but also the durability of playfulness and sheer possibility that interact with the contingent and also manage to transcend it (at least relatively). It should be rather obvious that Goethe's *Faust* fits such a criterion in ways in which none of Heinrich Zschokke's writings does. I will mention one more feature, more often overlooked than the others, but at least as important, because it confirms my view of the canons as an outcome of democratic pressures. I refer to canonical works as *mediating* between highbrow and lowbrow, or between curricular and commercial works. Chaucer's *Canterbury Tales* contains both courtly and popular literature, Shakespeare was imposed by popular demand against academic demurral, Homer is more obviously canonical than Mallarmé, Tolstoy than Hölderlin. It is not the case that canonical authors are imposed by oppressive elites. On the contrary, it is exactly when and if canonical authors come to be maintained by curricular elites and become their exclusive possession, that they are in danger of losing their canonical status.

III

The levels of meaning inside canonicity reveal themselves to us, I believe, by the force of self-evidence and the description offered above should not be too difficult to accept as a conveniently simplified picture of an actually existing state of affairs. The truly difficult questions emerge in two more practical areas: What is (or is thought to be) the relationship between the curricular and the canonical levels of literature and what is the status of canonical affirmation inside an accelerated and globalized sociohistorical process at the end of the twentieth century? At bottom, these, rather than knowledge about canons in themselves, are the questions that have stirred the critical and academic community in the last few years. I will address them in turn and in reporting about the second of them, I will also try to examine more carefully that first – most superficial and yet most relevant and visible – my three levels of canonical meaning.

In order to define how the curriculum refers to the canon, I think it is appropriate to point to such relationships as those between *langue* and *parole,* between "deep structure" and "surface structure," or between "competence" and "performance." This is not to say that canons are literally the *langue* of which curricula are the *parole,* but merely to indicate an analogous type of relationship. The canon is invisible, undefined, flexible, with a continuous slow movement inside it: ultimately an unknown realm, perceptible but not precisely measurable, or difficult to capture exactly. Its internal slidings are, by contrast, amplified and multiplied in the curriculum, where they are translated into jerky and discontinuous activities, at a simplified and more cognizable level. Curricular choices are heavily influenced by political institutional factors, particularly in interpretation, but sometimes even in selection. By contrast canons are shaped by deeper and less easily formalized categories: sensibilities, communitarian orientations, broad axiological decisions, tacit preferences, modes of behavior and being.

A good small example is provided by the aforementioned Curtius discussion. The full *curricular* list used by Conrad von Hirsau or some other twelfth-century author may seem inept or funny. Yet underneath it we may easily recognize the long-haul and durable *canonical langue:* the Scriptures with their hermeneutic and imaginative extensions, along with the central formulations of classical antiquity. The canonical *langue* remained stable for approximately 1000 years (500-1500) even while the curricular *parole* could undergo serious variations. And, of course, even before 500 and after 1500, well into our days, certain parts of that canon still hold, even while curricula may have widely oscillated.

The paradox of real canons is easily pinpointed in the elementary question of size. T.S. Eliot, as devoted as any modern intellectual we can think of to an ideal order of masterpieces with an almost Platonically firm reality, was compelled by his own earnest search to reduce finally the canon of classicity to a single work – Virgil's *Aeneid* – as a measuring rod for the whole of European literature in all its variety.[7] It is easy to see that from Eliot's extreme restraint to the idea of the canon as absence there is but one small step. In stark opposition there is the experience of anybody trying to teach a "masterpieces" semester course: the number of plausible authors and works is always considerably larger than the number of works and authors that can actually be studied in the classroom (or, as a matter of fact, even mentioned). Despite limitations of cultural geography ("Western" or "European language"), time period, field ("literature"), and so forth, the concrete syllabus will be a mere utterance – one among many other possible and credible ones – informed and controlled by an idiom (canonical literariness) that is much larger. This contradiction is rooted in the doubly gradual and transitional nature of the deep-structure canon. Hierarchically there is a very gradual transition from the position of Homer to that of John Donne or Montaigne, to Grimmelshausen, Leopardi and Elizabeth Barrett Browning, to Shadwell, Annette von Droste-Hülshoff, and Knut Hamsun, from there to John Hawkes, H. Sienkiewicz, Gala Galaction, and Grazia Deledda, and perhaps lower still towards the worlds of Michener, Sheldon, Jean Plaidy, and Maurice Egan, and the thousands of popular authors past and present. Such star-studded statistical curves are fun to produce and can be manufactured in almost unlimited numbers. What is interesting is of course that at each step the order is debatable. Why should John Hawkes not be placed higher than Shadwell? Droste-Hülshoff than Barrett-Browning? Leopardi than John Donne? and so forth. In the usual run of things, however, few would seriously argue that Montaigne's essays are less substantial and relevant than the novels of Deledda and Sienkiewicz, or that Grimmelshausen's *Simplicissimus* has more universal appeal and significance than Homer's *Odyssey*. It is one of the curious features of the canon's ineffability that even though it is contestable at each given point, its general outlines are quite firm and substantial.

The other side of the transitional mode of existence of the canon is its slow movement in time. Perhaps from this point of view an apter analogy than the linguistic set of doubles is one of center and periphery in an almost urban (or suburban) sense of moving, removing, and returning.[8] Sophocles and Euripides were canonical figures in antiquity (even *this* is a simplification, because in the centuries of the Empire their stock declined), they largely disappeared from view in the Middle Ages, only to revert to a central position from the seventeenth century on. Were they "uncanonical" authors in the fourteenth century, for example? It would be difficult to affirm this in any objective sense, but clearly their position was more peripheral. Many other examples can be adduced. The ups and downs of Milton's or Pope's fortunes are too well known to be recounted here. Most French critics and a good part of the public held the French Romantics in low esteem during the nineteenth and early twentieth centuries. When André Gide, compiler of a much-discussed anthology of French poetry,[9] was asked who the greatest French poet was, he answered: "Victor Hugo, hélàs!" Even more radical was the Romantic enterprise of establishing an alternative tradition of great aesthetic values: Dante, Shakespeare, Cervantes, and Calderón as opposed to the Latin and French classicist authors. The result, we can say after almost 200 years, was ambiguous: extension rather than displacement.

What is incontestable is the slow and continuous and multidirectional movement inside the canonical body. Outside pressures – as I will also argue a little later – are frequent and continuous, but their weight and decisiveness is questionable. Turbulent adjustments and readjustments inside the canonical sphere are a more powerful internal force. Those who establish the communication between the internal organs of canonicity and external pressures are not chiefly scholars, but new writers and works, that is, the *producers* of aesthetic events. They are the ones who both collect outside influences (political, social, religious, etc.) and process them or adapt them into the kind of patterns of sensibility and imagery, value and cognition (or into the kind of exercises of nuance and imperfection) that have the chance to penetrate the canonical world and set in motion the series of indirect effects that in turn may or may not modify existing canonical structures.

Serious attempts to uncover patterns of canonical change could well end up – given the undulating recurrences that can be observed – with a renewed version of the much-compromised and scorned theory of pendular literary change. In days of yore, respectable figures such as Eugenio d'Ors, Fritz Strich, Pierre Legouis, among many others, had embraced the concept of a classical and a romantic (or baroque) pole between which literary tastes, preferences, and production waver more or less inevitably and regularly. It is not impossible to imagine a version of it in which the amniotic waters of the canonical world move in their own ebbs and flows, generate their own contractions and expansions and thus maintain in the canon movements and modifications that often do not correspond with outside pressures and the strivings of curricular pedants.

IV

The most striking thing – and, for resolute anticanonical activists, the most troubling – is that at the very center of the canon there seems to be, despite tidal changes, Brownian motilities, and quicksilver rearrangements, a certain constancy. Slowly and calmly, the centuries seem to accumulate a small number of stubbornly recurrent authors and works in which literate humans recognize themselves more often and better than in all others. Homer and Aeschylus, Dante and Shakespeare, Tolstoy and Goethe and Kafka are surely among these recurrent names no matter how Milton and Pope, Racine and Rabelais, Strindberg and Eliot otherwise change places. Why is this center relatively stable or why does it seem difficult to displace?

In a recent book[10] George Steiner outlines an intriguing – almost a fantastic – hypothesis. He contemplates the continuity of pagan mythological figures and archetypes – a Narcissus, an Echo, a Prometheus, an Antigone and others – and the shock of recognition we have in the face of these figures even after 2000 and 3000 years. He wonders whether this significance and continuity are not due to the power of these myths and archetypes to engender basic modes of thoughts and expression of the human race and ultimately grammar itself. Is not the Narcissus myth a counterpart of the "long history of the demarcation of the first person singular," or is not the Prometheus myth connected with a thought-grammar capable of linguistically employing futurity, Steiner asks?[11] Similarly Freud could have asked whether the Oedipal myth did not engender basic psychological structures. Steiner's metaphorical outrageousness cannot obscure his brilliance and his profundity. If few will begin to believe that literally Narcissus and Prometheus are tales that produced grammatical changes (and of course Steiner himself never argues in such unsubtle terms) it will be less difficult to argue in more general terms and still in the spirit of Steiner's proposal. If language had some kind of beginning, then certainly it was preceded by and founded on some still inchoate structures of thought and narrativity, some figures and outlines that were fated to be given impact and indeed reality by the very expression they were engendering. It is this process that finds itself repeated in the relationship between myth and language and in the slight, in the relative, in the tiny dialectical precedence of the former over the latter. Thus reformulated and tamed Steiner's aggressive and visionary statement becomes for some of us more plausible or more debatable. Myths appear as later formulations of processes that are always already going on, and of relations that are always already being engaged in, points hovering on the brink between definitely unplumbed depths of time and the better-marked and lit stretches that we begin to call history; they do not belong to either but, if Steiner is right, they begin to make historical language possible. George Steiner's proposal is also interesting, it seems to me, because it offers an explanation for the relative stability of the canonical core of Western culture. Like Steiner's mythical figures, some key canonical works may be said to function as expressions/engenderers of a grammar of imaginative values and of models of that special intricacy and multipurposiveness that is unique to the literary discourse.[12] If Umberto Eco is right to define the functions of literary fiction as the cultivation of abilities such as: "perceptual alertness, rapid induction, construction of hypotheses, positing of possible worlds, moral sophistication, liguistic proficiency, value awareness,"[13] then surely it is easy to understand that such functioning can be recognized as exemplary, well done, and durable in some few instances more than in many others.

A particularly eloquent defense of the "classics" (by which he clearly understands what others have come to call "canonical" writers) is offered by Italo Calvino. I do not want to repeat it here, merely to point out that Calvino concentrates on rereading and the freshness of discovery inherent in that rereading, that is, the thickness of the utterance ("A classic is a book that has never finished saying what it has to say").[14] But Calvino also makes two points that are worth considering in some detail a little later. One regards the hermeneutic accretions that enhance and expand certain works and endow them with canonical weight. The other is the shrewd and subtle observation that canonical works persist "as a background noise" despite and against the power of the present. The latter argument blends nicely with arguments on the contrastive, recessive, and diversionary energies of literature in general.[15]

Calvino's felicitous phrase of "background noise" also connects with another reality of fully canonical works: their choice is due to democratic pressures, not to scholarly conspiracies (which can affect only curricula) or even to elite taste preferences. Both the latter factors are highly important in the construction and maintenance of literary institutions but their true effectiveness begins only after a certain communitarian consensus has set in. The examples are overwhelming in number. Homer or "Homer" was for a long time a purely popular author or phenomenon before being adopted by Alexandrian scholars, streamlined, adapted, and canonized. Shakespeare was an author of huge popular appeal and constant, recurring interest before being reluctantly accepted by the intellectual classes. Even in the late seventeenth century, Dryden still thought of Shakespeare as barely more than *primus inter pares* and found many faults in him,[16] and as late as the middle of the eighteenth century Dr. Johnson was sharply dismissive of parts of the Shakespearian legacy.[17] In the interval Thomas Bowdler, Nahum Tate, and others thought that sanction and approval should be bestowed only on sanitized versions of the plays. Only by the end of the eighteenth century, with Coleridge and Hazlitt in England, with the Schlegels and Tieck in Germany as standard-bearers, does Shakespeare obtain full academic and intellectual approval. In a word, it is democratic pressure, not aristocratic and ideological patronage that establish the special status of Shakespeare. Nor is Goethe's situation entirely dissimilar. His *Werther* was an early bestseller that made his name a household word all over Europe; this in turn was the consequence of an uncanny capture of widely shared sentimental patterns. Other works of Goethe's were German bestsellers. Literary canonization followed soon after 1830, and it was a rather conscious process,[18] but the point is surely that it would have been impossible in the absence of a prior popular choice.

V

What emerges from even a cursory look at purely canonical authors is that unconscious factors play a much more important role than factors derived from conscious manipulation and institutional pressures. This of course is one of the well-kept secrets in the history of criticism and literary theory: that there is very rarely a direct line of connection between "society" and criticism. Critical practitioners take their cues from literary producers who, in turn, are part and parcel of a sociocultural continuum: criticism and theory are usually just the codification of already established tenets of taste and literary practice. Leavis, Empson, and Richards became plausible and influential because Eliot and Pound had already cleared the ground. Derrida is impossible to understand historically without full awareness of the impact of Robbe-Grillet and Nathalie Sarraute in the fifties as novelists, but also (and emphatically) as essayists. Among the German and English Romantics critical theorizing always followed in the

wake of poetry. Valéry and Poe, Dryden, Lessing, and Tolstoy are greater
critical figures than pure critical scholars. Deconstruction, structuralism,
hermeneutic, psychoanalytic, and archetypal criticism, reader-response, all
find their sources in literature. Marxism is an exception, apparently, and
that would provide a good explanation for its failures, as well as for its
endemic hostility to literature.

If criticism is produced by literature rather than acting as its shaper
and guide, it is quite clear that its ability to "canonize" must not be over-
rated by us. By the same token the influence of "society" and of its conscious manipulations is limited. In an unexpected way, *non Caesar supra
grammaticos*. A number of examples can be adduced, the most striking of
which – almost a full-scale sociological experiment – occurred in Soviet
Russia. In 1936 the Stalin regime launched its thunders of disapproval on
Dostoevsky and his works. The novels were no longer published and existing editions were widely withdrawn from accessible public libraries.
Scholarship on Dostoevsky, or at least its possibility of public expression,
was virtually discontinued. An earnestly consistent nationwide censorship
struck out references to Dostoevsky from public texts or limited them to
occasional negative remarks. This situation continued for twenty years, a
long stretch of time for our century. Owing to the totalitarian nature of the
system that initiated it, this campaign had at its disposal possibilities that
were beyond the wildest imagination of modern European manipulators.
A convenient comparison is provided by R. Ohmann's analysis of the ways
in which publishing concerns in America influence the substance of the
modern novel. After a long, and more than once questionable or forced
demonstration, he concludes that "monopoly capitalism" manages to impose (very indirectly) some vague scheme of reconciliation, movement
"toward happiness," and an emphasis on individual consciousness on modern novels eligible for canonical status; most educated readers would consider these vague features as resulting from the internal momentum of
narrativity.[19] In direct contrast, the Soviet experiment was sharply focused,
executed with full control of all social levers, and implemented with un-
flinching decisiveness. It lasted twenty years: after 1956 the different bans
were gradually relaxed or dropped. This experiment in conscious and pur-
poseful canon-modification was a complete failure. Nothing allows us to
conclude that the canonical position of Dostoevsky was at all shaken in the
minds of the readership; perhaps on the contrary, it was slightly strengthened.[20]

Somewhat shorter and less decisive experiments took place in the "Second World" with other writers. In Romania after 1948 most of the classical and modern writing of the pre-Communist era was banned. The ban on the expressionist Lucian Blaga or the hermeticist Ion Barbu was in effect (with very small exceptions) between 1948 and 1962.[21] Most of the poems of the Romantic Mihai Eminescu were removed from public circulation for five to ten years. Simultaneously, government authorities with full control over anything published or publicly read, over all schools and all media, massively pressed for imposing the nineteenth-century proletarian poet D.Th. Neculuţă and the twentieth-century Communist poet A. Toma as canonical authors. None of this made even a slight dent upon the general recognition and prestige of these authors. As soon as the artificial barriers were removed, the canon snapped elastically back into position, indeed the authors earmarked for elimination may be said to have gained in authority.

The second half of the twentieth century provides dozens of similar examples proving that conscious and deliberate modification of the canonical traditions is most unlikely. Why did these and other attempts fail utterly?[22] The answer is plain: the initiators misunderstood the patterns of existence of literary canons, their emergent impulses, conditions of disappearance, and in particular, their chaotic stabilities. Administrative interventions and rational intentions fall short of reaching the levels on which canons dwell.

If administrative rationalists are not enough (they reach only curricula, non canons), it is perhaps ideological pressures that will do the trick. This is a widely held opinion, based upon the misconception that, in the past, it was ideologies that impelled the prominence and eventual selection to canonical status of particular authors and works. The image evoked for us is that of an academic search committee, followed by promotion deliberations. Or, in a more sinister vein, a version of the conspiratorial theory of history: secret huddles of fat, cigar-puffing capitalists, "the gnomes of Zurich" in their bank vaults, the Knights of the Round Table in dark Gothic chambers, the slave owners carousing in dissolute symposia and deciding the future of the literary profession. Or, again, we are cajoled into picturing the sly sycophantic wordsmith sniffing out the preferences of the mighty and quickly concocting the desired objects.

It is all too easy to dispel these little fantasies by looking at the facts around us. In the twentieth-century West, whose social and political ideology has been ruled by a steadily increasing pressure towards equality and democracy, uniformity and interchangeableness, unifying communication and simplifying abstraction, the writers that have been adopted as canonical seem directly opposed to the dominant ideologies: Joyce and Kafka, Proust and Mann, Yeats and Pound. If anything, the connection of these authors to the hegemonic progressive ideology of Western societies during the century is one of opposition. T.S. Eliot, the central English language poet, was a seriously conservative figure during his lifetime, even as a young man, indeed *more* so as a rebellious young man than by the time he had gained wide official recognition, when he moderated many of his views and positions. For the last half-century attempts to displace Eliot were frequent and energetic, almost desperate sometimes. The ineffectiveness of these campaigns is easily measured against Eliot's enormously increased appeal as a consequence of the worldwide popularity of the musical *Cats*. The way in which phrases such as "April is the cruellest month" or "Not with a bang but a whimper" and others were adopted in current usages are indices of a deep-rooted society-wide acceptance of Eliot as a stable major figure of the literary canon, even against the express wishes of the scholarly elites and their ideological tenets.

The canonization of Evelyn Waugh is, likewise, proceeding apace. Any partisan of the efficacy of ideological motivations must surely disbelieve the evidence of so improbable a chain of events. It is something that by rights should not have happened. Waugh's writings embody much of what the hegemonic intellectual classes castigate as being opposed to accelerated social and political progress in the twentieth century: a conservative love of tradition, outspoken elitism, intense loathing of equality and many similar features (including a hefty burden of prejudices). Under the very noses of academic watchdogs who actively struggle to establish curricula in conformity with late twentieth-century ideologies, a ground swell of public opinion and the multitudinous work of scholars imposed Waugh as a major writer. This position had been denied to him by "official" critics ever since the publication of *Brideshead Revisited* (1944); Edmund Wilson's fiery denunciation must be considered the turning point in condemnation.[23] Neither the huge American audiences (TV and readership) nor the small army of specialists (who patiently integrate Waugh in his contemporary context, in the mainstream of past literary and intellectual traditions and in the relation to modern and future developments)[24] are by any means, in their vast majority, sympathetic to the prejudices enacted in

Waugh's prose. Rather they respond in a very immediate way (as readers or as critics) to the richness of meanings and possibilities embedded in Waugh's texts. They also respond favorably, I would argue, even though unconsciously, to the need for contrastive imaginative relief provided in narrations whose premises are resolutely different from those of the prevailing social discourses.

Even more extreme cases are those of Louis Ferdinand Céline and Ernst Jünger. The first whose views (at least as expressed in some of his books) – and unlike those of Waugh – are truly despicable by almost any standards, has nevertheless achieved the breakthrough necessary for canonical status. Céline's writing voice has established a mode of literary (and essayistic) communication widely adopted in France and has then pulled up along with it his own writings. The case of Ernst Jünger is different. A very articulate and substantial traditionalist conservative, he was erroneously associated with national socialism. The battle over his access to canonicity has been waged for decades with inconclusive results; it is a case in which ideology has fought literature to a standstill. It will be very interesting to see if after the author's death the relative suppression of his work will still be possible. The case of Jünger presents some similarities to that of Bulgakov, a Soviet author who died in 1940 and whose work was thereafter banned for approximately twenty years (unlike Dostoevsky, Bulgakov was a contemporary and nonestablished author); despite institutional opposition, Bulgakov is quickly emerging as a leading figure of the twentieth-century canon of Russian literature. By contrast, ideologically well-aligned authors such as Graham Greene, Mikhail Sholokhov, Louis Aragon, and Archibald MacLeish tend to dwindle towards the status of the purely local and illustrative.

VI

If not rational and institional pressures, and if not ideological conformity, then what can be at last approximately designated as a mechanism for entry into the subliminal fluidities of the canonical domain?

My first conclusion, suggested above, but one that I would like to emphasize as strongly as possible, is that canonization is primarily a democratic process. Scholars, institutions, ideologies, groups of writers, or (last but not least) individuals may propose, initiate, pressure, and manipulate as much as they wish. The power to dispose is reserved to a much wider reading public which, standing for the community as a whole, over longer stretches of time adopt certain works and authors as representative for themselves. It is simplifying, but not false, to say that canonical works are the bestsellers of historical majorities as against those of local temporal minorities: Shakespeare against Horace Walpole, Virginia Woolf against Cronin and Warwick Deeping.

As to how exactly literate communities select their narrative and imaginative providers, perhaps it is best to think of it by analogy with the theory of chaos in modern physics and mathematics. Inextricable collaborations of rational and predictable factors with irrational and sudden developments lead to stabilities and turbulences that alternate irregularly, or to nonperiodical regularities and recurrences. In literature we generally group such processes under the headings of sensibility and taste. These terms do not only indicate the metarational level on which decisions are taken, they also indicate the thin and pervasive nature of the value judgments involved, as well as a randomized, carefree, and unfocused interaction with all kinds of material interests and existential choices.

Works that can hope to achieve and maintain a canonical status over a longer period of time must first of all be endowed with a certain intrinsic thickness and multiplicity. They must be able to respond to numerous and diverse solicitations, they must be capable of shouldering the burden of contrastive interpretations. In other words, they must in their very texture partake of heterogeneity:[25] not in the declared intentions of authors or characters, not in the overt signals of the text, but rather in their silent behaviors. The durability of Homer's *Iliad* is explained by how it is many things at the same time: a narrative of defeat, an examination of seesawing right and wrong, a thematic treatment of polarities essential to all human beings (war and peace, the gods and the human race, the masculine and the feminine, chance and design, law and compassion, reason and sentiment, and others yet), a history of human memory, a history of freedom, a gallery of persons and situations. It is also, not first among these many other important things, a record of local sociohistorical events and behaviors.

Or consider the *Chanson de Roland*. Its contemporary political and historical relevance is, few could doubt it, modest. Its enactment of moral values such as courage, loyalty, and sacrifice and their relationship to the chivalric-feudal version of Western Christendom in which they grew can expand to some extent the reach of its validity. Real contemporary interest however will be sparked by an understanding of Roland's last stand as the struggle of a small rural culture against a brilliant and overwhelming imperial power: with the piquant role-reversal of a pre-Romanesque Europe defending its identity against a society that nowadays, as "Third World," would seem to be mostly in need of sentimental encouragement. The interaction of these and other facts must lead to a text complexity that cannot be experienced in separate treatments of each of the strands woven into it, a complexity that is intuitively recognized as such by large nubmers of readers over the centuries who as a consequence rightly place the text over and above many others.

This is to say that – as I said before – not only is a reduction of *Macbeth* to Shakespeare's relationships with King James a piece of insignificant pedantry,[26] not only is ideological discipline irrelevant, but a key element for canonical status is a sizable degree of opposition to the *ephemera* of historical flow. Masterpieces do not gain quasi-universal appeal *because of,* but *in spite of* their ideologies and world views. Dante survived, as opposed to Brunetto Latini, or to (the Sicilian Ghibelline) Piero della Vigna, or to the Franciscan Giacomino da Verona (author of *De Babilonia infernali* or *De Jerusalem celesti,* poems much within the thematic range of the *Divine Comedy),* not to speak of the multitude of hagiographical writings, because he transcended the mere local ideological confines. Once the free pass is gained to a wider circulation (Chaucer as Medieval and Renaissance, Goethe as conservative and liberal, Euripides as classical and romantic, etc.) they begin to constitute not only a "cultural grammar for interpreting experience"[27] as Altieri once quite aptly described them but an effective opposition against, for instance, the economic greed, pressures, and manipulations that go into the making of a bestseller. They are equally effective in limiting the absolutist tendencies of ideologies in their historical succession and the covetous anarchy of personal ambitions and generational tantrums.

The point must also be made that while affirmations of canonical status are made originally and then finally sanctioned by the general preference of the readership, informally expressed, in between other factors intervene. Scholarly and critical opinions do play a role, although a smaller one than often believed: Samuel Johnson could exert decisive influence because he intuited justly the desires and tastes of society, Irving Babbitt did not because he was much less attuned to general sensibility. Compatibility of a work or author with some general coherence of the canonical domain also plays a certain role. Hugh Kenner may be somewhat over-stating the case when he speaks of the canon as being actually "a narrative of some intricacy" or as a "shapely story" that is "complexly coherent,"[28] but there is no question that as gatekeepers go, works previously canon-ized are considerably more effective than bookselling interests or academ-ic snobbishness. Joyce's *Ulysses* relates in multiple ways not only to Homer and Dante, but to the picaresque novel, or to Thackeray and Tennyson, or to Chaucer (*Wife of Bath*). Another decisive factor of selection is, as I already said, the literary mode of production of the day: what and how and why writers are writing in a certain way at a certain given time is much more important than what critics are saying about these things. The writers are – as it were – the stand-ins for both the community and the elites and at the same time the places where these entitites meet and com-bine in a creative way, with future-oriented openness. One last factor is the weight itself of the hermeneutic applied. To quote Kenner once more (quoting Borges): "Writers invent their predecessors."[29] Yes, but once this has been done, it becomes soon almost impossible to *disinvent* them. The accretions around given works amplify them to formidable proportions and often change them decisively (as Italo Calvino indicates). Industrious hermeneutic activities spin out strong and subtle ties between works, meshings, and intertextualities. "We are the result of reinterpretations of life, death, consciousness, creativity, and so forth, elaborated since the pre-Socratics, and even before (since the discovery of agriculture and met-allurgy for example)."[30] The results of *literary* hermeneutic activity are no less real and massive than the results of the *existential* hermeneutic Eliade is talking about. The first, and still the most prototypical canonical work of Western culture, the *Iliad,* is in most important ways an absence: there is no consensus on its authorship, on its date of publication, on its genesis, or on its text. The *Iliad* as we know it is the result of successive layers of her-meneutic activity, much as the onion-like reality of the philosopher in Carlyle's *Sartor Resartus*. And yet the results of such slow and constructive literary hermeneutics are quite palpable and solid. They maintain tradi-tions already established and they fashion options and limitations of future growth.

VII

After these rather obvious and simple truths, let me return to the canonical debate currently raging in American academic institutions, with all its disquieting and yet perhaps symptomatic aspects, in other words let me return to what I called above the first level of canonical meanings. Before I briefly address the issues, let me dismiss quickly a number of motivations that are in themselves of the highest sociological interest and would deserve detailed scrutiny, but that are not immediately relevant to our discussion here. Many of these motivations are connected to a comical over-evaluation of classroom power, or the confusion of curriculum with canon. Others derive from overspecialization and the exacerbated nominalism that can understandably lead even the stoutest heart to despair. The least excusable motivation is the widespread brattishness that enjoys chastising the past and that uses anticanonical slogans in order to attack culture and "society" in general. I say it is the least excusable, and strongly doubt its critical seriousness because objectively it is a move towards the disciplining and alignment of literary tradition with the prevailing *Zeitgeist*, that is, an effort to homogenize and impose uniformity. This type of argument does not differ in its essence from the Victorian moral regimentations that sought to discipline Flaubert, Baudelaire, and Wilde, from the Puritan banning of Shakespeare, from Medieval distrust and punishment of the literary, and ultimately from Socrates' trial and execution; literature should be a tool for betterment and social action, or it should not be at all. At a time when a certain tension between intellectuals and their society (between communication and production) is widely regarded as a healthy prerequisite for the good functioning of advanced human communities, the "attack against literature" is clearly deleterious and regressive in its very nature.

I will, however, leave aside these motivations and instead deal with the sensible core of the "anticanonical" argument on the "first" (or foregrounded) level and with the qualifications that can reasonably be suggested to it. Essentially the objections against the present "canon" (and its defenses) are not too different from the inchoate but decisive assault of the romantics against the human model put forward by the eighteenth-century Enlightenment, in its neoclassical and rationalist variants. It will be remembered that with the loudly proclaimed benevolent and progressive intention of obliterating the deep differences (social, religious, cultural) between humans, seventeenth- and particularly eighteenth-century writers and thinkers rallied around standards of behavior and being that were diurnal, solar, social, activist, temperate, virtuous, and reasonable. Such standards could assure, it was widely held, human improvement and liberation from injustice and superstition. By the end of the eighteenth century, there was increasing mistrust in and dissatisfaction with this human model as one too restrictive. The specificities not only of femininity and the extra-European (in the guise of the primitive and exotic, as they were then extolled) but also of infancy and old age, as well as of all kinds of deviance (up to and including insanity and crime) were advocated and described as against a stale or old-fashioned adherence to neoclassical proprieties and timorously standardized humanism. Cainite and demonic figures, special imaginative states, and national and regional identities proliferated in the discourses of the time. It would be superfluous to recap here the history of that confrontation: all the social and intellectual (and specifically literary) good that came of it, no less than the dark consequences (collectivist and nationalist among others) that beset the West later, as well as different interesting compromises and syntheses that ensued.

I am firmly convinced that the current dilemmas are in important ways analogous to the confrontations of 200 years ago, now projected on a global (or globalizing) scale. They can be grouped under three broad dichotomies: Western/non-Western, male/female, and elite/popular discourses. Of these three the last one seems comparatively the least tractable. Let us consider each of them briefly.

VIII

Criticizing Western canonical patterns for their lack of non-Western openness is in the majority of cases as simple as answering these critiques. It borders on the frivolous or the inane to accuse Shakespeare of not having enough "colored people" in his plays, as some have done: one might as well complain about the lack of Scandinavians in the *Ramayana*, or of Cervantes's failure to describe refrigerators or telephones in his writings. On a more serious level are the curricular questions: how much integration between courses in Western literature and courses in world literature is possible or desireable? Disputes along these lines sprang up following the increasing globalization of education, an issue that arises only well into the second half of the twentieth century. On the face of it, solutions should be easy to propose: there is no reason why a course on *Western* literature and thought should include Confucius, much as there is no excuse for a course in *world* literature and thought to ignore Confucius and *Gilgamesh*. From this point on, departments and universities can decide by themselves (and from case to case) the number or proportion or status of such courses, according to local circumstances and aims.

The triviality of the issue hides serious complexities. Well over 150 years ago Goethe had proposed *Weltliteratur*[31] as a kind of high plateau on which the best of the best can meet each other in Olympian serenity over national, linguistic, and cultural distinctions. (Nor was his view Eurocentric: as we know, Persian, Hebrew, and Sanskrit were well within his purview.) This is a noble ideal, but one may wonder how the Olympians will coexist up there. Comparative literature, a young discipline, barely has the tools to establish connections between European national literatures, and despite its brave amateurish attempts in the last ten years or so, is still very far from generating many categories useful for universal critical and literary interactions. On an even more basic level there are hardly more than a handful of scholars in the world today with the intimate and multilateral knowledge in *several* cultures that is necessary if any common grounds for a *Weltliteratur* (in the Goethean sense) are to be outlined. Moreover the principals in the affair do not seem themselves too eager to enter into cooperative agreements. The proud self-confidence of Western literature and thought is almost always held up for opprobrium in discussions of this kind (often in the most strident tones) and not without some justice. It is equally just to point to an Islamic culture that is not entirely convinced that literature is tolerable at all, let alone eager to engage in integrative ar rangements with non-Islamic literatures. It is no less just to point to a Chinese culture that perceives its own identity as dependent upon a much more formalized canon and requires a thorough acquisition of that canon by even technical and scientific students, in ways that are rather strictly exclusionary of "supplementary" Western values and information.

One can easily subscribe to quick curricular modifications: splendid literary works like Amos Tutuola's *The Palm-Wine Drinkard*, Derek Walcott's poems, or V.S. Naipaul's *A Bend in the River*, as well as (probably) writings by Soyinka, Achebe, Césaire, or Y. Ouologuem (perhaps more than the Afro-American school of novelists) can be integrated in Western literary curricula without much difficulty simply because they are *written* in

European languages. Whether they will eventually reach canonical integration must remain for the moment an open question: as I argued before, this kind of promotion is not dependent on MLA committee decisions. Rather it may hinge – to speculate for a moment – on the acceptance of a gradually more integrated *Weltliteratur*: the pressure of other works in or around a putatively new canonical field can push them towards a renewed centrality.

To continue in the same speculative vein, it seems almost impossible to imagine a global literary canonical field outside some frameworks established in the Western tradition. It is irrelevant where the power centers of the future will be located – Tokyo or Moscow, Habana or Nairobi, Peking or Cairo – the Third World no less than the "Second" World has as its main program the famed "catching up," that is, its own alignement to the sociopolitical values and the economic patterns established in the nineteenth century in Western Europe and in the twentieth century in North America. Capitalist democracy, Biblically molded conceptual modes, and a consumerist hedonism now provide – for the better or the worse – the common denominators for global interactions. These, along with communicative and relational foci of cognition, are all modes of existence engendered in and identified with Western civilization. It seems quite unlikely that literary canons will represent an exception to this pattern of development and that Western literary experiences will suddenly become peripheral as an expression of humanness. Moreover such an improbable event would be of dubious desirability. The transition of vast areas of the globe from traditional and organic ("biological" as some historians have called them) modes of existence to the atomized and rapid existence of modernity is traumatic and deeply painful at its best, and accompanied by such disasters as revolutions, wars, and economic misery. The kind tolerance and interrogative humanness of Western literary thought canons provide the smoothest and most decent avenue towards the new horizons of social being. This is proved by the choices and testimonies of intellectuals involved in the change ("Third World" radicals and writers for instance), but it can also be deduced: after all, a key component of the key pieces of the canon deal precisely with the process of grappling with a coming modernity in given circumstances, and with the anxieties and hopes of this process. In the absence of any familiarity with Western cultural canons, modernization descends no less inevitably upon the world, but without the protective and mediating energies emitted by that familiarity.

Somewhat similar dilemmas are raised by the male-female polarity when inserted in a discussion of literary curricula and canons. The central rational argument of *literary* feminism is quite strong and sound. It says that the male-female problematic in literature and thought (no less than in society or in any human life) is at least as important and central as other oppositions defining humanness – such as individual versus society, immanent versus transcendent, young versus old – and that it should receive no less, or even more attention than these other polarities.[32] Very few can, I believe, doubt the legitimacy of this position. Around this fully justified center militant connotative circles emerged. We have to ignore here the predictable parasitic role of a moribund Marxist teaching: it replaces social class with gender and then launches itself into the well-known dialectic of suspicion and hate. This is a methodology widely spread in American universities, but of no intellectual respectability. Only slightly weightier is the proposition that Western literary history is a tale of mere patriarchal suppressions and wrongful selections:[33] a hypothesis that to survive at all will probably have to accommodate serious modifications.

From a canonical point of view, the feminist problematic becomes more interesting when it requests a revised canonical structure on the grounds that only thus can a truly complete and balanced image of humanity be obtained. The linear progress and mechanic rationalism of "maleness" requires completion by the rounded comprehensiveness and emotional depth and subtlety of the "feminine" cultural psyche.[34] This valid argument can often deteriorate into mere statistical quibbling with no substantial qualitative backing. It also brings back memories of earlier attempts to tie literary worth to racial characteristics (hair and eye pigmentation, skull shape, etc.):[35] different as gender features might be from these, resorting to them and privileging them implies a reduction of the aesthetic and cultural to merely genetic material that must surely give pause. Despite these serious objections, there is much soundness in efforts to gain a canonical image in which gender dialectics should be adequately presented. Using a curricular leverage to effect canonical changes ought not to be rejected out of hand.

Nevertheless any such enterprise has to consider two outstanding facts. The first is that if critical and hermeneutic operations in the last century or so have certainly fallen woefully short in interpreting the gender-related values of the West's great canonical works, the same is simply not true of the canon itself. One wonders how many true feminists would indeed be ready to dispense with Antigone and Penelope, Cassandra and Iphigenia, the Wife of Bath and Molly Bloom, Cordelia and Kriemhild, Moll Flanders and Emma Bovary? (Surely the pale artificialities of, for example, *Harlequin*-type literature, often written by women authors, give a more distorted and demeaning image of femininity.) While criticism has often failed to underline or work out the implications of female-male polarities, the canonical order itself was chosen – one cannot but infer – because the tastes, instincts, and sensibilities of the reading and writing community had recognized early on the human richness of these works at levels that the prevailing ideological paradigms took much longer to acknowledge.

The second is that the "radical pedagogy" often intended by anticanonical movements is apt to backfire cruelly in the case of feminine literature. The canon was selected on the basis of liberal and pluralist value choices, central and commonly human experiences, on the basis of openness and complexity. The radical values of subversion and rebellion, of questioning and process are deeply interwoven in the texture of Western canons, curricula and privileged literature. The distortive and mechanical inclinations of the professional ideologue's mind will expect that by exploring the strata of "suppressed" and "marginalized" writing it must uncover true revolution (social or sexual). Nothing of the kind is likely to happen. The whole field of marginalized literature (written by men or women) is replete with acquiescence, formalized harmonies, and translations of obsolete ideologies: noncanonical literature is *par excellence* the domain of conservatism.[36] One example is Felicia Hemans, public, prominent, and popular in her own day, slowly declining into obscurity later, certainly an excellent representative of the "tamed romanticism" of the 1820s and 1830s. This "marginalized feminine" turns out to be a repository of and tireless extoller of the values of family, tradition, stability, religion, and hierarchy, an embodiment of the most orthodox Biedermeier. Such curricular surprises are the rule more than the exception. Literature chosen on the basis of authorial gender alone can reveal itself as conformist, predictable, and well behaved. Canonical works, even products of heroic- patriarchal mentality as the *Nibelungenlied* and the *Odyssey*, are so imbued with dialectics and ambiguities that serious readers genuinely had to ask themselves whether their authors are not women. In this, as in everything else, there are numbers of exceptions, on both sides, but I think it can be said that many key ethical and critical aims of feminist methodologies are achieved as well (and better) by working with the canonical domains than outside (or against them).

IX

Ultimately, however, the problematic and objectives discussed above seem to converge into the broader and more philosophical question of the admissibility of a "high canon" under circumstances when equalization seems a pressing historical (no, almost evolutionary) priority.

There are several ways in which this objection can be answered, of which I will quickly mention only four. The first is that canonical works are precisely those located at the intersection of popular and elite preferences. Shakespeare is canonical in a different way from Mallarmé and G.M. Hopkins, because the multiplicity of his readings encompasses some that are on the level of manufactured predictability (TV sitcom), some that are geared to satisfying archetypal and purely narrative needs, and others that are involved in the sophisticated, exploratory, and ambiguous domain of possibility and multiplicity that allows the human race to move and advance. The former set of interpretations (popular) supports the latter (elitist) and is continuous with it. To proclaim a conflictual situation between them and to try to abolish canonical literature in the name of popular literature is incongruous and counterproductive. The values of popular literature in all ages have been dependent on powerful master-texts – Biblical or oral-mythical – that have had a privileged and authoritative role freely and passionately (fanatically?) accepted. It is hypothetically possible (though to me personally, horrifying) to contemplate a future in which such master-texts will be of commercial-advertising or political-manipulative origin. But this very possibility emphasizes the elegance and flexibility of the state of human mind and society in which literary canons could at the same time be and not be master-texts. This is not an idealization of literary canons, but a coldly factual description, one confirmed by the situation in, say, music or painting (or even philosophy), where canons are supported by "popular demand" even while sniped at by elites, and where their role as regulating factors in the ecology of the intellect seems well understood.

The second has to do with the oft-repeated prediction that historical morphologies and symbolic traditions are likely to be dissolved in the general informational soup of a post-historical human organization. Literature ought to disappear and will disappear in the light of a more abstract and humanly-devised environment. Demolishing the canon, the implied argument runs, is a progressive duty of right-thinking people. It is not for me to say whether indeed this will be the course of human evolution. Assuming however that it will, then literature in general and the canonical domain in particular must become of greater rather than lesser import. A cognitive environment based on quasi-universal relationships between indifferent and replaceable bits of information inevitably leaves unsatisfied the human need for immediacy, concreteness, and physicality. To offer an analogy: as the sensorial involvement and the contacts with nature of an increasingly urbanized and insulated society dwindled in the twentieth century, the importance of and reliance upon sexuality as a channel of naturalness and physicality were enhanced. It seems that the valuation of literature as an intermediary between the concrete and the abstract will be likewise strengthened rather than weakened in a similarly abstract intellectual and sensorial context. Popular literature with its archetypal and cliché-ridden modes, and devoid of inbuilt contradictory and subversive mechanisms, can satisfy such needs less well than sophisticated works. Literature (as well as other aesthetic productions) is uniquely positioned to maintain and transfer archaic features in discourses that are available to postcontemporary abstract and transactive organizations.[37]

The third point is somewhat related to the one made above. If indeed a post-historical and even anomic state of affairs were to install itself, would it not be the case that such a human society would still be in need of self-understanding? Or is it not conceivable that such a human community would want to have a better grasp of the mechanisms and roads that led to its own constitution? The argument of "historical grammars" was developed by Charles Altieri with more eloquence that I can hope to muster and I will simply point readers to his essays.[38]

Finally, my fourth and – I believe – strongest point is again one that is developed at length elsewhere. It is simply that literature in its internal and aesthetic substance is opposed to historical progress with its velocity and callously unrestrained single-mindedness. It is literature in its broadly canonical domains that – as much as anything else – allows for and even calls for qualification, digression, delay, and admission of imperfection.[39] It is literature that opens up heteronomy and alternative. The attacks against literature – under the guise of offensives against "hegemonic" canonicity – are not rebellions but operations of repression and liquidation. The convenient elitist label hides the more sinister purpose of erasing difference. At the same time, canonical literariy functions as a release for the needs of memory and tradition that are ingrained in human existence. Blocking this release is no less unhealthy than other forms of repression; allowing it to function is like inoculation against vastly more dangerous social urges of stagnation and return, and can contribute to a defense against them.

The canonical domain is, at bottom, coextensive with literature itself, so imperceptible are the shades marking transitions from periphery to core. Demolishing one part is not possible without gravely endangering the whole. How likely is it that the banning of Mallarmé will result in the massive and informed reading of eighteenth-century testaments and political pamphlets? Will the appreciation of Felicia Hemans be enhanced by the neglect of or contempt for John Keats? One can only shrug at such naiveties. Rather we should recognize what any reader with some passion and patience always knew: that the abrupt and categorical opposition between "elite" and "popular" literature is contrived and spurious. The importance and desirability of literary works and values is a very gradual continuum from the more peripheral to the most central. The parts need each other. Moreover there is movement here, communication, change, replacement, musical chairs on a local and on a general scale. Not only is the canonical domain shaped by democratic choice (as I have argued earlier) it also seems democratically governed and organized.

X

I sincerely hope that none of the above considerations can be deemed as supportive of the idea of an ironclad, stable, or eternal "canon." Except for a handful of uninfluential pedants nobody expressed such a view in the last few decades: it is one clearly alien to literature and its worlds. Moreover, even though I have argued at length against the probability that manipulative processes will result in quick and deep-going changes, this does not mean at all that I exclude the possibility of such changes in other ways. A human race geared to the visual and oral/aural communications is not an impossibility. Either a complete ecological, or a manmade disaster, could lead to regression to a prehistorical state. Alternatively, advances into an anomic, regularized, and totally controlled post-historic future are not a complete impossibility either. In both these broad categories of cases human society and *all* its agencies, expression, or communications can change so much as to lead to rapid and decisive modifications of the imaginative and narrative needs of humanity. The latter can disappear, I believe, only with the very disappearance of humanness, but their modes of satisfaction can obviously vary depending on the state of societies. Canonical domains, in a word, are intimately linked with history itself and are not likely to disappear before it. Nor are their patterns of behavior – and particularly their continuous but sluggish mode of movement – apt to change much even under the impact of an age in which the weight of consciousness and self-consciousness is tremendously increased, as ours seems to be.

The most interesting and most worrisome question is the one with which I started these considerations and that can now be articulated more fully. What happens in an intermediary and transitional situation in which accelerated change seems to bring us closer to anomic states and controls without actually plunging us in cataclysmic alterations? In that kind of gray area literature would find itself diminished and constricted and it is precisely in such a historical environment that hard and simple canons arise, as shorthand versions for literature. Or, to use the terminology of this very essay: curricular and properly canonical planes tend to collapse and fuse. The reduction of literature to a limited and reified list of names and works (no matter what criteria are used in its selection) would seriously, perhaps irreparably harm literature, as well as impair humane modes of interaction. Canons, if not accepted in all their irregular breadth, and if not seen in their organic solidarity with all kinds of literacy, are fearsome and unlovable creatures indeed. In a curious and paradoxical way it is precisely the more delicate cultivating of the canonical domains that is our chance for avoiding the low perspectives of reified canonical oppressions.

Notes

1. Søren Kierkegaard, *The Present Age*, transl. A. Dru, 1940 (New York: Harper and Row, 1962), pp. 89 and 94. The distinctions between the aesthetic, the ethical, and the religious pervade Kierkegaard's whole work beginning with *Enten/Eller* of 1843.

2. Irving Kristol, *Reflections of a Neo-Conservative* (New York: Basic Books, 1983), pp. 318-19.

3. Arthur Quinn, *Broken Shore: The Marin Peninsula* (Peregrine Smith: Salt Lake City, 1981), p. 165.

4. Ernst Robert Curtius, *European Literature and the Latin Middle Ages* (Germ. version 1948; Princeton, N.J.: Princeton University Press, 1973), pp. 49-53.

5. Alastair Fowler, *Kinds of Literature* (Cambridge, MA: Harvard University Press, 1982), p. 232.

6. Harold Bloom, *Ruin the Sacred Truths* (Cambridge, MA: Harvard University Press, 1989).

7. T.S. Eliot, "What is a Classic," in *On Poetry and Poets* (London: Faber, 1957). An essay written in 1944.

8. I am grateful to my colleague Rosemary Gates for suggesting this comparison.

9. André Gide, *Anthologie de la poesie française* (Paris: Gallimard, coll. Pleiade, 1949).

10. George Steiner, *Antigones* (1984; Oxford: Oxford Univeristy Press, 1986).

11. Steiner, *Antigones*, pp. 134-39.

12. Charles Altieri, "An Idea and Ideal of a Literary Canon," in Robert von Hallberg, ed., *Canons*, (Chicago: University of Chicago Press, 1984), pp. 41-64.

13. Umberto Eco, *The Role of the Reader: Explorations in the Semiotics of Texts*, (Bloomington, IN: Indiana University Press, 1979), apud Thomas Pavel, *Fictional Worlds* (Cambridge, MA: Harvard University Press, 1986), p. 141.

14. Italo Calvino, "Why Read the Classics," *New York Review of Books*, October 9, 1986, pp. 19-20.

15. Charles Altieri, *op. cit.*; Virgil Nemoianu, *A Theory of the Secondary: Literature, Progress and Reaction* (Baltimore: Johns Hopkins University Press, 1989).

16. I have in mind *An Essay of Dramatic Poesy* of 1668 with its calmly superior comparison of Jonson, Shakespeare, and the Beaumont and Fletcher team.

17. Samuel Johnson in his 1765 preface to Shakespeare's works is generally censorious, and by turns enthusiastic and patronizing in ways that were very, very rare after 1800.

18. Peter Uwe Hohendahl, *Literarische Kultur im Zeitalter des Liberalismus 1830-1870* (Munchen: Beck, 1985), pp. 202-206, actually (though unwittingly or unwillingly) confirms my point. It was continuing popular support of Goethe that was crucial to

his canonical survival despite the reluctance of radical intellectual elites. Institutional measures followed, by decades, community taste decisions.

19. Richard Ohmann, "The Shaping of A Canon: U.S. Literature 1960-1975," in *Canons*, pp. 377-402. I say the argument is forced not only because it is very indirect, but for other reasons also. The "gatekeeping journals" quoted by him are liberal and radical rather than conservative. The combination of "large circulation and gatekeeping" on which Ohmann relies fails in at least one-third of the cases quoted by him (since some books achieved only small circulations). The theory of managerial society was expounded by James Burnham long before John and Barbara Ehrenreich (Ohmann's derivative sources). Segal's *Love Story* is one case that flagrantly contradicts Ohmann's speculative analysis.

20. For a detailed description see Vladimir Seduro, *Dostoevski in Russian Literary Criticism 1846-1956* (1957; New York: Octagon Books, 1969), pp. 95-99, 133, 183-85, 236-40. See also Gleb Struve, *Russian Literature Under Lenin and Stalin 1917- 1953* (Norman, OK: University of Oklahoma Press, 1971), pp. 363, 374, and 258, and in general, Parts V and VII as background.

21. They were allowed to publish translations, but no work of theirs was in print and only occasional negative critical comments were allowed. The counterproductive effects of direct (administrative) canonical manipulation in Russian, Romanian, Hungarian literature among others are confirmed, for example, in America by the attempts to censor out Mark Twain. Indirect, slower, and more insidious efforts, against a general background of social downplayinig of literature, as pursued by Western societies since 1960 or so, may be more effective in the long run: the jury is still out.

22. The vagaries of intellectual and cultural politics in post-1949 China are fascinating. For a period of time attempts were made to suppress Lao Tze as being too idealist, while Confucius was seen as partly confirming the structured purposiveness of Maoist order.

23. Edmund Wilson wrote in glowingly appreciative terms about Waugh in 1943, 1944, and later, but in the *New Yorker* of January 5, 1946, he launched a blistering attack against Waugh who was henceforward a marked and labelled man for establishment criticism for several decades.

24. As one personally involved in Waugh criticism and acquainted with many of those contributing patiently to his "canonization," I know that these critics are by no means sympathetic to Waugh's ideological biases.

25. Frank Kermode, *The Classic* (1975; Cambridge: Harvard University Press, 1983) makes the point several times.

26. "Speaking for the Humanities," *Chronicle of Higher Education*, January 11, 1989.

27. Altieri, *op. cit.*

28. Hugh Kenner in *Canons*, pp. 373 and 375.

29. Kenner, *Canons*, p. 363.

30. Mircea Eliade, *No Souvenirs* (New York: Harper and Row, 1973), pp. 289-90.

31. The typical case adduced is the conversation with Eckermann of January 31, 1827. But for a complete account see Fritz Strich, *Goethe and World Literature* (New York: Hafner, 1949).

32. Toril Moi, *Sexual/Textual Politics: Feminist Literary Theory* (London: Methuen, 1985).

33. Dale Spender, *Mothers of the Novel* (London: Pandora Books), 1986. See the relevant observations of Pierre Walker, "Arnold's Legacy: Religious Rhetoric of Critics on the Literary Canon," *Stanford Literature Review* 5 (1988), *1-2*, pp. 169-174.

34. Ellen Messer-Davidow, "The Philosophical Basis of Feminist Literary Criticisms," *New Literary History* 19 (1987), *1*, pp. 63-104, and *ibid.* the response of Gerald Graff, pp. 135-38. See also Martha Nussbaum, and some of the writings of Luce Irigaray.

35. For instance Josef Nadler, *Literaturgeschichte des deutschen Volkes*, 4 vols. (1912; Berlin Propyläen, 1939) with its emphasis on the biological sources of cultural regionalism and, of course, in a much broader and sweeping sense of the "raceological" philosophy of culture of Hans F.K. Gunther.

36. The French conservative-monarchist author Jacques Bainville thought that the greatest strategic mistake of the returning Bourbons after 1815 was not to have granted universal suffrage, since the latter was and is a factor of stability and conservation, unlike the elite-oriented franchise that led to the revolutionary upheavals of 1930 and 1948. See J. Bainville, *Histoire de France*, 2 vols. (Paris: Tullandier, 1926), pp. II, 154, 165-67, and 189.

37. There are numerous other arguments that could be adduced. For instance, canons in painting and music. Musical programs on radio and in concert halls have to be based in large part upon audience preferences. These go massively towards a canonical tradition and there is a continual tug of war between directors/interpreters/programmers chafing at the bit and desirous to innovate and experiment and the conservative opera-and-concert-audiences. In painting and in other arts such canonical choices are translated in financial figures and are thus much more measurable. Another point to be kept in mind is that national identities are often – for the better or the worse – expressed in terms of cultural achievements, and particularly in smaller nations. Does it seem likely that Ireland will renounce Joyce and Yeats, Greece its great authors and so forth, for the sake of canonical levelling and the overturning of hierarchies? The obvious answer is again the result of democratic pressures, not of institutional impositions.

38. Altieri, *op. cit.* See also article in this volume.

39. Virgil Nemoianu, *A Theory of the Secondary*.

Contributors

Charles Altieri

Charles Altieri is a Professor in the Department of English and Comparative Literature at the University of Washington. He has written books on act and quality – a theory of interpretation, and has volumes forthcoming on abstraction in modernist poetry and painting, as well as a collection of essays on canons and consequences that tries to develop the issue of a pragmatic aesthetics of idealism.

Yves Chevrel

Yves Chevrel is Professor of General and Comparative literature at the University of the Sorbonne in Paris. His latest publication is "La Litterature comparée" in the prestigious collection *Que sais-je?* (Paris).

Christopher Clausen

Christopher Clausen, Professor of English at the Pennsylvania State University, is the author of *The Place of Poetry* (University Press of Kentucky, 1981) and *The Moral Imagination* (University of Iowa Press, 1986). He has published many poems, essays, and reviews in the *American Scholar*, the *Times Literary Supplement*, the *Georgia Review*, and other periodicals.

Michael G. Cooke

Michael G. Cooke, now deceased, was the Bird White Housum Professor of English Literature at Yale University. Born and reared in Jamaica, he took his Ph.D. at the University of California, Berkeley. He was awarded a Woodrow Wilson Fellowship in 1957, a Morse Fellowship in 1966, a Guggenheim Fellowship in 1972, and received Griswald awards in 1975, 1979, and 1984. In addition to Yale, he taught at the University of Iowa and at Boston University, where he also served as editor of *Studies in Romanticism*. His most recent book is *Afro-Amer-*

ican Literature in the Twentieth-Century: The Achievements of Intimacy. He was director of The Common Wealth of Letters at Yale University and special consultant to the University of Houston's multi-cultural program on "Texts and Tradition: The Common Ground."

Lilian R. Furst

Lilian R. Furst is the Marcel Bataillon Professor of Comparative Literature at the University of North Carolina at Chapel Hill. Born in Vienna, Austria, and educated in England, she has taught at many institutions including Dartmouth College, William and Mary, Stanford, and Harvard. She has also held ACLS, Guggenheim, and National Humanities Center Fellowships. She has published articles and books on European literature from the eighteenth to the twentieth century, notably *Romanticism in Perspective, Romaticism, Naturalism, Counterparts*, and *Fictions of Romantic Irony.*

Glen M. Johnson

Glen M. Johnson is an Associate Professor of English at the Catholic University of America. He received his Ph.D. in American studies at Indiana University. He previously taught at Grinnell College and the University of Louisville. He is the editor of *Emerson's Journals, Notebooks*, and *Works*, and has published articles on nineteenth- and twentieth-century American writers, literary scholars and biographers, popular culture, and film.

Virgil Nemoianu

Virgil Nemoianu is Professor of English and Comparative Literature at the Catholic University of America. His latest books are *The Taming of Romanticism* (1985) and *A Theory of the Secondary* (1989).

Rosa E.M.D. Penna

Rosa E.M.D. Penna is Licenciada en Letras, is Assistant Professor of English and American literature at the Universidad Católica Argentina in Buenos Aires since 1969; and Assistant Professor of English literature at the Universidad de Buenos Aires since 1980. She has served as bibliographer (Spanish literature) for the

MLA International Bibliography since 1983. She worked with Jorge L. Borges from 1970 until 1975.

Raymond A. Prier

Raymond A. Prier received his Ph.D. at Yale in 1970. He has taught at the Universities of Southern California and Houston. His latest book is *Thauma Idesthai: The Phenomenology of Sight and Appearance in Archaic Greek* (Florida State University Press, 1989).

Robert Royal

Robert Royal is vice president for research at the Ethics and Public Policy Center, Washington, D.C., and a doctoral candidate at the Catholic University of America in comparative literature. He holds a B.A. and M.A. from Brown University and spent 1977 in Italy as a Fulbright Scholar. He has taught at Brown, Rhode Island College, and Catholic University. From 1980 to 1982 he was editor-in-chief of *Prospect* magazine in Princeton, New Jersey. His articles have appeared in a number of magazines and newspapers, among them the *Washington Post*, the *Washington Times*, *National Review*, the *American Spectator*, and *Crisis*.

Roger Shattuck

Roger Shattuck is author of *The Banquet Years, The Forbidden Experiment, The Innocent Eye*, and two books on Marcel Proust. He teaches in the University Professors Program at Boston University.

Pierre Walker

Pierre Walker completed his Ph.D. at Columbia University. He is Assistant Professor of English at the University of Minnesota at Duluth, and he is currently working on a book on Henry James and French Culture.

Index

In the series CULTURA LUDENS (CL) the following titles have been published:

1:1. SPARIOSU, Mihai and Giuseppe MAZZOTTA (eds): *Mimesis in Contemporary Theory, Vol. 1: The Literary and Philosophical Debate*. Philadelphia/Amsterdam, 1985.

1:2. BOGUE, Ronald (ed.): *Mimesis in Contemporary Theory, Vol. 2: Mimesis, Semiosis and Power*. Amsterdam/Philadelphia, 1991.

2. GUINNESS, Gerald and Andrew HURLEY (eds): *Auctor Ludens: Essays on Play in Literature*. Philadelphia/Amsterdam, 1986.

3. HANS, James S.: *Imitation and the Image of Man*. Philadelphia/Amsterdam, 1987.

4. NEMOIANU, Virgil and Robert ROYAL (eds): *The Hospitable Canon. Essays on literary play, scholarly choice, and popular pressures*. Amsterdam/Philadelphia, 1991.